Quakers & Slavery

Quakers & Slavery

A DIVIDED SPIRIT

JEAN R. SODERLUND

PRINCETON UNIVERSITY PRESS
PRINCETON, NEW JERSEY

ISBN 0-691-04732-4

Publication of this book has been aided by the
Governor Alfred E. Driscoll Publication Prize of the
New Jersey Historical Commission

This book has been composed in Linotron Monticello

Clothbound editions of Princeton University Press books
are printed on acid-free paper, and binding materials are
chosen for strength and durability

Printed in the United States of America by
Princeton University Press
Princeton, New Jersey

FOR RUDY

CONTENTS

FIGURES

Maps

Graphs

TABLES

ACKNOWLEDGMENTS

When one works on a project for ten years it is impossible not to accumulate a massive number of debts. In my case, the accounting must start even before my actual research began, because both my parents, Joyce and John Ruth, and my students at Deptford Township High School and Camden County College, guided me to the conclusion that we must learn more about the history of relations between blacks and whites in America if we are to understand the evolution of our society. P.M.G. Harris of Temple University directed the dissertation on which this book is based. He helped me devise the research plan to test my hypotheses and provided good advice and encouragement throughout my work. Marianne S. Wokeck listened patiently to the partial results of my research and raised many questions that had not occurred to me. While our thesis topics overlapped only slightly, we were able to share insights on eighteenth-century colonial society that have substantially improved my work. Emma J. Lapsansky and J. William Frost cheerfully read several drafts of my dissertation, helped me look at the topic from different perspectives, and directed me to additional sources. Marilyn Campbell, Paul Clemens, Richard Dunn, Gary Nash, Joyce Ruth, Lucy Simler, Rudy Soderlund, Gail Ullman, Lisa Waciega, and John Wilson read the entire manuscript and made valuable suggestions for improving its content and presentation. Jon Butler, Mary Dunn, Jack Michel, Richard Ryerson, and members of the Philadelphia Center for Early American Studies seminar provided helpful criticism of portions of the work. I am grateful to everyone for sharing their thoughts and expertise.

My research was partially funded by fellowships from the Philadelphia Center for Early American Studies, the New Jersey Historical Commission, and Temple University. The Bernard C. Watson Dissertation Award of Temple University and the Governor Alfred E. Driscoll Publication Prize of the New Jersey Historical Commission enabled me to do further research for preparing the manuscript. The staffs of several libraries and archives were especially gracious in meeting my research needs. Albert Fowler, Patricia Neiley, Nancy Speers, Jane Thorson, and Ramsay Turberg of Friends Historical Library, Swarthmore College, deserve special thanks. The staffs of the Burlington County Historical Society, the Chester County Archives, the Chester County Register of Wills

Office, the Historical Society of Pennsylvania, the New Jersey Division of Archives and Records Management, the Quaker Collection of Haverford College, Paley Library of Temple University, the Stewart Collection of Glassboro State College, and Van Pelt Library of the University of Pennsylvania were also very helpful.

Above all, I am indebted to my husband Rudy. Throughout the years I have worked on this project, he has sustained a keen interest in my work and has provided steadfast encouragement and support. I have benefited greatly from discussing my ideas with him and receiving his forthright criticism and advice.

Grenloch, New Jersey
October 1984

ABBREVIATIONS

BCHS	Burlington County Historical Society, Burlington, New Jersey
FHL	Friends Historical Library, Swarthmore, Pennsylvania
HSP	Historical Society of Pennsylvania, Philadelphia, Pennsylvania
JNH	*Journal of Negro History*
MM mans.	Monthly Meeting manumissions
MM mins.	Monthly Meeting minutes
PMHB	*Pennsylvania Magazine of History and Biography*
PYM mins.	Philadelphia Yearly Meeting minutes
QM mins.	Quarterly Meeting minutes
WMQ	*William and Mary Quarterly*

Quakers & Slavery

INTRODUCTION

In 1770 nearly half a million men, women, and children of African origin or descent toiled on plantations and farms, in shops, houses, and shipyards throughout the British North American mainland. Few Americans challenged slavery before that year. For most Anglo-American colonists, the move toward slavery was an economic decision. When enslaved Indians died off and the number of white indentured servants proved insufficient, British Americans turned to Africa to supply their labor needs. Initially, differences in the legal status of white and black bondsmen were unclear. During the seventeenth century, however, colonial legislators in a piecemeal fashion established a fully articulated caste system. By 1730, most of the American colonies had legal frameworks for perpetual servitude that rested on the generally accepted view that blacks were inferior to whites.[1]

Against this backdrop of pervasive racial prejudice and oppression, persons speaking out against slavery were uncommon. Just a handful of Americans demanded abolition before the conflicts with Great Britain in the 1760s and 1770s popularized the notion that liberty was a natural right. Most of these abolitionists belonged to or considered themselves members of the Society of Friends. Beginning with George Fox, the English founder of Quakerism, individual Friends had voiced their uneasiness about slavery. In 1657, soon after the Quaker movement got started, Fox reminded his slaveowning followers in America that everyone was equal in the sight of God. Later, when he visited Barbados in 1671, Fox preached to the blacks and urged Quaker masters to limit their slaves' terms and to educate them. Probably the first Quaker to denounce slaveholding outright was William Edmundson, who accompanied Fox to Barbados in 1671 and issued his own indictment of slavery from Newport, Rhode Island, in 1676.[2] The center of Quaker abolition-

---

[1] U.S. Bureau of the Census, *Historical Statistics of the United States, Colonial Times to 1970* (Washington, D.C., 1975), 2:1168; Winthrop D. Jordan, *White over Black: American Attitudes toward the Negro, 1550-1812* (Chapel Hill, N.C., 1968), 44-98.

[2] J. William Frost, ed., *The Quaker Origins of Antislavery* (Norwood, Pa., 1980), 31-68; Thomas E. Drake, *Quakers and Slavery in America* (New Haven, Conn., 1950), 4-10; David Brion Davis, *The Problem of Slavery in Western Culture* (Ithaca, N.Y., 1966), 307-309. In the English-speaking world, before 1750, just a few non-Quakers opposed slavery: the English Presbyterian Richard Baxter, the Anglican Morgan Godwyn, and Samuel Sewall, the Massachusetts jurist. Davis, *Problem of Slavery in Western Culture*, 338-348.

ism then moved to Pennsylvania, where other Friends, such as the four signers of a 1688 Germantown antislavery petition, the outspoken radicals William Southeby and Benjamin Lay, and the renowned abolitionists John Woolman and Anthony Benezet, demanded an end to the slave trade and slavery itself. These reformers believed that slaveholding was inconsistent with Christianity and urged the Society to ban members from holding blacks. Philadelphia Yearly Meeting, to which Quakers of Pennsylvania, New Jersey, and parts of Delaware and Maryland belonged, in 1754 published a statement against slavery and in 1776 finally agreed to prohibit slave ownership among its members.[3] Many Friends then helped to foster the growth of abolitionism in American society at large.

Although Delaware Valley Quakers were the first unified group to oppose black slavery—and in fact their movement became the primary wellspring of American social reform—Philadelphia Yearly Meeting achieved the unity necessary to prohibit slaveholding with great difficulty. Until the 1750s, most Friends probably had about the same attitudes on slavery as other colonists: they either owned slaves and saw nothing wrong with their behavior as long as they treated their chattels well, or they thought little about slavery at all. They were more likely to oppose the slave trade than members of other religions because of the violence inherent in the trade, and relatively few Pennsylvania and New Jersey Quakers actually imported blacks, but the Yearly Meeting was unable to agree even to punish slave traders until 1758. They would not prohibit slaveholding itself for another eighteen years.

For anyone interested in the history of racism and slavery in the Americas, the Delaware Valley Friends pose a number of challenging questions. Most obviously, why did the Quakers come to oppose slavery when practically all other whites saw nothing wrong with the institution? The answer often given is that the Friends were an extraordinary group, cut off from mainstream colonial society, whose beliefs in the equality of all humans before God and in nonviolence mandated acceptance of abolitionism. This solution serves on only the most superficial level. For if Quaker theology led inevitably to opposition to slavery, why did the meeting not forbid slaveholding in 1671, when George Fox spoke out, rather than a century later

---

[3] Philadelphia Yearly Meeting was the first American yearly meeting to speak out against slavery and to prohibit buying and selling slaves, but the New England and New York yearly meetings forbade slaveholding in 1770 and 1774, respectively, before Delaware Valley Friends took that step. Arthur J. Worrall, *Quakers in the Colonial Northeast* (Hanover, N.H. and London, 1980), 161-163.

in 1776? Why did it take so long for the pacifist and reputedly egalitarian Friends to denounce the oppression of blacks? We can find out by looking at the local growth of abolitionism among Quakers, by investigating the positions Friends held in society and their involvements with slavery, if any. In doing this, we do not find that the Quakers were a weird group who enhanced their separateness from other colonists by opposing slavery. Rather, in Pennsylvania and New Jersey at least, the Friends were often substantial slaveholders who, because of the egalitarian strand in their religion, had to face a difficult choice between giving up a valuable source of labor or continuing to resist the arguments of abolitionist members of the meeting. Philadelphia Yearly Meeting thus provides an excellent opportunity for us to study the process by which values changed among one group of early Americans. We can see how religious belief and economic interest interacted in the growth of abolitionism among these Friends.

BEFORE investigating the growth of antislavery reform within Philadelphia Yearly Meeting in the eighteenth century, it is useful to take a look at the history of the larger body to which that meeting belonged, the Society of Friends. The Society was born in northern England in the early 1650s when George Fox gathered a small following from among the Seekers, one of the radical Protestant groups spawned by the English Civil War.[4] Quakers shared many beliefs with the Puritans, who held power during the Commonwealth period under Oliver Cromwell, and even with the Church of England, whose authority was restored when Charles II took the throne in 1660. But the theology of Friends also departed from these groups in several significant respects. The central concept of Quakerism was that potentially anyone could experience God directly and inwardly, regardless of gender, nationality, or social status. Friends rejected the Calvinist concept of predestination, and instead believed that all people who sought to lead blameless lives could receive the Light and be saved.[5]

Fox's followers adopted several other principles that set them off from the dominant churches of seventeenth-century England and

[4] William C. Braithwaite, *The Beginnings of Quakerism*, ed. Henry J. Cadbury, 2d ed. (Cambridge, 1955), 78-97, 553.

[5] J. William Frost, *The Quaker Family in Colonial America* (New York, 1973), 10-26; Frost, ed., *Quaker Origins*, 2; Frederick B. Tolles, *Meeting House and Counting House: The Quaker Merchants of Colonial Philadelphia 1682-1763* (Chapel Hill, N.C., 1948), 4-11.

her colonies in America. They rejected all violence, including just wars, and refused to perform various social graces that symbolized subservience to authority, such as doffing one's hat, and using "you" to address a single person. Quakers also denounced a paid ministry and would not offer tithes or take oaths.[6] Though the moral code of Friends was essentially like that of the Puritans,[7] and members of the Society repeatedly assured their English rulers that they had no intention of overthrowing the government,[8] early Quakers were persecuted throughout Great Britain and America for their beliefs and for not attending the established church. Nevertheless, ministers called "First Publishers of Truth" traveled widely, making converts in Scotland, Ireland, Europe, the West Indies, Massachusetts, New York, and elsewhere, as early as 1660. They saw themselves as true descendants of the early Christians and accepted persecution as proof of their lineage.[9]

The Quakers at first had little organization beyond the gathered meetings for worship and the leadership of esteemed ministers, or "public Friends," like George Fox, Francis Howgill, and Edward Burrough. Then in the late 1660s Fox recognized that a church based primarily on personal revelation could easily spin apart, and began to set up the hierarchical system of meetings that still exists in the Society today.[10] Fox traveled throughout the British Isles and in 1671 visited America. Everywhere he established local meetings to supervise marriages and oversee the behavior of Friends.[11] The Society of Friends remained outside the law in England until the Toleration Act of 1689; it survived mainly because the authorities only sporadically enforced the statutes requiring conformity. The threat—and at times the reality—of harsh persecution continued to exist into the late 1670s and early 1680s, however, and thus many Friends, along with people of other disfavored beliefs, hearkened to

[6] Frost, *Quaker Family*, 24-25, 190-193; Tolles, *Meeting House*, 5.

[7] Frost, *Quaker Family*, 207-208, 217; Hugh Barbour, *The Quakers in Puritan England* (New Haven, Conn., 1964), 1-32.

[8] For example, see the petition to Parliament, April 1671, from William Penn, Jasper Batt, John Boulton, Theophilus Green, and Patrick Livingstone, published in Mary Maples Dunn et al., eds., *The Papers of William Penn* (Philadelphia, 1981-), 1:205-208.

[9] William Wayne Spurrier, "The Persecution of the Quakers in England: 1650-1714" (Ph.D. diss., University of North Carolina at Chapel Hill, 1976), 111-112.

[10] See Appendix A for a discussion of the meeting structure and disciplinary procedures of the Society of Friends.

[11] William C. Braithwaite, *The Second Period of Quakerism*, ed. Henry J. Cadbury, 2d ed. (Cambridge, 1961), 251-268.

the twin promises of religious freedom and economic prosperity and migrated to West Jersey and Pennsylvania. There Friends found themselves in an altered situation, for instead of an embattled minority, they were now the ruling group.[12]

Most Quakers who immigrated to the Delaware Valley came directly from the British Isles, but others had lived in the West Indies, Maryland, New York, and Rhode Island. Some were very wealthy and arrived with gangs of slaves or purchased blacks after they arrived. These affluent merchants and plantation owners brought the capital as well as the contacts with London and the West Indies that stimulated Philadelphia's rapid growth during the very first years. Others better fitted the stereotype of the plain, hard-working English immigrant who found adequate prosperity on a farm carved out of the wilderness in the New World.[13] Although Friends remained a majority of the population only until about 1720 or 1730 at the latest, Quakers in Pennsylvania kept control of the Assembly until 1756 and both Pennsylvania and West Jersey Friends held considerable power in their respective colonies until the Revolution. In both provinces the Quaker elite constantly faced a dilemma—how to adhere to their religious testimony and at the same time make their fortunes, maintain their control or influence in government, satisfy the Crown's demands for military support, and quell the cries of non-Quaker colonists for defense. As Frederick B. Tolles skillfully showed, Friends in Pennsylvania walked a tightrope of compromise for over seventy years until the Seven Years' War broke out in 1754. Conscientious members of Philadelphia Yearly Meeting then withdrew from a government that raised troops and distrained goods from Quakers who refused to pay taxes for military purposes. Though some devout Friends returned to the Pennsylvania Assembly when the war ended, the Revolution subsequently brought to a close the era of Quaker power within the governments of both New Jersey and Pennsylvania. When the new nation formed, the Society's role was limited to pressuring federal and state governments from the outside for specific reforms.[14]

[12] Tolles, *Meeting House*, 11-44.

[13] Gary B. Nash, *Quakers and Politics: Pennsylvania, 1681-1726* (Princeton, N.J., 1968), 48-67; Tolles, *Meeting House*, 29-44; my own analysis of probate records in four local areas of the Delaware Valley. See Appendix B.

[14] Richard Alan Ryerson, "Portrait of a Colonial Oligarchy: The Quaker Elite in the Pennsylvania Assembly, 1729-1776," in *Power and Status: Essays on Officeholding in the American Colonies*, ed. Bruce Daniels (Middletown, Conn., forthcoming); Thomas L. Purvis, "The New Jersey Assembly, 1722-1776" (Ph.D. diss., The Johns Hopkins

Most scholars of Pennsylvania Quakers have followed Tolles's lead in focusing on the Crisis of 1755 as the crucial turning point in the Yearly Meeting's history. Dramatic changes did indeed take place in the meeting during the 1750s, and not the least of these was the Friends' adoption of a firm antislavery stance. Historians interested in slavery and racism in early America have naturally turned their attention to this accomplishment of Philadelphia Quakers as the exception to the generally dreary record of black-white relations in the British colonies. Winthrop Jordan showed that racism was deeply rooted in Anglo-American culture, evidenced by the imagery of the language, even before the English had contact with sub-Saharan Africans. Only some Quakers and a few persons of other religions were able to break the shackles of ethnocentrism that held blacks in contempt as inferior beings whose just and natural fate was to work as slaves.[15] For Edmund S. Morgan, the pervasive eighteenth-century acceptance of slavery stemmed less from any cultural baggage that the English brought with them from the mother country than from the way colonists built their society in the new land. Morgan hypothesized from the experience of colonial Virginia that, ironically, slavery and racism became the foundation for America's free society (for whites) because oppression of blacks has bound white Americans together, permitting a master class of both rich and poor whites to participate in government on equal terms.[16]

Why then did the mid-Atlantic Quakers decide to prohibit slaveholding within their Society when the institution was an accepted practice among most eighteenth-century Americans? To answer this question, most observers have stressed the period of the 1750s crisis when the Quaker Philadelphia elite lost control of the Pennsylvania government during the Seven Years' War. Historians have viewed the abolitionism of Philadelphia Yearly Meeting as a product of the unique beliefs of the Friends tempered by the unique circumstances of the "crucial decade." Each scholar took a somewhat different

University, 1979); Tolles, *Meeting House*, 11-28, 230-243; Richard Bauman, *For the Reputation of Truth: Politics, Religion, and Conflict among the Pennsylvania Quakers, 1750-1800* (Baltimore, 1971), 19-33, 228-229.

[15] Jordan, *White over Black*, 3-43, 193-198.

[16] Edmund S. Morgan, *American Slavery American Freedom: The Ordeal of Colonial Virginia* (New York, 1975), 295-387. For other views on slavery's beginnings in British America, see Oscar and Mary F. Handlin, "Origins of the Southern Labor System," *WMQ*, 3d ser., 7 (1950), 199-222; and Carl N. Degler, "Slavery and the Genesis of American Race Prejudice," *Comparative Studies in Society and History* 2 (1959), 49-66.

direction in his explanation, but all focused on the Philadelphia leadership during these years.

For example, Thomas Drake emphasized the importance of the witness of individual Quaker abolitionists who tried to convince fellow Friends that slavery was wrong. Of these spokesmen, John Woolman was ultimately successful in convincing the Yearly Meeting leaders that the Society should ban slaveholding. According to Drake, Woolman achieved this feat, whereas his predecessors had failed, both because his manner was more gentle and acceptable to the Friends and because events were on his side. Many Quakers were ready to accept the reformers' argument that the Seven Years' War was God's punishment for adopting sinful ways like slaveholding.[17] Sydney James, on the other hand, saw the actual beliefs of Friends as less important in adopting an antislavery stance than their desire to maintain their status in colonial society after they withdrew from the Pennsylvania Assembly. James believed that the Philadelphia elite experienced a crisis of identity when they were forced to give up control of the Pennsylvania government and that they turned to philanthropic causes such as opposing slavery and working for peaceful relations with the Indians in order to keep their influence without violating their creed.[18] In *The Problem of Slavery in Western Culture*, David Brion Davis also viewed Quaker abolitionism as a product of the Crisis of 1755. He argued that before 1750, opponents of slavery throughout Europe and America were outcasts from the society in which they lived. Abolitionism was "an outlet for deviant personalities." Pennsylvania Friends accepted antislavery in the 1750s because they had become a persecuted sect; in his view, they expressed their newly acquired peculiarity by supporting a controversial reform.[19] Later, in *The Problem of Slavery in the Age of Revolution*, Davis took a somewhat different tack to stress the influence of an increased acceptance of natural law among people of all religions in the mid-eighteenth century. Quaker abolitionists gained support from the growing opinion that freedom was a basic right of all humans.[20] Gary B. Nash, finally, focused on the economic aspects of the issue and believed that a short-term rise

[17] Drake, *Quakers and Slavery*, 1-113.

[18] Sydney V. James, *A People among Peoples: Quaker Benevolence in Eighteenth-Century America* (Cambridge, Mass., 1963), 1-2, 103-168, 216-239.

[19] Davis, *Problem of Slavery in Western Culture*, 291-332, 483-493; quotation on p. 324.

[20] David Brion Davis, *The Problem of Slavery in the Age of Revolution, 1770-1823* (Ithaca, N.Y., 1975), 213-254.

in the demand for black labor during the Seven Years' War affected the Yearly Meeting's policy on slavery in two ways. Increasing importation once again made reforming Quakers keenly aware of the issue, while many other Friends invested in blacks because white servants were scarce and the wages of free laborers were high. The opposition of these slave-owning Quakers postponed a decision to ban slaveholding within the meeting for almost twenty years.[21]

Without question, these historians have advanced provocative hypotheses about the growth of abolitionism in Philadelphia Yearly Meeting. But their stress on the change of opinion that occurred among the meeting's elite during the 1750s has prevented us from understanding how opposition to slavery developed among the whole membership of the meeting over the eighteenth century. It remains unclear, for instance, how the Crisis of 1755 influenced Friends living *outside* Pennsylvania to accept antislavery reform. Who supported and opposed abolitionism, and how were their attitudes related to the importance of slavery in their daily lives? Were the leaders of the Yearly Meeting a true oligarchy who could work their way at will? Could they simply respond to their own psychological requirements, as argued, by instituting changes that governed the entire Yearly Meeting? Or did the reforming elite merely execute the decision of the rank and file and change their position on slavery along with—perhaps even after—the majority of the Society?

Further, emphasis on the decade of the 1750s makes it very difficult to determine exactly what events or factors engendered abolitionism within the Yearly Meeting. Possible influences encouraging antislavery reform at this time include the Great Awakening among Calvinists and the reform movement among English Friends, the psychological effects of the Seven Years' War crisis on the Society in the Delaware Valley, the rise in importance of John Woolman and Anthony Benezet within Philadelphia Yearly Meeting, increased acceptance of Enlightenment thought, and the burst of investment in slaves by Friends during the wartime labor shortages. Each scholar has argued for the preeminence of one factor, but in the end, it is really not possible to separate the impact of any one of these elements from that of the others as long as we focus on the change in attitudes during that one decade. Therefore we must look at Friends living in contexts other than Philadelphia in the 1750s,

[21] Gary B. Nash, "Slaves and Slaveowners in Colonial Philadelphia," *WMQ*, 3d ser., 30 (1973), 253-254.

and at several aspects of their lives simultaneously and systematically. The impulse against slavery, for instance, clearly emerged in certain local meetings at times when the Yearly Meeting was not interested in the issue or avoided it. An exploration of these seminal local meetings and the concerns of their members can suggest the forces that fostered the development of antislavery reform.

This study seeks to go beyond the present literature in two ways: 1) by looking closely at the development of abolitionism within local monthly meetings as well as in the Yearly Meeting; and 2) by suggesting ways in which the early movement against slavery can be compared with later drives for reform in American society. The first chapter describes the prolonged debate over slavery within the Yearly Meeting from the earliest petitions to the decision in 1758 to discipline buyers and sellers of slaves. Chapter 2 examines the changing composition of the Yearly Meeting leadership, especially in respect to slaveholding, wealth, residence, and government officeholding. This chapter delineates the extraordinary change in attitudes toward slavery that occurred among leading Friends during the first half of the eighteenth century.

To describe the change in Friends' values and to explain why they came as a group to oppose slavery are two different matters, so Chapter 3 takes a first step toward understanding the growth of abolitionism by investigating the practical value of slavery for Friends and their neighbors in colonial Pennsylvania and New Jersey. Evidence about all heads of household (regardless of their religion) from probate records and tax assessment lists shows wide variations in slaveholding from one part of the Delaware Valley to another, as well as over the century from 1680 to 1780. Chapter 4 then returns to the Quaker meeting records to examine how the local meetings executed the Yearly Meeting's 1758 decision against slave trading and moved toward the more stringent ban against slaveholding itself in 1776. In Chapters 5 and 6, we then look closely at the very varied development of antislavery stances in four monthly meetings—Shrewsbury and Chesterfield in New Jersey and Philadelphia and Chester in Pennsylvania. In each locality, Quakers either were less likely to own blacks or freed their slaves earlier than residents of other faiths. Nevertheless, Friends in some meetings pushed much faster against slavery than the Yearly Meeting, while other meetings lagged behind. These chapters investigate the sources of these differences, including involvement in slavery and varying interpretations of Friends' beliefs.

The conclusion points out the limits of Quaker abolitionism. In executing the Society's ban on slaveholding, most Friends treated blacks with paternalism. The meeting failed to welcome the ex-slaves as full-fledged members of their religion. Eighteenth-century Quakers in this way became the forebears of later white abolitionists and even some liberal white reformers of the civil rights era who wanted an end to the stark oppression of blacks but who did not really view Afro-Americans as social equals.

Examining the development of antislavery reform in the local Quaker meetings as well as in the Yearly Meeting shows clearly why the Friends deliberated the question of slavery for an entire century. Many members owned slaves, and as long as slaveholders dominated a meeting, no agreement could be reached to ban the practice. By moving away from a single focus on the Philadelphia elite, we can see in one meeting after another how Friends struggled to come to grips with the issue. The eighteenth-century Friends were indeed a "peculiar people" because their drive to eradicate slavery among themselves was a success. Nevertheless, the process of building support for the reform within Philadelphia Yearly Meeting had the same elements that can be found in later movements for social change. Slaveholding Americans of other religions and other eras confronted the same choice between conscience and socioeconomic concerns when challenged by abolitionist thought.

SOCIOLOGISTS John D. McCarthy and Mayer N. Zald have devised the term "conscience reform" to describe a common thread among a long line of American reformers.[22] These scholars differentiate reformers who strive to alleviate injustices that they themselves endure from those who try to help others. The latter are conscience reformers, "outsiders" who mobilize to fight inequities suffered by another group. There are numerous examples of these activists in American history: white abolitionists of any religion (or none) during the eighteenth and nineteenth centuries, male supporters of woman's suffrage, women and older men who opposed the military draft, and the whites who joined the civil rights movement of the 1960s. None of these groups had an immediately apparent direct interest in the reform they advocated. All, on the surface at least, were altruistic, wanting to make the world a better place in which to live. The conscience reformers often worked alongside other reformers who were members of groups that would benefit more

[22] John D. McCarthy and Mayer N. Zald, "Resource Mobilization and Social Movements: A Partial Theory," *American Journal of Sociology* 82 (1977), 1222, 1231-1232.

personally from the changes sought. For instance, the antislavery movement of the nineteenth century included the whites, William Lloyd Garrison, Wendell Phillips, Angelina and Sarah Grimké, and Theodore Weld, who believed that southern slavery was a blight on the nation, as well as ex-slaves Frederick Douglass, Sojourner Truth, Henry Highland Garnet, and Harriet Tubman, who had experienced bondage and wanted to free their families and fellow blacks. In the case of the 1960s civil rights movement, the conscience reformers included the northern white students who joined the much larger contingent of Afro-Americans to fight discrimination in public accommodations, jobs, housing, education, and voting. Across the centuries, a shared goal bound the early Quaker abolitionist to the white civil rights activist—a professed desire to improve society by ending the subjugation of blacks.

As we shall see with the example of Philadelphia Yearly Meeting, conscience reformers were not at all united on the methods of achieving reform or even on the precise goals of their efforts. Some Delaware Valley Friends focused their entire lives on eliminating slavery, while others joined the movement only after much coaxing. The earliest spokesmen were more radical and, considered eccentrics, revolutionaries, or both, were largely ignored. Then along came John Woolman who couched the same "radical" message in moderate language. Aided by other circumstances that made reform more attractive, he and his fellow abolitionists began to reach a wider audience. In the process of securing greater support, however, they found it necessary to set more limited short-term goals. Instead of demanding outright emancipation in 1758, the reformers settled for the ban on buying and selling slaves. Over the next eighteen years they worked at convincing other Friends that slavery was wrong. By 1776, the abolitionists garnered enough support from "second string" reformers to prohibit slave ownership among Friends, but that is essentially as far as the meeting would go. They would not permit blacks to join their religion on an equal basis until the 1790s, and the Yearly Meeting did very little to bring about general emancipation in society at large. In this way we can see some parallels with the 1960s civil rights movement. After black leaders like Martin Luther King, Jr., and white activists like James Peck had demonstrated the absolute necessity of improving the conditions in which blacks lived, many whites (led by Presidents John F. Kennedy and Lyndon B. Johnson) supported passage of such laws as the Civil Rights Act of 1964 and the Voting Rights Act of 1965. These laws were valuable in protecting basic civil rights, but they did not begin to alleviate the economic inequities that most blacks endure. Again, the people brought in with the tide of reform were content when apparent sizable gains had been made. They did not have the long-term commitment needed to bring about true equality for blacks and whites.

THE purpose of this study is to show the process by which one movement for conscience reform, abolitionism, grew among eighteenth-century Delaware Valley Friends. The circumstances of this change in values were complex. For almost a century, Quakers with divergent attitudes debated the issue of slavery: that the Yearly Meeting in 1776 united in spirit to prohibit slaveholding hid the fact that in the end members felt varying degrees of enthusiasm for the decision and obscured the pushes and pulls individual Friends experienced as they contemplated whether to give up their slaves. All members of Philadelphia Yearly Meeting ostensibly accepted the fundamental Quaker beliefs that underlay antislavery thought, but close analysis indicates wide differences in their willingness to oppose slavery. Friends who owned slaves and who wanted to hold on to them because they needed labor or because they wanted the blacks as symbols of social status either refused or took a long time to agree that the institution was inconsistent with Friends' beliefs. Abolitionists in the Society—like whites who fought southern slavery a century later or those who opposed racial discrimination another century after that—used varying strategies to support their case. Though the Delaware Valley Quakers fought their battle within the confines of a single religion, we can gain important insight into the process by which a reform movement is born, grows, and withers away, by examining Philadelphia Yearly Meeting's long debate over slavery and investigating the soul-searching of individuals caught between the dictates of their consciences and the demands of their daily lives.

· 1 ·

ABOLITIONISTS CONFRONT THE
MEETING

In September 1738, the town of Burlington bustled with Friends from every part of the Delaware Valley. Representatives to Philadelphia Yearly Meeting, who met in alternate years in this West Jersey town and in Philadelphia, came from as far away as Duck Creek (Delaware), Lancaster (Pennsylvania), and Cape May (New Jersey). Devout Quakers from all walks of life—men, women, and children—gathered to worship with friends they had not seen since the previous year. And in the business meeting, "weighty" or well-respected Quakers who were sent as representatives from their local meetings, deliberated problems of discipline and questions of policy that their monthly and quarterly meetings sent to the central body for consideration.

Despite all of the activity outside the meeting house, Yearly Meetings for business in the 1730s were rather stolid affairs. The Philadelphia and Burlington Quakers who guided the meeting were leaders in provincial government and commerce as well. Most were wealthy, and many owned slaves. Their philosophy and practice in both government and religion were preeminently conservative; their interest lay in keeping policies as they were and in maintaining control in their own hands.

Thus, when the small hunchbacked abolitionist, Benjamin Lay, walked into the 1738 Yearly Meeting, he was hardly a welcome visitor. The Friends knew him well. In fact, he claimed to be a member of their Society although his monthly meeting in England had disowned him years before. Originally of Colchester, Lay had immigrated first to Barbados and then to Philadelphia around 1731. He hated the system of slavery he had first experienced in the West Indies and set out to eradicate the less extensive, though still well-entrenched, institution he found in the Delaware Valley. His efforts earned him much enmity among the Quaker slaveholders who held sway in the Society in the 1730s and 1740s but probably helped to encourage the budding opponents to slavery who would gain support and take control of Philadelphia Yearly Meeting early in the 1750s.

Lay's tactics were as varied as they were provocative. He ha-

15

rangued local Friends' meetings, and was ejected from them forth-with. He kidnapped a Quaker child to illustrate the grief suffered by African families when their children were stolen by enslavers. He stood with one bare foot in deep snow to publicize the ill-treatment suffered by blacks, especially in the winter. Lay's most famous exploit, however, was his "bladder of blood" demonstration at the 1738 Yearly Meeting. He arrived dressed in a military costume, complete with sword, hidden under a plain coat, and carrying a hollowed-out book that resembled a Bible but actually contained a bladder of red juice. According to one account, Lay rose to speak to the meeting at a propitious moment and said, "Oh all you Negro masters who are contentedly holding your fellow creatures in a state of slavery, . . . you might as well throw off the plain coat as I do . . ."—at which time Lay took off the overcoat and disclosed his military garb to the surprised gathering. He continued, "It would be as justifiable in the sight of the Almighty . . . if you should thrust a sword through their hearts as I do through this book!" Lay then dramatically drew his sword, stabbed the book and bladder, and sprinkled "blood" all over the Friends sitting nearby. The Yearly Meeting was outraged; the members decided that all connection between this radical and their meeting must be cut. Therefore, they directed John Kinsey, the clerk (or presiding officer), to advertise publicly that Friends took no responsibility for Lay's conduct (which also included speaking without invitation in other churches), and they repudiated his book, *All Slave-Keepers, That Keep the Innocent in Bondage, Apostates* (1737). Benjamin Lay subsequently dropped from public view, but some Friends visited him from time to time at the cave in which he lived near Abington, and he lived to see Philadelphia Yearly Meeting take substantial steps against slavery in the 1750s.[1]

[1] C. Brightwen Rowntree, "Benjamin Lay (1681-1759)," *The Journal of the Friends' Historical Society* 33 (1936), 3-19; Roberts Vaux, *Memoirs of the Lives of Benjamin Lay and Ralph Sandiford; Two of the Earliest Public Advocates for the Emancipation of the Enslaved Africans* (Philadelphia, 1815), 17, 25-28; Benjamin Lay, *All Slave-Keepers, That Keep the Innocent in Bondage, Apostates* . . . (Philadelphia, 1737), 63; Thomas E. Drake, *Quakers and Slavery in America* (New Haven, Conn., 1950), 45; Philadelphia Yearly Meeting minutes (hereafter PYM mins.), 16-20/7M/1738. These minutes, and other records of Friends' meetings cited below, are available on microfilm at the Friends Historical Library, Swarthmore College, Swarthmore, Pennsylvania. All are minutes of men's meetings for business, unless noted. Minutes are cited by the exact dates under which they appear in the manuscripts because they are all organized chronologically and can be found most expeditiously in this way. The system of dating may need some explanation. Before 1752, British Americans used the Julian, or Old Style, calendar in

Benjamin Lay did not convince the Yearly Meeting to ban slavery among its members in 1738. He was the wrong man at that time, just as John Woolman would be the right man in the 1750s. Lay's method was direct confrontation and he could not wait for the Friends to achieve a sense of the meeting (or general agreement that their judgment reflected God's will) to oppose slavery. He believed that God had manifested the Truth in him and expected others to see the Light immediately. The give-and-take of the meeting, in which the words and examples of abolitionist Friends over many years gradually convinced hesitant slave owners to give up their blacks, was not Benjamin Lay's milieu. Even Friends who opposed slavery as deeply as he—such as members of Shrewsbury Monthly Meeting in East Jersey—could never condone his extreme measures.

EARLY ABOLITIONISTS

For fifty years before Benjamin Lay stabbed the bladder of "blood" in the Yearly Meeting, abolitionists had tried various strategies to put forth their case. Most began their crusades by presenting papers to their local meetings, who usually decided that the subject was beyond their jurisdiction and referred the proposals to the Yearly Meeting. When the reformers were rebuffed—as were all who wanted the Yearly Meeting to ban slave trading or slaveholding before 1750—they had to make a difficult choice. Those who wanted to remain Quakers in good standing were forced to accept the sense of the meeting and simply work quietly within the Society to convince others of their views. To move outside the meeting and publish antislavery tracts was a breach of unity, a disownable offense. Before 1753, the Quaker overseers of the press prohibited publication of all papers against slavery; thus anyone who issued such a pamphlet was in effect denouncing Friends as well as slavery. John Woolman is the foremost example of an abolitionist who labored within the meeting until the time was ripe for reform. Benjamin Lay took the other route—and Friends cut him off from the Society as a result.

Quakerism offered three basic tenets that proponents of abolitionism could employ to support their case. The first was that all people were equal in the sight of God. Friends who were not sympathetic to abolitionism argued that this simply meant that everyone was capable of receiving God's Light, not that all humans should

which the year started on 25 March. Quakers referred to months by number rather than by their "heathen" names. Thus, until 1752 the first month was March and the twelfth month was February.

be equal socially, politically, and economically. Probably no Quaker abolitionist believed that blacks were the social equals of whites, and most reformers accepted without comment the hierarchical social and political structure of the eighteenth century. They believed that slavery was wrong because under the system of involuntary bondage one person could force another to do his or her will; thus masters could prevent their slaves from reaching God. Slave owners, for example, often separated husbands from wives, and thereby practically forced them to commit adultery. The second tenet that Quaker abolitionists used to back their case was nonviolence. Proslavery apologists argued that they treated their slaves well and of course never beat them, but activists pointed out that Africans were captured by force and that the system of slavery could not exist without the use or threat of violence. The third relevant Quaker doctrine was that Friends should avoid ostentation and sloth in their daily lives. Abolitionists accused slaveholders of using their blacks as symbols of conspicuous consumption; they also thought that slavery made both masters and their children lazy.

The earliest known antislavery appeal of Pennsylvania Quakers was signed in 1688 by Gerrit Hendricks, Derick op den Graeff, Francis Daniel Pastorius, and Abraham op den Graeff of the Germantown meeting. These men opposed the slave trade on the grounds that it encouraged theft and adultery, raised the possibility of rebellion, gave Pennsylvania and the Society of Friends bad reputations, and was contrary to the Golden Rule, that is, to do unto others as you wish others to do unto you (Luke 6:31). The Yearly Meeting refused to consider this epistle because it believed that Pennsylvania and New Jersey Friends could not outlaw slave trading as long as Quakers living elsewhere were involved in the trade.[2] As far as we know, the Germantown petitioners raised no further objections to the institution.

Nevertheless, the Yearly Meeting elite could not avoid the issue for long, for only five years later an anonymous group of George Keith's Christian Quakers published *An Exhortation and Caution to Friends Concerning Buying or Keeping of Negroes* (1693). As might be expected, the Yearly Meeting did not respond favorably to this appeal, since the Keithians were schismatics who had demanded changes in key tenets of Quaker theology and had disrupted the

---

[2] "A Timely Proposal," *JNH* 18 (1933), 99-101; PYM mins., 5/7M/1688. See Chapter 3 on the importation of slaves into Pennsylvania and New Jersey at this time. Darold D. Wax discussed Quaker involvement in this trade in "Quaker Merchants and the Slave Trade in Colonial Pennsylvania," *PMHB* 86 (1962), 143-159.

Yearly Meeting.[3] But in 1696 the writing of two weighty Friends did convince the Yearly Meeting to take a small step in cautioning members against importing slaves. In this case, William Southeby, who was active in Philadelphia Monthly Meeting and had lived in Maryland and Delaware before moving to Pennsylvania, and Cadwalader Morgan of Merion, demanded a ban on slave ownership and importation.[4] In response, the meeting advised Friends to "be Careful not to Encourage the bringing in of any more Negroes, & that such that have Negroes be Careful of them, bring them to Meetings, or have Meetings with them in their Families, & Restrain them from Loose, & Lewd Living as much as in them lies, & from Rambling abroad on First Days or other Times."[5] Southeby and Morgan were without doubt unsatisfied by this first advice of Philadelphia Yearly Meeting on slavery because it had no teeth for disciplining slave owners and traders. Nevertheless, the ruling was important because it established several precedents for later decisions. The meeting clearly stated that blacks should be taught the principles of Christian religion and morality—a concern that remained strong even after Friends freed most of their slaves in the late 1770s. The meeting also for the first time in 1696 rooted itself firmly in an antislavery stance, even though it would only denounce slave importation at this time. Morgan apparently kept silent on this issue after he wrote the one paper, probably limiting his activities to speaking in private to weighty Friends. Southeby issued no more tracts until 1712 when, as we shall see below, he petitioned the Pennsylvania Assembly for general emancipation.

The Yearly Meeting's advice of 1696 carried very little weight: Quakers continued to import and own slaves. Therefore in 1698 Robert Pyle, a prominent member of Concord Monthly Meeting in Chester County, echoed previous arguments against slaveholding and suggested that quarterly meetings oversee manumissions. His paper, which recounted a dream in which blacks were represented by a "black pot" that must be set aside in order to reach heaven,

---

[3] Drake, *Quakers and Slavery*, 15-16. There is no evidence of a strong link between Keithians and antislavery reform; several prominent Keithians owned slaves.

[4] Phila. MM mins., 1682-1720; PYM mins., 23/7M/1696; Kenneth L. Carroll, "William Southeby, Early Quaker Antislavery Writer," *PMHB* 89 (1965), 416-427; Drake, *Quakers and Slavery*, 19-20; J. William Frost, ed., *The Quaker Origins of Antislavery* (Norwood, Pa., 1980), 70; Thomas E. Drake, "Cadwalader Morgan: Antislavery Quaker of the Welsh Tract," *Friends Intelligencer* 98 (1941), 575-576.

[5] Henry J. Cadbury, "Another Early Quaker Anti-Slavery Document," *JNH* 27 (1942), 210; PYM mins., 23/7M/1696.

had racist overtones that were absent in the writings of other Quaker abolitionists.[6] There is no record that Pyle's paper was discussed or even read at the Yearly Meeting, but in the same year Philadelphia Monthly Meeting followed the Yearly Meeting's 1696 advice by asking Friends in Barbados to send no more blacks to Pennsylvania.[7]

The next protest, this one aimed specifically against buying slaves imported into Pennsylvania, emerged in 1711 from Chester Monthly Meeting. That petition was significant because it came from an entire meeting, not just one or two individuals. Chester was the first monthly meeting, as far as we know, to demand new measures designed to stop the expansion of slavery in the Delaware Valley. For the first time in America, an organized body decided with unanimity or near unanimity that the slave trade was wrong and that it should be eliminated by disciplinary action. The Chester Friends believed that the policy of Philadelphia Yearly Meeting then in force, simply that Quaker merchants should discourage their correspondents from sending additional blacks to Pennsylvania and New Jersey, was too weak. They could see that many Friends and their neighbors of other religions were importing slaves. Slavery would grow, the Chester Quakers believed, as long as members continued to purchase slaves brought into the Delaware Valley.[8] Again the central meeting tried to avoid further restrictions, contending that they did not have the power to forbid slave trading outright. Thus in 1712 the Delaware Valley Friends asked London Yearly Meeting to consult with other American meetings and decide whether or not Quakers should import and own black slaves, "detaining them and their Posterity as such without any Limitation or Time of Redemption from that Condition."[9] The next year, the English meeting refused to ban members' participation in the African slave trade though they admitted that it violated the Golden Rule. The Delaware Valley Friends had also asked the London Quakers to protest the queen's veto of the 1712 Pennsylvania law that placed a prohibitive tax on slave imports, but the English meeting again refused. However, two years later, in 1715, the London meeting did go so far as to warn Friends to stop participating in the trade.[10]

[6] Cadbury, "An Early Quaker Anti-Slavery Statement," *JNH* 22 (1937), 488-493.

[7] PYM mins., 21/7M/1698; Phila. MM mins., 30/7M/1698.

[8] Chester QM mins., 6/6M/1711; PYM mins., 18/7M/1711 and 21-24/7M/1712.

[9] PYM mins., 21-24/7M/1712.

[10] The Pennsylvania Assembly placed a £20 per head duty on imported blacks at the urging of numerous, unnamed petitioners who feared a slave uprising similar to one that

London's lukewarm response neither satisfied nor quieted the abolitionists of Chester Quarterly Meeting. Spurred on this time by both Chester and Newark monthly meetings, they complained in 1715 that "some Friends be yet in the practice of importing, buying and selling of negro slaves." The Yearly Meeting merely reiterated its 1696 decision and even rebuked the Chester Friends, suggesting in its epistle to local meetings "that all do forbear judging or reflecting on one another either in publick or private concerning the detaining or keeping them [blacks] Servants."[11] Chester Monthly Meeting was disappointed with this decision because it believed that the former minute was not sufficient to stop importation. So in the next year it suggested a rule that would in the future bar Friends from buying any imported blacks. The Yearly Meeting answered sternly that this petition was little different from the one Chester had sent in 1715, and that the central meeting was content with its limited decision of the year before. Nevertheless, the representatives in the Yearly Meeting decided "in Condescention to such Friends as are streightnd in their minds against the holding them, it is desir'd that friends generally do as much as may be avoid buying such Negroes as shall hereafter be brought in, rather than offend any friends who are against it. Yet this is only caution and not Censure."[12] Thus, at the insistence of Chester meeting, Philadelphia Yearly Meeting now took another step by cautioning Friends to avoid buying imported slaves. Again, this minute was only a mild warning, not a rule of discipline.

During the fourteen years following 1716, Philadelphia Yearly Meeting's stance on slavery remained unchanged. In the 1719 Book of Discipline, the Society prohibited the importation of blacks and the buying or selling of Indian slaves ("to avoid giving them occasion of discontent"),[13] but the meeting still strongly resisted pressure from individual Quakers for additional reform. During the 1710s,

---

occurred in New York in April 1712. The Crown repealed this legislation. Darold D. Wax, "The Negro Slave Trade in Colonial Pennsylvania" (Ph.D. diss., University of Washington, 1962), 267-269. PYM mins., 18-22/7M/1714; Drake, *Quakers and Slavery*, 25; Anne T. Gary, "The Political and Economic Relations of English and American Quakers (1750-1785)" (Ph.D. diss., St. Hugh's College [Oxford], 1935), 182. It is relevant that England was awarded the *asiento*, or monopoly to provide African slaves to the Spanish American colonies, in 1713.

[11] Chester QM mins., 1/6M/1715; PYM mins., 18-22/7M/1715.

[12] Chester QM mins., 6/6M/1716; PYM mins., 16-19/7M/1716.

[13] The 1719 Book of Discipline was included verbatim in the PYM mins., 19-24/7M/1719. There is no evidence in the minutes that the monthly meetings dealt with Friends for disobeying these sections of the discipline.

William Southeby renewed his crusade. In 1712 he had petitioned the Pennsylvania Assembly for the emancipation of all slaves, a move the Quaker-dominated legislature promptly rejected (though it did pass a restrictive tariff that was subsequently disapproved by the Crown). Then in 1716, Southeby published several papers against slaveholding without securing permission from the Quaker overseers of the press. Philadelphia Monthly Meeting censured and threatened him with disownment for this breach of discipline. Still, he died apparently in good standing in 1722.[14] John Farmer, an English Quaker visiting Friends in America, called for the liberation of all slaves owned by members of the Society. The Newport, Rhode Island, Friends disowned him because he refused to be still, and when he appealed to Philadelphia Monthly and Quarterly Meetings they also condemned him for publishing papers "tending to division and contrary to good order used among friends." Philadelphia Yearly Meeting made the final decision in 1718 and agreed with the others about his publications, "being fully sensible of the ill Consequences of such pernitious practices."[15] John Hepburn of East Jersey, possibly a follower of the schismatic George Keith who continued to consider himself a Quaker even after other Keithians joined the Anglicans, also published an abolitionist tract, *The American Defence of the Christian Golden Rule*, during these years.[16]

The issue of slavery did not come up again in Philadelphia Yearly Meeting until the late 1720s. In 1727, London Yearly Meeting reported in its epistle that "it is the Sense of this Meeting, that the Importation of Negroes from their Native Country and Relations by Friends, is not a Commendable nor Allowable Practice; and that Practice is Censured by this Meeting," and asked the Delaware Valley Quakers if they were involved in the trade. The Philadelphia Meeting of 1728 replied that "no Friends that we know of within the Extent of this Meeting, are concern'd in that practice," although Darold D. Wax has found in his study of the Pennsylvania slave

[14] Carroll, "William Southeby," 426-427.

[15] Drake, *Quakers and Slavery*, 31; PYM mins. 20-24/7M/1718. According to Arthur Worrall, Farmer and other antislavery proponents in New England and New York found support in the rural meetings such as Nantucket Monthly Meeting, but not in the urban meetings of Rhode Island and New York. *Quakers in the Colonial Northeast* (Hanover, N.H. and London, 1980), 156-157. Further study of the growth of abolitionism among New England and New York Friends is needed.

[16] Henry J. Cadbury, "John Hepburn and His Book against Slavery, 1715," *Proceedings of the American Antiquarian Society*, n.s., 59 (1949), 89-102.

trade that a few Quakers were in fact still importing blacks at that time.[17]

The next year Ralph Sandiford and Chester Monthly Meeting broke open the controversy once again. Sandiford, a Philadelphia merchant, was terribly disturbed about the increase in slave importation that resulted when the per capita duty on blacks dropped to forty shillings in 1729. He wrote a pamphlet attacking Friends for holding slaves and published it even though the Quaker overseers of the press denied him permission. As might be expected by this point, the Philadelphia Friends condemned him for his actions.[18]

While Sandiford chose to attack the Quaker leadership in public (and thereby threaten the unity of the meeting), the Chester Friends used another strategy to force the Yearly Meeting to reconsider its position on purchasing imported slaves. In August 1729, prompted once again by Chester Monthly Meeting, representatives from Chester Quarterly Meeting reported that they had been "for some time under a Concern, by reason of the great Quantity of Negros fetched, and imported, into this Country and finding by our discipline That we as a Society are Restricted from being concerned therein do think it as reasonable that we should be restricted from being concerned in the buying of them when imported." The Yearly Meeting referred the petition to its constituent meetings; their answers, sent back in 1730, map out the wide range of attitudes about buying imported slaves that Quakers from various parts of the Delaware Valley held at this time. The Philadelphia Quarterly (see Map 1) reported it had thoroughly debated the subject and decided that the earlier decisions of 1715 and 1716 were sufficient. Bucks could not agree among themselves and left the decision up to the Yearly Meeting. Burlington Friends felt that Quakers should neither import slaves nor buy those brought in, but thought the Society should only advise its members and not censure them. Gloucester-Salem and Shrewsbury quarterly meetings agreed with Chester that

[17] Benjamin Bourne, trans., "Christian and Brotherly Advices Given Forth from Time to Time by the Yearly Meeting in London Alphabetically Digested," MS (London, 1756), 203, FHL; PYM mins., 14-18/7M/1728; Wax, "Quaker Merchants," 157.

[18] Drake, *Quakers and Slavery*, 43; Ralph Sandiford, *A Brief Examination of the Practice of the Times* ... (Philadelphia, 1729); Lay, *All Slave-Keepers*, 21. In his book, Lay discussed the Yearly Meeting's condemnation of Sandiford. At about this time, in 1733, a Nantucket Quaker, Elihu Coleman, received permission from New England Yearly Meeting to publish a paper against slavery. Perhaps he received approval because he avoided denouncing slaveholders outright, but more investigation is needed to compare the situation in New England Yearly Meeting with that of Philadelphia Yearly Meeting. Worrall, *Quakers in the Colonial Northeast*, 158-159.

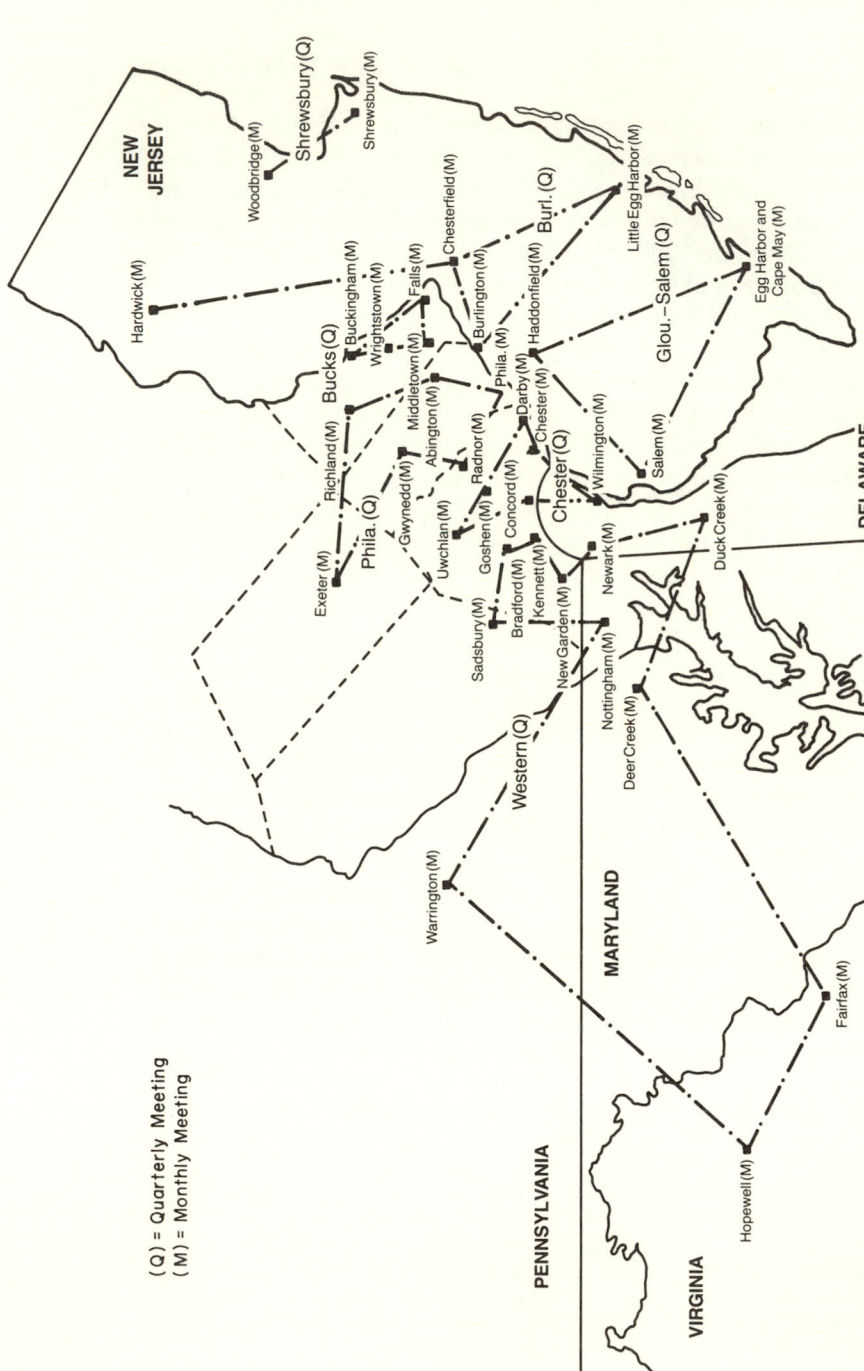

(Q) = Quarterly Meeting
(M) = Monthly Meeting

MAP 1. THE PHILADELPHIA YEARLY MEETING, 1770

Friends should be restricted by discipline from buying imported blacks.[19]

Probing deeper to find out how monthly meetings stood on this issue yields only partial results. Nevertheless, the information we can obtain from meeting reports or by deducing local positions from quarterly meeting decisions indicates which meetings were leaning toward abolitionism at a fairly early date. Only two monthly meetings recorded their decisions on Chester's proposal: Chesterfield Monthly Meeting sent a statement to Burlington Quarterly Meeting rejecting Chester's petition, while Salem Monthly Meeting submitted a favorable report that was echoed by their quarterly meeting.[20] The attitudes of some other local meetings are also clear. Because Friends formulated new policy only after reaching a unified sense of the meeting, the unequivocal stances taken by Chester, Gloucester-Salem, and Shrewsbury quarterly meetings in favor of restricting the purchase of imported blacks suggest that all of their constituent monthly meetings agreed. On the other hand, in Burlington Quarter, Chesterfield's opposition made a decision in favor of the ban impossible; thus we cannot determine exactly what the other monthly meetings thought. This last holds true for most local meetings of Bucks and Philadelphia quarters. Philadelphia Monthly Meeting—given its condemnation of Ralph Sandiford—likely opposed further antislavery reform at this time.

With its constituents far from united on the subject, the Yearly Meeting of 1730 strengthened only slightly its testimony against buying imported slaves. The meeting agreed that Friends should be "very Cautious" of making such purchases, "it being Disagreeable to the Sense of this Meeting," and recommended that monthly meetings admonish and caution any members who engaged in the practice.[21] For the next twenty-three years, this is as far as the Yearly Meeting would go. Not even Benjamin Lay could rouse them from their torpor. At the same meeting in 1738 during which he performed his "bladder of blood" demonstration, several members expressed satisfaction that few Quakers were importing blacks.[22] These "blood"-spattered Friends were content with the then current official policy of the Society and made no further changes until 1753. During the 1730s and early 1740s, though, the central meeting did

---

[19] Chester MM mins. 28/5M/1729; Chester QM mins., 11/6M/1729; PYM mins., 20-24/7M/1729, 19-23/7M/1730.

[20] Chesterfield MM mins., 6/6M/1730; Salem MM mins., 31/6M/1730.

[21] PYM mins., 19-23/7M/1730.

[22] PYM mins., 16-20/7M/1738.

ask quarterly meetings to report whether Friends were adhering to its 1730 decision; and in 1743 it included a question on slave trading in the queries that local meetings answered each year.[23] Several quarterly meetings recorded their answers in the minutes, reporting that a few members had disobeyed the Yearly Meeting's advice. But while a number of Friends clearly violated the Society's ban during this period, monthly meetings did not discipline their members for importing or purchasing imported blacks because the Yearly Meeting had not yet made slave trading a disownable offense.[24]

REFORMERS TAKE CONTROL

The 1750s, however, witnessed a significant change in the policy of Philadelphia Yearly Meeting toward slavery. Early stirrings on the issue came in 1753, when Buckingham Monthly Meeting asked Bucks Quarter what they should do about Friends who bought imported blacks. The Yearly Meeting policy on this, dating back to 1730, was that the monthly meetings should "admonish" slave buyers. The fact that Buckingham raised the question may mean that they wanted to go further and discipline the purchasers of slaves in some way,[25] but the quarterly meeting only echoed the Yearly Meeting's earlier position. "It is the sense of this Meeting," they wrote, "that such who have or may be guilty therein ought to be dealt with in a brotherly and loving manner, as disorderly persons & censured according to the nature of the offense." Bucks did not take the issue to the Yearly Meeting.[26]

The first signal that the Yearly Meeting would alter its direction on slavery was the approval of John Woolman's essay, *Some Considerations on the Keeping of Negroes*. Woolman (1720-1772), who is probably the best-known Quaker abolitionist and has been credited by a number of historians for persuading the Yearly Meeting to prohibit slave owning, was a minister of Burlington Monthly Meeting in West Jersey. He was a successful tailor, shopkeeper, and farmer, but cut back on his business activities in order to avoid the temptations of wealth, and also to devote much of his time to

[23] PYM mins., 20-24/7M/1735, 18-22/7M/1736, 17-21/7M/1737, 16-20/7M/1738, 15-19/7M/1739, 19-23/7M/1741, 18-22/7M/1742, and 17-21/7M/1743.

[24] Chester QM mins., 11/6M/1738 and 8/6M/1743; Gloucester-Salem QM mins., 15/7M/1738; Burlington QM mins., 29/6M/1743; Goshen MM mins., 18/5M/1743.

[25] Buckingham MM mins., 3/6M/1753-3/9M/1753. The minutes do not give the reason for this inquiry.

[26] Bucks QM mins., 30/8M/1753; PYM mins., 15-19/9M/1753.

the ministry. He had written his tract seven years earlier, but knew in 1746 that he could not get permission to publish it from the hostile overseers of the press. As we shall see in the next chapter, the membership of this committee changed significantly by 1753 and so he then submitted it for review. In his 1754 essay, Woolman avoided attacking slaveholders directly and instead entreated Friends to work for the good of all mankind, not their own self-interest. He reminded his readers that blacks are equal to whites in God's eyes.[27]

At the next Yearly Meeting, Friends agreed to publish an anti-slavery tract of their own, *An Epistle of Caution and Advice, Concerning the Buying and Keeping of Slaves*. This paper, which had originated in Philadelphia Monthly Meeting, represented an important shift in the Society's policy.[28] For the first time the Yearly Meeting suggested to its members that slaveholding *itself*, and not just importation, was an un-Christian practice. The letter mourned a recent increase in slave ownership among Friends, and warned members to live according to the Golden Rule and remember that blacks were enslaved through theft and war. The epistle further asked owners to care for their slaves kindly, teach them "the Fear of God," and train them in preparation for freedom, if or when they received it. And it warned masters "to weigh the Cause of detaining them in Bondage," for if they held slaves for personal gain it was quite likely that "the Love of God and the Influence of the Holy Spirit" did not guide them in their daily lives and that their "Hearts [were] not sufficiently redeemed from the World."[29]

In 1755 the Yearly Meeting appointed a committee to rewrite its queries to local meetings. The query concerning slaves now read: "Are Friends clear of importing and buying Negroes and do they use those well which they are possessed of by Inheritance or otherwise endeavouring to train them up in the Principles of the Christian Religion?" The same meeting also directed local meetings to "treat"

---

[27] PYM mins., 15-19/9M/1753; Phillips P. Moulton, ed., *The Journal and Major Essays of John Woolman* (New York, 1971), 44, 198-209.

[28] The authorship of the *Epistle* of 1754 is disputed. Frost shows that Janet Whitney in *John Woolman, American Quaker* (Boston, 1942), had no basis for her claim that Woolman wrote the paper. See J. William Frost's review article, "The Origins of the Quaker Crusade against Slavery: A Review of Recent Literature," *Quaker History* 67 (1978), 49-50. According to the Phila. MM mins., 25/1M/1754, Anthony Benezet laid the proposal to publicize Friends' opposition to slave trading before the meeting, which then appointed a committee to revise it and prepare it for publication.

[29] PYM mins., 14-19/9M/1754.

with, or try to convince that they had acted wrongly, any Friends who imported or bought slaves.[30]

This directive caused problems for the monthly meetings because it did not specify exactly what kind of offenses were included in the prohibition—or what means, if any, should be used to punish offenders. Each time a member bought a slave, his or her meeting was faced with a decision. Most meetings apparently simply talked with the offender or ignored the offense; they recorded no action on the subject. Two monthly meetings, however, asked for and received clarification from their quarterly meetings. In 1756 Middletown Friends asked Bucks Quarterly Meeting whether the ban on buying slaves included all blacks or only those brought from other countries. The quarterly meeting decided the new rule restricted the purchase of all slaves.[31] Another question arose in the following year in Shrewsbury Quarter, when Shrewsbury Monthly Meeting inquired how Friends who imported or bought blacks should be punished. This quarterly meeting decided, without prior approval of the Yearly Meeting, that the monthly meeting had the authority to disown such offenders.[32]

By 1758, it became clear that the Yearly Meeting's decision of 1755 must be reconsidered. Rank-and-file Quakers raised further questions that quarterly meetings could not answer on the basis of the 1755 minute. Woodbridge Monthly Meeting, for instance, wondered in January 1758 whether hiring the labor of slaves for a number of years was prohibited. Shrewsbury Quarter referred this question to the Yearly Meeting.[33] Members of Philadelphia Monthly Meeting, at the same time, asked their quarterly meeting whether they could punish those who bought and sold slaves. This monthly meeting had dealt with several slave purchasers during 1757, and had referred the case of David Clark, who had bought a slave but now promised that he would buy no more and that he would treat his slaves well, to the quarterly meeting.[34] On a somewhat different note, Gwynedd Monthly Meeting, also of Philadelphia Quarter, asked who, if anyone, was blameworthy when one Friend sold a slave to another Friend.[35]

---

[30] PYM mins., 20-26/9M/1755.

[31] Bucks QM mins., 25/11M/1756.

[32] Shrewsbury QM mins., 25/7M/1757.

[33] Shrewsbury QM mins., 30/1M/1758 and 24/4M/1758.

[34] Phila. MM mins., 26/8M/1757 and 25/11M/1757; Phila. QM mins., 6/2M/1758.

[35] Phila. QM mins., 7/8M/1758. The quarterly meeting believed both Friends had done wrong, but referred the question to the Yearly Meeting for its opinion.

In February 1758, Philadelphia Quarterly Meeting appointed a Committee on Negroes, which resolved by August that the Society should take any step within its power to stop the current increase in buying, selling, and keeping slaves. The committee urged the Yearly Meeting to reconsider and elucidate the minute of 1755, "a hope being raised among us, that the Renewing the Consideration thereof in the Yearly Meeting may tend to Strengthen the Exercise in the minds of Friends in general." The quarterly meeting agreed with the committee's report.[36]

Thus the question of slavery once again came before Philadelphia Yearly Meeting. This time it threatened to shake the Society to its roots. Since the outbreak of the Seven Years' War in 1754, the Yearly Meeting had been wrestling with a number of perplexing questions of which the most fundamental was whether Friends should withdraw from the Pennsylvania government. This issue was especially traumatic for the Quakers because they had governed the colony for over seventy years, but they believed that they could not raise the troops and supplies that the English government required and remain faithful to their religious principles. The reality of war in their own province and their forced withdrawal from Pennsylvania government led increasing numbers of Friends to wonder what their place in colonial society should be. Reformers like John Churchman (1705-1775) of Nottingham, Chester County, and John Woolman warned Friends that the war was God's punishment for their worldliness and sin. The Yearly Meeting, in 1755-1757, instituted a number of reforms tightening the discipline on plainness in dress, speech, and personal belongings, taking oaths, participating in government, and marrying outside the Society.[37]

The drive to abolish slave trading and slaveholding in Philadelphia Yearly Meeting was part of this reform movement and was extremely controversial because many Friends owned, or would have liked to own, slaves. John Pemberton (1727-1795), the wealthy Philadelphia reformer, wrote immediately following the 1758 annual gathering, "I am Sure I even dreaded the meeting, least some Debates might arise, that might prove painful."[38] Anthony Benezet believed that the situation within the Society was so tumultuous

[36] Phila. QM mins., 6/2M/1758, 1/5M/1758, and 7/8M/1758.

[37] Frederick B. Tolles, *Meeting House and Counting House: The Quaker Merchants of Colonial Philadelphia 1682-1763* (Chapel Hill, N.C., 1948), 234-243; Jack D. Marietta, *The Reformation of American Quakerism, 1748-1783* (Philadelphia, 1984).

[38] Moulton, ed., *Journal . . . of John Woolman*, 310; John Pemberton to William Reckitt, 2/10M/1758, Reckitt MSS, FHL.

during this period in the late 1750s "that a thoughtful Person might well query. What is Truth? and will find it necessary to recurr to the ancient Standard of Truth in themselves."[39] John Woolman wrote his impressions of the 1758 Yearly Meeting's discussion on slavery in his journal. He observed that at first "though none did openly justify the practice of slavekeeping in general, yet some appeared concerned lest the meeting should go into such measures as might give uneasiness to many brethren, alleging that if Friends patiently continued under the exercise, the Lord in time to come might open a way for the deliverance of these people." Woolman, supported by others he did not name, responded to these conservatives that God, who is just, had heard the cries of oppressed slaves. He continued, "Should we now be sensible of what he requires of us, and through a respect to the private interest of some persons or through a regard to some friendships which do not stand on an immutable foundation, neglect to do our duty in firmness and constancy, still waiting for some extraordinary means to bring about their deliverance, it may be that by terrible things in righteousness God may answer us in this matter." Woolman believed that his side of the argument—which pressed for measures against slavekeeping—eventually prevailed in the meeting. He noted that "many Friends declared that they believed liberty was the Negro's right, to which at length no opposition was made publicly."[40]

In fact, the Friends did move quite forcefully against slave trading in 1758 and even set into motion a campaign against slavery itself. The minutes report that at the end of the discussion, "an unanimous Concern [prevailed] to put a stop to the Increase of the practice of Importing buying selling or keeping Slaves for term of Life or purchasing them for such a Number of Years as manifests, that such purchasers do only in Terms and not in fact avoid the Imputation of being keepers of Slaves." The Yearly Meeting cited the Seven Years' War as a possible divine consequence of Friends keeping slaves, and like abolitionist writers earlier in the century, reminded slave owners to do unto others as they wished others to do unto them.[41]

The formal ruling of the meeting was that monthly meetings should place under discipline Friends who imported, bought, or

[39] Anthony Benezet to Jonas Thompson, 28/8M/1759, Misc. MSS, FHL.

[40] Moulton, ed., *Journal . . . of John Woolman*, 92-93. John Pemberton in the letter to William Reckitt cited above also stated that the meeting ended in concord and "to Very General Satisfaction." Pemberton to Reckitt, 2/10M/1758.

[41] PYM mins., 23-29/9M/1758.

sold slaves. It was left up to each local meeting whether members could serve as executors, guardians, or trustees when their duties would involve buying or selling slaves. The form of discipline now used against slave traders was a kind of partial disownment that meant a Friend could not sit in business meetings, contribute funds, or serve as a leader or representative in the Society. He or she was still considered a member, however. Thus, the meeting did not ban slaveholding itself, nor did it remove slave owners from positions of authority at this time. It did, however, denounce slavery unequivocally and urge Friends to manumit their blacks. Five respected ministers, John Woolman; John Sykes (1682-1771), a farmer of Chesterfield Monthly Meeting who had been active in the Yearly Meeting since 1728; John Scarborough (1704-1769), a farmer of Buckingham Monthly Meeting; John Churchman; and Daniel Stanton (1708-1770), a Philadelphia joiner, were appointed "to visit and treat with all such Friends who have any Slaves" and report to later meetings on their progress.[42]

The decision of 1758 was a major step in the progress of antislavery reform in Philadelphia Yearly Meeting even though it did not ban slavery completely. It provided abolition-minded local meetings with the power to discipline slave traders, and prodded other meetings, which had little interest in ending the institution, to do the same. The central meeting's stand against slavery, made evident to all Friends by the appointment of the five-man visitation committee, established a precedent for later, stronger steps in the 1770s.

[42] Ibid.; Moulton, ed., *Journal . . . of John Woolman*, 308, 310-312; Richard Bauman, *For the Reputation of Truth: Politics, Religion, and Conflict among the Pennsylvania Quakers, 1750-1800* (Baltimore, 1971), 236-239.

· 2 ·

LEADERSHIP AND CONTROL OF
THE YEARLY MEETING

In the period between 1738, when weighty Friends threw Benjamin Lay out of the Yearly Meeting, and 1754, when the Society itself denounced slavery, an important change occurred. Leadership of Philadelphia Yearly Meeting passed from a predominantly conservative, slave-owning oligarchy controlled by Philadelphia and Burlington Friends to a more reform-minded and geographically diverse group. Many Society leaders active before 1750 were slaveholders, explaining to a great extent why the Yearly Meeting repudiated all petitions calling for firm action against members who imported or owned slaves. A considerably smaller percentage of weighty Friends owned slaves by the 1750s; thus John Woolman's tract *Some Considerations* found a much friendlier reception than the arguments of William Southeby and Ralph Sandiford had obtained several decades before. Although we cannot know from the following evidence alone *why* the meeting leaders came to oppose slavery, we can see how direct interest in slavery was present to influence the early leaders' views on the issue, and we can sketch out changes in the power structure of the meeting between the 1730s and 1750s that subsequently facilitated antislavery reform.

Use of the term "Yearly Meeting leader" is problematic because Quakers did not formally recognize the concept of meeting leadership. Ostensibly the entire meeting made decisions communally with God's guidance (or reached a "sense of the meeting") and Friends appointed committees of two or more persons to perform almost all job assignments (such as to write epistles to local meetings, revise the Book of Discipline, and hear appeals of disciplinary cases). Nevertheless, some Friends took a more active role in creating policy than others, and on a practical level dominated the meeting. In this chapter anyone who was assigned to four or more Yearly Meeting committees over the years he was a representative, or who served as an officer (including the clerk, collector of the yearly stock or treasurer, correspondent to London Yearly Meeting, overseer of the press, or representative to the Meeting for Sufferings) is considered a leader. Two hundred and eighty-seven of approximately 1,700 men who represented the quarterly meetings during the years 1681-1780 meet these criteria.

Before examining the data shown in Table 2.1, it is necessary to explain how the evidence was compiled and to consider the limitations of this analysis. In the table, the 287 Yearly Meeting leaders are assigned to one or more periods of about twenty-five years each in which they served. For example, if a man was active in Philadelphia Yearly Meeting from 1725 to 1760, he was counted as a participant during the second, third, and fourth periods. Probate wills and inventories provided information on levels of wealth and slave ownership among the Quaker leaders who died prior to 1775, and tax assessment lists and manumissions fill in data for those still alive at that time.[1] Additional information comes from Darold D. Wax's list of Quakers who imported slaves into Pennsylvania prior to 1767,[2] and most meeting minutes report persons who bought or sold slaves after 1757. The figures for slaveholding are conservative because, with a few exceptions, they do not include any of the leaders who died before 1775 having already sold or manumitted all of their blacks. In the case of Friends still alive in the mid-1770s, there is no surviving evidence if they freed slaves before the monthly meetings started recording manumissions.

A note of caution is thus necessary. The decline in slave ownership among the Yearly Meeting elite after 1730 was probably less dramatic than the data in Table 2.1 show. This is because information on whether or not they owned slaves is available for many Friends only in the 1760s and 1770s, after the Yearly Meeting decided to oppose slavery. Data on slave ownership among leading Quakers who were active before 1730 are more complete because probate records exist for most of these leaders. This means that while we can identify a large proportion of the early slaveholders, we do not know which of the later leaders owned slaves in the 1740s and 1750s but freed or sold them before they would show up in tax lists and meeting records. Nevertheless, we do know that many of these later leaders had antislavery sympathies because they gave up any slaves they owned before the 1760s and 1770s, and because many were leaders of local meetings that opposed slavery and were members of local committees that dealt with slave traders and owners. Though we cannot say, based on this evidence alone, that the Phil-

[1] See Appendix B for information on these sources and how they have been used.

[2] "The Negro Slave Trade in Colonial Pennsylvania" (Ph.D. diss., University of Washington, 1962), 372-373.

adelphia Yearly Meeting leadership of the 1750s opposed slavery because they had no economic interest in the institution, we can pinpoint sources of resistance to abolitionism and chart changes in the balance of power between Friends who were utterly resistant to and those who were favorably inclined toward the Society's drive for antislavery reform.

As Table 2.1 demonstrates, the early leadership of Philadelphia Yearly Meeting was heavily involved in slaveholding. During 1681-1705, 70 percent of those for whom probate records exist, owned slaves, and in the period 1706-1730, about 60 percent still held blacks. The proportion of these weighty Friends who owned slaves then dropped to about one-third in 1731-1753 and to one-tenth in the last period. Table 2.2 shows that slave owners held the same sway over the committee of the press, the men who decided whether or not antislavery writings should be approved for publication. We can see why John Woolman's *Some Considerations* (1754) was the

TABLE 2.1. SLAVE OWNERSHIP AMONG
PHILADELPHIA YEARLY MEETING LEADERS, 1681-1780

	1681-1705	1706-1730	1731-1753	1754-1780
No. for whom evidence exists on slave owning	30	58	76	176
Slave owners	70.0%	58.6%	34.2%	10.2%

SOURCES: PYM mins., 1681-1780; probate records; tax assessment lists

TABLE 2.2. SLAVE OWNERSHIP AMONG
OVERSEERS OF THE PRESS, 1681-1756

	1681-1705	1706-1730	1731-1751	1752-1756
No. for whom evidence exists on slave owning	3	17	9	14
Slave owners	66.7%	76.5%	66.7%	28.6%

SOURCES: PYM mins., 1681-1780; probate records; tax assessment lists

first abolitionist tract to meet their approval. Over two-thirds of the men appointed to this committee during the years 1681-1751 owned slaves. They consistently forbade the publication of antislavery works, including those of William Southeby, John Farmer, Ralph Sandiford, and Benjamin Lay. As late as 1746 the overseers deleted a passage from Thomas Chalkley's journal that described the sight of a dog eating the flesh of a dead black man in Barbados in 1717.[3]

The Yearly Meeting leaders active in the period from 1681 to 1753 were a surprisingly small group and included the major commercial and political powers of Pennsylvania and New Jersey. About three-fourths of the 1681-1730 leaders ranked in the wealthiest 20 percent of surviving inventories and tax assessment lists, and over 50 percent ranked in the top tenth. Of the 1731-1753 group, 68 percent were in the wealthiest 20 percent and almost half in the upper 10 percent.[4] Many of these early leaders also held high governmental posts in their respective colonies. In the first period, 1681-1705, thirty of the thirty-six Yearly Meeting leaders (83 percent) were assemblymen or held other provincial offices. In 1706-1730 this proportion declined, but only to about 64 percent. Of the 1731-1753 Yearly Meeting leaders, 34 percent held high governmental office, while only a modest 11 percent of the 1754-1780 group served in provincial government. Most of this last period followed

---

[3] Some Account of the Life & Travels of Tho: Chalkley, Pt. 2, 53, MS, HSP; PYM mins., 20-24/7M/1746; Thomas E. Drake, *Quakers and Slavery in America* (New Haven, Conn., 1950), 49. George Willauer has found that the Barbados story was only one of many passages stricken from Chalkley's journal before publication. He believes that the overseers did not indicate any special proslavery bias, because they deleted all portions of the author's manuscript that did not deal directly with his spiritual life. George J. Willauer, Jr., "Editorial Practices in Eighteenth-Century Philadelphia: The Journal of Thomas Chalkley in Manuscript and Print," *PMHB* 107 (1983), 217-234.

[4] Wealth probably did not account for the decline in slaveholding among the 1754-1780 leadership, as 69 percent of this group ranked in the upper 20 percent, and 40 percent were in the highest tenth.

Since these data on wealth were obtained from two different sources, probate inventories and tax assessment lists, percentile rankings were assigned in order to make the evidence roughly comparable. Leaders with inventories were included in the percentile in which their gross personal wealth (total inventoried wealth before debts were subtracted but including no real estate) ranked among all Philadelphia inventories of the same decade. Leaders whose wealth was obtained from tax assessment lists were ranked in relationship to others on the same county tax list. Because evidence for most leaders in the earlier periods comes from inventories and data for most later Friends come from tax lists, the decline in average wealth over the century was probably greater, but not significantly greater, than these percentages suggest. See Appendix B for more information on these sources.

the withdrawal of many Quaker leaders from the Pennsylvania government during the Seven Years' War.

For the first seventy years of Pennsylvania history, the same men often ran both the Yearly Meeting and the colony. Some of the earliest leaders bought their land directly from William Penn, and with the proprietor made the first decisions about what shape the government should take and how the colony should develop. Samuel Carpenter (1649-1714), for example, was a merchant and First Purchaser of 5,000 acres who emigrated from Barbados in 1683. He built the first wharf in Philadelphia and invested heavily in mills, lumbering, and land. He served on the Pennsylvania Provincial Council for twenty-one years and was an assemblyman and provincial treasurer. In the Yearly Meeting, he represented Philadelphia Quarter from 1692 to 1711, served on thirty-four committees, and was appointed correspondent to London Yearly Meeting in 1713. At his death he owned at least seven blacks and three white servants who helped run his mill, smithy, and plantation in Bristol, Bucks County.[5] Another weighty Friend was Anthony Morris I (1654-1721), who served as overseer of the press, clerk, and collector of the Yearly Meeting stock. He represented Philadelphia Quarterly Meeting from 1691 to 1721, and served on forty-three committees. Morris was a wealthy brewer and merchant who sat on the Pennsylvania Supreme Court and served in the Assembly. He owned a black slave when he died.[6]

The list of Quaker slaveholders who dominated both the Yearly Meeting and the provincial government is quite impressive. Thomas Lloyd (1640-1694), whom Penn left in charge as president of the Provincial Council when he departed for England in 1684, helped write the Yearly Meeting's epistles to London Yearly Meeting during the 1680s and early 1690s.[7] Nicholas Waln (ca. 1650-1722) was a long-term representative to the Assembly, and Phineas Pemberton (1650-1702), clerk of the meeting, served as Speaker of the

[5] Mary Maples Dunn et al., eds., *The Papers of William Penn* (Philadelphia, 1981-), 2:542; Phila. Co. Wills, Bk. D, No. 1. Data on activities in the Yearly Meeting of Carpenter and other leaders discussed below are from my analysis of the Philadelphia Yearly Meeting minutes, 1681-1780. Information on Pennsylvania officeholding is from *Pennsylvania Archives*, 2d ser. (1880), 9:639-657, 691-818; J. Thomas Scharf and Thompson Westcott, *History of Philadelphia 1609-1884* (Philadelphia, 1884), 2:1557-1578.

[6] Phila. Co. Wills, Bk. D, No. 227; Frederick B. Tolles, *Meeting House and Counting House: The Quaker Merchants of Colonial Philadelphia 1682-1763* (Chapel Hill, N.C., 1948), 43.

[7] Dunn et al., eds., *Papers of William Penn*, 2:555, Phila. Co. Wills, Bk. A, No. 105.

House.[8] James Logan (1674-1751), Penn's secretary and chief representative in Pennsylvania, was an overseer of the press. Isaac Norris I (1671-1735) held a long string of offices in both the Society and Pennsylvania government: he was clerk of the Yearly Meeting from 1711 to 1729 and served as assemblyman, Speaker of the House, and provincial councilor.[9] Israel Pemberton I (d. 1754), who served in the Assembly for twenty years, sat on over fifty Yearly Meeting committees and was an overseer of the press. Other leading Pennsylvania Friends were James Fox, assemblyman for Philadelphia; Edward Shippen, who held a number of government positions; Nicholas Pyle, a Chester County assemblyman; and David Lloyd, the outspoken leader of the anti-Penn faction and chief justice of the Supreme Court. All of these men owned slaves.[10]

Significantly fewer meeting leaders came from New Jersey than from Pennsylvania during the early period (see Table 2.3), but like their colleagues from Pennsylvania, many of the Jerseyans were members of their colony's ruling elite. For example, Samuel Jennings (d. ca. 1708), a Burlington merchant, served as deputy-governor, Speaker of the Assembly, and provincial councilor of West New Jersey. In the Yearly Meeting he was an overseer of the press and collector of the yearly stock, and sat on thirty-one committees. There is no evidence about whether he owned a slave.[11] However, we know that most other Yearly Meeting leaders from New Jersey owned blacks. Thomas Gardner (d. 1712), also of Burlington, was treasurer of West Jersey, Speaker of the Assembly, and a provincial councilor; he owned four slaves when he died. Bartholomew Wyatt (ca. 1670-1727) of Salem County, an assemblyman, had five blacks

[8] Dunn et al., eds., *Papers of William Penn*, 2:532; Phila. Co. Wills, Bk. D, No. 240; Phineas Pemberton to Phebe Pemberton, 2 April 1695, Pemberton Papers, 2:106, HSP.

[9] Phila. Co. Wills, Bk. I, No. 314; Bk. E, No. 412. Albert Cook Myers, ed., *Hannah Logan's Courtship* (Philadelphia, 1904), 9-24, 131; Isaac Sharpless, *Political Leaders of Provincial Pennsylvania* (1919; reprint Freeport, N.Y., 1971), 102-103; Tolles, *Meeting House*, 16.

[10] Phila. Co. Recorded Wills, Bk. K, 143. Phila. Co. Wills, Bk. B, No. 41; Bk. C, No. 241. Bucks Co. Wills, No. 161; No. 409. Chester Co. Wills, No. 52; No. 394. Tolles, *Meeting House*, 15-16.

[11] Dunn et al., eds., *Papers of William Penn*, 2:481. Evidence of New Jersey office-holding for Jennings and other Yearly Meeting leaders discussed below comes from "Tables of the Sittings of the Provincial Assemblies, with the Names of the Members," *Proceedings of the New Jersey Historical Society* 5 (1850), 19-33; Thomas L. Purvis, "The New Jersey Assembly, 1722-1776" (Ph.D. diss., The Johns Hopkins University, 1979), 264-311; Donald L. Kemmerer, *Path to Freedom: The Struggle for Self-Government in Colonial New Jersey, 1703-1776* (Cos Cob, Conn., 1968), 356-365.

TABLE 2.3. DISTRIBUTION OF YEARLY MEETING LEADERS

	1681-1705	1706-1730	1731-1753	1754-1780	Assessments for yearly stock, 1757[a]
Leaders (No.)	36	71	90	202	
% from each Quarterly Meeting:					
Philadelphia	41.7%	31.0%	28.9%	19.8%	32.5%
Chester	13.9	22.5	15.6	26.7	25.0
Bucks	8.3	7.0	13.3	12.4	10.0
Burlington	19.5	22.5	22.2	14.3	17.5
Glou.-Salem	8.3	8.5	10.0	13.4	11.0
Shrewsbury	8.3	8.5	10.0	13.4	4.0
Total	100.0	100.0	100.0	100.0	100.0

SOURCE: PYM mins., 1681-1780
NOTE: "Leaders" include representatives appointed to four or more committees and officers
[a]PYM mins., 23-29/9M/1758

listed in his estate.[12] Jedidiah Allen of Shrewsbury, another member of the Assembly, was a wealthy slave owner, as were Speaker of the Assembly John Kinsey I of Woodbridge, assemblymen Samuel Smith (1672-1718) of Burlington, and Thomas Lambert of Nottingham Township, Burlington County, and provincial councilors Richard Smith I and John Rodman of Burlington.[13]

The sons of several of these leaders from both sides of the Delaware carried on the governing—and slaveholding—traditions of their fathers. Isaac Norris II (1701-1766), member of the Pennsylvania Assembly after 1734 and its Speaker from 1750 to 1764, was a Quaker overseer of the press. Anthony Morris II (d. 1763) was active in Philadelphia city government and an assemblyman; he was treasurer of Philadelphia Yearly Meeting for twenty years and an overseer of the press.[14] Samuel Preston (1665-1743), while not a

[12] Burlington Co. Wills, 349C, 1120-1126C; Salem Co. Wills, 256Q.

[13] N.J. Unrecorded Wills, 11:311; 12:310-318. Middlesex Co. Wills, 933-935L, 1003-1006L. Burlington Co. Wills, 785-787C; 2573-2582C; 4867-4870C, 10681C; 5754-5768C. Myers, ed., *Hannah Logan's Courtship*, 25-26.

[14] Myers, ed., *Hannah Logan's Courtship*, 131; Richard Bauman, *For the Reputation of Truth: Politics, Religion, and Conflict among the Pennsylvania Quakers, 1750-1800* (Baltimore, 1971), 244; Richard Alan Ryerson, "Portrait of a Colonial Oligarchy: The Quaker Elite in the Pennsylvania Assembly, 1729-1776," in *Power and Status: Essays*

son of a Yearly Meeting leader, was the son-in-law of Thomas Lloyd. He served as the central meeting's clerk, correspondent to London, treasurer, and overseer of the press, and was an assemblyman, provincial councilor, and Philadelphia mayor. Richard Hill (d. 1729), another son-in-law of Thomas Lloyd, served on fifty-six Yearly Meeting committees and was correspondent to London and overseer of the press. He was a Pennsylvania Supreme Court justice, Speaker of the Assembly, and provincial councilor.[15] Across the Delaware, Richard Smith II (1699-1751), son of Samuel Smith and nephew of Richard Smith I, sat in the New Jersey Assembly from 1730 until his death. He was treasurer and overseer of the press in the Yearly Meeting.[16]

Most influential of the Yearly Meeting leaders before 1750 was John Kinsey II (1693-1750). Indeed, he managed both the Yearly Meeting and the Pennsylvania Assembly in similar fashion; his death brought change to the way in which both bodies accomplished their work. Kinsey practiced law and served as an assemblyman in New Jersey during the 1720s and early 1730s. He moved to Philadelphia in 1730, and was immediately elected to the Pennsylvania Assembly. He held seats coterminously in the New Jersey and Pennsylvania legislatures during the 1730s. Then in 1739 he became Speaker of the Pennsylvania House, a post he held till his death in 1750, and also served as attorney general and chief justice of the Supreme Court during these years. In addition, he was acting trustee of the Pennsylvania Loan Office, a position that carried with it much patronage and led to scandal after his death when it was discovered he had mishandled more than £3,000. At the same time he held these secular offices, Kinsey was clerk of the Yearly Meeting from 1730 to 1749, correspondent to the London meeting, and overseer of the press.[17]

---

on *Officeholding in the American Colonies*, ed. Bruce Daniels (Middletown, Conn., forthcoming); Wax, "Negro Slave Trade," 373; Phila. Co. Tax List, 1767, Northern Liberties East, MS, Rare Book Room, Van Pelt Library, University of Pennsylvania; Phila. Co. Wills, Bk. N, No. 25.

[15] Phila. Co. Wills, Bk. G, No. 41; Bk. E, No. 128. Tolles, *Meeting House*, 17, 44; *A Collection of Memorials Concerning Divers Deceased Ministers and Other of the People Called Quakers in Pennsylvania, New Jersey, and Parts Adjacent, from Nearly the First Settlement Thereof to the Year 1787* (Philadelphia, 1787), 70-73, 126-127.

[16] Purvis, "New Jersey Assembly," 288; Myers, ed., *Hannah Logan's Courtship*, 24-27; Burlington Co. Wills, 4875-4878C.

[17] Middlesex Co. Wills, 2327-2328L, 2653L; Purvis, "New Jersey Assembly," 264; Ryerson, "Portrait of a Colonial Oligarchy"; Alan Tully, *William Penn's Legacy: Politics and Social Structure in Provincial Pennsylvania, 1726-1755* (Baltimore, 1977), 20-21;

Several historians, notably Frederick Tolles, Alan Tully, and Richard Ryerson, have argued convincingly that these Quaker politicians formed an oligarchy that controlled the Pennsylvania government. These Friends ensured that all legislation conformed with their interpretation of Quaker ideals. For instance, the Pennsylvania government established no militia and authorized no direct military spending before the Seven Years' War. Instead, when the British authorities insisted on Pennsylvania's support for various wars, Friends reached a compromise by appropriating funds "for the King's use."[18] The Assembly proceedings throughout the colonial period resembled a Quaker meeting: the minutes record very few votes on legislation, debates were closed to outsiders and often consisted of periods of silence, and when discussion was over the Speaker sometimes declared "the sense of the House" instead of asking for a vote.[19] William Penn boasted in April 1683 that "the general assembly about a month since passed 83 laws, & all but 3 & those trivial without any nay: —the living word in testimony & prayer opening & closing our assemblies in a most heavenly manner, like to our general Meetings."[20] An anonymous observer visiting the House about ninety years later on 21 July 1774, found the scene substantially unchanged. He wrote, "there was not a speech made the whole time, whether their silence proceeded from their modesty or from their inability to speak I know not."[21]

Since we know that many of the weighty Friends who dominated both the Assembly and the Yearly Meeting owned slaves, and suspect that at least some of the others for whom there is no evidence (such as John Kinsey) did as well, it should not come as a surprise to find that the Pennsylvania legislature passed a series of laws establishing the legal basis for slavery during the early eighteenth century. Together these statutes created a slave code that was not as harsh as those of other colonies but was perhaps more stringent than one would expect in the Quaker province. For over a decade after the province's founding, slavery was not specifically sanctioned in Pennsylvania law; Pennsylvanians simply adopted the customs

---

Edwin B. Bronner, "The Disgrace of John Kinsey, Quaker Politician, 1739-1750," *PMHB* 75 (1951), 400-415. Kinsey's will and inventory, which might have provided information on whether or not he owned slaves, have not been found.

[18] Tolles, *Meeting House*, 17-28.

[19] Tully, *William Penn's Legacy*, 95.

[20] Actually the March-April 1683 Assembly rejected at least six laws in their original form. Dunn et al., eds., *Papers of William Penn*, 2:376-377.

[21] Quoted in Ryerson, "Portrait of a Colonial Oligarchy."

and rights associated with slave ownership in other colonies. In a law passed in 1700, however, the assemblymen formally recognized differences between the terms of slaves, who served for life, and servants, who served for a specified number of years; and in 1705 they set up separate courts for blacks.[22] About twenty years later, the Assembly went further and established a code that not only tightened restrictions on slaves but limited the freedom of free blacks as well. The law banned intermarriage between whites and blacks, required a £30 surety bond for manumission, empowered justices to bind out free black children with or without their parents' permission (boys until they reached age twenty-four and girls until they were twenty-one), and placed restrictions on the liberty of all blacks to travel, drink liquor, and carry on trade.[23] The first two decades of the eighteenth century were a period of quite high importation of Africans and West Indian blacks into Pennsylvania, and the Assembly established this code in an effort to control the relatively large Afro-American population.[24]

In New Jersey, Quakers had less influence in the Assembly than in Pennsylvania, but still they formed a sturdy bloc. Thomas L. Purvis finds that about one-third of the assemblymen who served between 1722 and 1776 were Quaker: most of these men represented West Jersey, but some came from Middlesex and Monmouth counties as well. From 1727 until 1754 at least ten, and usually eleven or twelve, of the Assembly's twenty-four members were Friends. Further, 40 percent of the men who performed the largest share of committee work in the Assembly were Quakers. As in the case of Massachusetts, Pennsylvania, and Virginia legislators, the Burlington Friends achieved high positions because they lived near the seat of power. The New Jersey Assembly alternated its meeting place between Burlington and Perth Amboy, and most of its leaders

[22] William M. Wiecek, "The Statutory Law of Slavery and Race in the Thirteen Mainland Colonies of British America," *WMQ*, 3d ser., 34 (1977), 258-280. Before 1700 the Assembly passed only one law concerning blacks—the 1697 statute prescribing punishment for blacks committing rape and other capital offenses. Gail McKnight Beckman, comp., *The Statutes at Large of Pennsylvania in the Time of William Penn* (New York, 1976), 34, 225; Edward Raymond Turner, *Slavery in Pennsylvania* (Baltimore, 1911), 17-23; "An Act for the Better Regulation of Servants in This Province and Territories" (1700), and "An Act for the Trial of Negroes" (1706), James T. Mitchell and Henry Flanders, comps., *The Statutes at Large of Pennsylvania from 1682 to 1801* (Harrisburg, 1896-1915), 2:54-56, 233-236.

[23] "An Act for the Better Regulating of Negroes in This Province" (1726), *Statutes at Large*, 4:59-64.

[24] See Chapter 3.

lived in Burlington and Middlesex counties. Among the Philadelphia Yearly Meeting leaders who served in the first rank of the New Jersey Assembly were John Kinsey I and II, Thomas Lambert, and Richard Smith II.[25]

Since Quakers did not dominate the New Jersey legislature during the first half of the eighteenth century in the same way Pennsylvania Friends controlled their state house, it is difficult to evaluate their role in devising New Jersey's legal code on slavery. There is no record that Friends (or anyone else) petitioned the Assembly for an end to the slave trade between the years 1721 and 1761, and apparently no motion was made for general emancipation before the 1770s.[26] As in Pennsylvania, slavery was legal in New Jersey from the earliest years. The Concessions of 1664 of Lord Berkeley and Sir George Carteret, the colony's first constitution, mentioned slaves as possible members of a settler's household.[27] At first, laws governing servants and apprentices applied to slaves as well, but gradually New Jersey legislators established the separate legal status of blacks. In 1714 they passed "An Act for Regulating of Slaves" that served as the colony's slave code before the Revolution. This law prohibited black, Indian, and mulatto slaves from traveling without their masters' permission, established special procedures for trying slaves accused of capital crimes (murder, rape, arson, and mutilation), set penalties for lesser crimes such as theft and attempted rape, and forbade whites from trading with slaves or entertaining them in their homes without the master's permission. The act further prohibited freed blacks from owning real estate, and required a £200 bond for manumission.[28] The same Assembly passed a duty of £10 on each slave imported for sale. This law expired after seven years

---

[25] Purvis, "New Jersey Assembly," 22-25, 32-35, 313-315.

[26] I am indebted to Thomas Purvis for this information.

[27] Aaron Leaming and Jacob Spicer, eds., *The Grants, Concessions, and Original Constitutions of the Province of New Jersey* . . . , 2d ed. (Philadelphia, 1881), 20-23. Some historians have believed, as did the eminent Rotterdam Quaker Benjamin Furly, that the West New Jersey Concessions (1676) forbade slavery. However, the statement "that all and every person and persons Inhabiting the said Province shall as farr as in us lies be free from oppression and slavery" was part of a section mandating open trials and was intended to protect whites only. Dunn et al., eds., *Papers of William Penn*, 1:399, 501; Jean R. Soderlund et al., eds., *William Penn and the Founding of Pennsylvania, 1680-1684: A Documentary History* (Philadelphia, 1983), 134-140; Henry Scofield Cooley, *A Study of Slavery in New Jersey* (Baltimore, 1896), 10.

[28] Cooley, *Slavery in New Jersey*, 11; Bernard Bush, comp., *Laws of the Royal Colony of New Jersey, 1703-1745, New Jersey Archives*, 3d ser., 2 (Trenton, 1977), 136-140; Wiecek, "Statutory Law," 258-280.

and was not replaced until the 1760s. During the period between 1722 and 1761 apparently little effort was made to change the New Jersey laws on slavery or the slave trade. Records of only two Assembly actions on the subject survive from the period before 1761. In 1739 and 1744 the Assembly passed bills to impose duties on imported slaves; most of the Quaker members of each session supported passage of the duty. The Provincial Council rejected both bills, however, and so they did not become law.[29]

In short, the leaders of Philadelphia Yearly Meeting before 1750 belonged to the highest governmental and socioeconomic circles of Pennsylvania and New Jersey. While participation in the Society was not restricted entirely to a wealthy, slave-owning oligarchy during the early eighteenth century, such men as Samuel Carpenter, Isaac Norris I, and John Kinsey II did have control. Relatively few men of modest means served on as many as four Yearly Meeting committees, even fewer held meeting offices, and most of the less affluent Friends who qualified for Yearly Meeting leadership played secondary roles. For example, Nicholas Fairlamb, John Lee, and Ephraim Jackson of Chester County, Hugh Roberts I of Philadelphia County, and Samuel Bunting and Thomas Scattergood of Burlington County, were among the few Yearly Meeting activists before 1750 whose inventoried estates totaled less than £300. None of these men was appointed to more than eight committees during his lifetime and none held a Yearly Meeting office.[30]

THE sharp drop in slaveholding among all Yearly Meeting leaders after 1731 and among overseers of the press appointed after 1751 (Tables 2.1, 2.2) suggests that many slave owners died or were removed from the meeting leadership by 1750 and were replaced by Friends who either never owned slaves or who became convinced that slavery was wrong by the 1760s. This in fact occurred. Table 2.4 shows that of the thirteen leading Quakers whose careers ended in the Yearly Meeting between 1742 and 1753 and for whom we have evidence concerning slave ownership, ten, or 77 percent, owned slaves. In contrast, of the fifty weighty Friends whose careers began between 1746 and 1755, including John Woolman, Anthony

[29] "An Act for Laying a Duty on Negro, Indian and Mullatto Slaves Imported and Brought into This Province" (1714), in Bush, comp., *Laws*, 163-164; Cooley, *Slavery in New Jersey*, 14-16; Thomas Purvis's analysis of roll call votes for 20 January 1739, and 15 October 1744.

[30] Chester Co. Wills, No. 155; No. 241; No. 485. Phila. Co. Wills, Bk. B, No. 99. Burlington Co. Wills, 1157-1160C; 3753-3758C.

TABLE 2.4. SLAVE OWNERSHIP AMONG
TURNOVER GROUPS OF YEARLY MEETING LEADERS,
1742-1755

	No. for whom evidence exists on slave owning	Slave owners
Leaders with careers *ending* 1742-1753	13	76.9%
Leaders with careers *beginning* 1746-1755	50	8.0
Leaders *continuing* from before 1746 and ending after 1753	40	20.0

SOURCES: PYM mins., 1681-1780; probate records; tax assessment lists

Benezet, and John and James Pemberton, only four (8 percent) owned slaves by the 1760s and 1770s when the evidence for most leaders in this cohort is first available. And of these four slave owners, two—William Logan and Samuel Preston Moore—either left by their own choice or were forced out of the Yearly Meeting leadership by 1756.[31] As for the overseers of the press, eight of the fourteen overseers active during the 1740s died or left the meeting before 1752. Of these eight, all six for whom we have evidence owned slaves. In contrast, only two of the six new appointees to the press committee in 1752 owned slaves by the 1760s and 1770s. The appointment of reformers Anthony Benezet and John Smith (1722-1771), of Burlington and Philadelphia, certainly changed the complexion of this committee.

While the turnover in the Yearly Meeting leadership around 1750 was considerable, antislavery reform was not solely the accomplishment of a cadre of new men. Rather, the group who entered the meeting for the first time around 1750 allied with already well-established non-slaveholders who had served under the old pro-slavery regime. Thus, of the forty continuing leaders for whom there

[31] Neither Logan nor Moore participated in the Yearly Meeting after 1756; according to the Manumission Book of the Three Philadelphia Monthly Meetings 1772-1796, Arch Street Meeting House, Philadelphia [Phila. MM mans.], both still owned slaves in 1776. The case of Logan provides an example of how the issue of slavery divided families as well as meetings. Logan's brother-in-law, John Smith, was a friend of John Woolman and an ardent abolitionist.

is evidence (Table 2.4), who began their Yearly Meeting careers before 1746 and continued after 1753, only eight, or 20 percent, owned slaves. Of the six overseers of the press who were appointed before 1752 and continued to serve in 1754, just two held blacks at that time.[32] Some of the men who took antislavery stances earlier than most Friends and who began serving in the Yearly Meeting before 1746 included Daniel Stanton of Philadelphia, John Sykes of Chesterfield, and John Scarborough of Buckingham, all of whom served with John Woolman on the 1758 committee to visit slave owners. Other abolitionists were Joseph Wardell II and Joseph Parker II of Shrewsbury, and David Ferris of Wilmington, who all came from those monthly meetings that most insistently opposed slavery in the 1750s and early 1760s. Both in the Yearly Meeting as a whole and among the overseers of the press, then, significantly fewer of the cohort to which Woolman and Benezet belonged owned slaves than the group they replaced; but these new men joined more experienced leaders continuing in the Yearly Meeting and in the committee of the press who were also much less likely to own unfree black labor than the weighty Friends who died or who left positions of power around mid-century.

The actions of the committee appointed to consider the *Epistle* of 1754 further illuminate the sources of opposition to and support for antislavery reform among Quaker leaders in the Delaware Valley. On 17 September 1754, the Yearly Meeting asked fourteen representatives to decide whether *An Epistle of Caution and Advice* should be approved for publication. Five, or 38 percent, of the original thirteen appointees for whom we have evidence owned slaves, and almost four-fifths (79 percent) had started their Yearly Meeting careers prior to 1746. Apparently a lively debate took place during the committee's deliberations over the next twenty-four hours, for when they recommended the next day that the tract be published, the committee membership had significantly changed. Seven of the original members failed to sign the report, including four of the five slave-owning appointees. None of the five men who took their places owned blacks by the 1760s and 1770s, and so only one of the eleven signers for whom we have evidence held slaves. It should be noted that the altered composition of the 1754 committee did not signify a takeover by new leaders, as nine of the twelve signers had begun their careers before 1746. Thus, while

[32] Israel Pemberton I had earlier offered freedom to his wife's black woman, so I did not count him as a slave owner in 1754. Phila. Co. Recorded Wills, Bk. K, 143.

the *Epistle* of 1754 was approved only when most of the die-hard slave owners left the committee, this landmark decision to oppose slaveholding was made largely by men who had been active in the Yearly Meeting before 1746.[33]

It is clear from this evidence, then, that antislavery ideals were gaining substantial support in the Yearly Meeting already between 1731 and 1753, although throughout that period the weighty Friends who continued to own slaves effectively discouraged any changes in the discipline. Even among the slave owners, however, there was a glimmer of abolitionist sentiment as an increased number freed their slaves in their wills. Of the eighteen Yearly Meeting leaders who died between 1681 and 1730 owning slaves, none freed all of his slaves, and only one, Samuel Smith I of Burlington, provided for the liberty of one of his black workers after an additional sixteen years of service. This pattern changed in the period 1731-1754, as five (or almost 30 percent) of the seventeen leaders who owned slaves at death freed all of their slaves, and one more, Thomas Marriott of Bucks County, freed one of his six bondsmen. These emancipators, who included Samuel Preston and Isaac Norris I of Philadelphia Quarter, and Richard Smith II and Jonathan Wright of Burlington Quarter, were convinced prior to their deaths that slavery was wrong, even if they waited until they died to give up their slaves. Israel Pemberton I, who had offered freedom to his wife's black woman years earlier only to have the slave refuse, freed the woman in his will and provided for her support.[34]

In summary, Philadelphia Yearly Meeting embraced the belief that slaveholding was sinful in 1753-1754, when the overseers of the press approved Woolman's *Some Considerations* for publication and the Yearly Meeting issued its own essay against the practice. At this point, antislavery proponents achieved a sense of the meeting, but did so only after most proslavery leaders died or left the meeting.

[33] Changes in the level of slaveholding between these two committees who considered so differently the *Epistle* of 1754, or between the groups who were overseers of the press before and after 1752 (as discussed above), cannot be attributed to differences in wealth. Over 60 percent of both 1754 committees (for the members for whom evidence exists) ranked in the wealthiest 20 percent, and four of the five new men who were not originally appointed but who signed the committee's report ranked in the top 20 percent. As for the overseers of the press, a higher percentage of 1752 committee members (66.7 percent) ranked in the wealthiest *10 percent* than did overseers of the 1730-1743 cohort who died before 1752 (60 percent).

[34] Burlington Co. Wills, 785-787C; 4875-4878C; 3557-3572C. Phila. Co. Wills, Bk. E, No. 412; Bk. G, No. 41. Phila. Co. Recorded Wills, Bk. K, 143. Bucks Co. Wills, No. 570.

Until 1753, at least one-third of the Yearly Meeting elite owned slaves; these men forestalled any move to ban slave trading or slaveholding. Over two-thirds of the overseers of the press who served between 1681 and 1751 owned blacks. These slaveholding Friends—among the most influential in the Yearly Meeting and in Pennsylvania and New Jersey government as well—simply could not agree that Friends should be banned from holding slaves. When these conservatives passed from the scene by the early 1750s, antislavery reformers made their move. Publication of the *Epistle* in 1754 and the ban on slave trading of 1758 were the work of young reformers like Woolman and Benezet who allied with more experienced leaders who had been fighting slavery with varied success in their local meetings for a long time. Philadelphia Yearly Meeting and its constituent meetings had been divided over slavery for many years. The Society's position changed as abolitionists silenced objections from recalcitrant slave owners and swayed the balance of opinion toward antislavery reform.

To begin to understand how abolitionism grew in Philadelphia Yearly Meeting we must look beyond the combined figures for all Yearly Meeting leaders and compare the frequency of slaveholding among weighty representatives from the six quarterly meetings (seven after 1758 when Chester Quarterly Meeting divided into Chester and Western quarterly meetings). We already know from Chapter 1 that as early as 1730 Delaware Valley Friends were split over the question of whether members should buy imported slaves. Table 2.5 illustrates one source of the disagreement: there were wide differences in the percentage who owned slaves among the

TABLE 2.5. SLAVE OWNERSHIP AMONG
REPRESENTATIVES TO THE YEARLY MEETING, 1681-1780

Quarterly Meeting	1681-1705	1706-1730	1731-1753	1754-1780
Philadelphia	81.8%	88.9%	64.0%	17.9%
Chester	40.0	26.7	18.2	5.0
Bucks	100.0	50.0	9.1	4.3
Burlington	40.0	53.8	29.4	10.7
Glou.-Salem	66.7	75.0	28.6	8.3
Shrewsbury	100.0	50.0	0.0	13.6

SOURCES: PYM mins., 1681-1780; probate records; tax assessment lists

leading delegates of the various quarterly meetings. These distinctions conform quite well to what we already know about the local meetings' positions on slavery.

In the first period from the 1680s to 1705, when antislavery writers made little headway in Philadelphia Yearly Meeting and no local meeting opposed slavery, two-thirds or more of the leading representatives from four of the six quarterly meetings owned slaves. The level of slave ownership was lower in Chester and Burlington quarters; but even among Yearly Meeting leaders from Chester during this early period, slaveholding was at the highest point it would reach for the entire century.

During the next era, 1706-1730, slave ownership actually rose among Philadelphia, Burlington, and Gloucester-Salem leaders, while it fell in Chester, Bucks, and Shrewsbury. The fact that a small and falling percentage of Yearly Meeting leaders from Chester owned blacks certainly helps explain why representatives from that quarter so forcefully advocated a ban on buying imported slaves in 1711-1716 and 1729-1730. Between the periods 1706-1730 and 1731-1753, however, ownership of blacks among the Chester leaders then declined more slowly than among weighty delegates from every other quarter except Philadelphia. Meanwhile, under the influence of several eminent slaveholders, Chester Friends began to take a less forward stance against slavery in the 1740s and 1750s, and—as we will see in Chapter 4—Chester and Western quarterly meetings included monthly meetings with quite varied views on slavery as late as the 1770s. On the other hand, the rather dramatic decline of slave ownership among Shrewsbury's leading delegates from 1681-1705 when all for whom there is evidence owned slaves, to 1731-1753 when none of the five representatives was a slave owner, gives some indication of why Shrewsbury Quarterly Meeting supported Chester's petition in 1730 and also actively pushed for antislavery reform in the 1750s.[35]

Representatives from Philadelphia and Burlington quarters were slower to give up slavery than their colleagues from Shrewsbury, but the percentage of Yearly Meeting leaders from Burlington who

[35] The increase in slave ownership among Shrewsbury leaders in the last period does not actually represent regression among that group. Two slave owners from Shrewsbury Quarterly Meeting who had leadership positions during the last period were Solomon Hunt and William Jackson, who were relatively unimportant leaders in the Yearly Meeting and who were not sent to represent the Quarterly Meeting after 1766. The third slaveholder was William Smith who freed his slaves in 1774, and represented the quarter only after that date.

owned slaves did drop substantially in 1731-1753. The proportion in Philadelphia remained very high—at 64 percent—in 1731-1753; and, in fact, representatives from that quarter were quite certainly the primary source of resistance to antislavery during that period. Most of the overseers of the press and other officers of the Yearly Meeting were members of Philadelphia Quarter. The proportion of leading delegates from both Philadelphia and Burlington who owned slaves then declined in 1754-1780 to levels that were the same as, or only slightly higher than, the other quarters. The development of abolitionist sentiment among Yearly Meeting leaders from the city coincided with the emergence of opposition to slavery by 1753 among the membership of Philadelphia Monthly and Quarterly meetings. Most Yearly Meeting leaders from Burlington Quarter in 1754-1780, in contrast, appear to have accepted abolitionism somewhat *before* their fellow members of Burlington and Chesterfield monthly meetings. While Burlington delegates like John Woolman and John and Anthony Sykes actively opposed slavery in the central meeting, they were not so successful in convincing weighty members at home that the institution was wrong. As we will see below, Burlington Monthly Meeting failed to discipline purchasers of slaves in a consistent manner until after 1765, and Chesterfield refused to condemn slave traders until the mid-1770s.[36]

A shift in the power structure of the Yearly Meeting in the 1750s facilitated the move toward antislavery reform. With the death of John Kinsey, leadership opportunities opened up significantly and many more men from outside Philadelphia and Burlington joined the Yearly Meeting elite. Kinsey's death seems pivotal because a similar change occurred in the Pennsylvania Assembly at the same time.[37] In his position as clerk of the Yearly Meeting from 1730 to 1749, as in his office as Speaker of the House from 1739 to 1750, Kinsey apparently restricted leadership to a relatively tight group of men. Under his guidance, the Yearly Meeting appointed few committees (after all one of the functions of committees was to consider new disciplinary policies, and the leaders of the 1730s and 1740s had little interest in making new restrictions), and most of the officers came from Philadelphia and Burlington.[38] Traditionally,

[36] Bucks and Gloucester-Salem quarterly meetings are not included in this discussion because my survey of meeting records revealed that they neither initiated nor resisted antislavery reform on their own, but rather generally conformed to Yearly Meeting decisions.

[37] Ryerson, "Portrait of a Colonial Oligarchy."

[38] A smaller percentage of the total number of representatives to the Yearly Meeting

since 1681, Philadelphia Friends had always held over three-fifths of the offices, while no officers came from Gloucester-Salem and Shrewsbury quarters (see Table 2.6). Burlington was even with Chester and Bucks in the earliest period, but moved substantially ahead in 1706-1730. During the approximate time of Kinsey's regime, 1731-1753, Philadelphia and Burlington Friends held 94.2 percent of the Yearly Meeting offices. The city Friends controlled these offices for a number of practical reasons. With few appointed committees, these clerks, treasurers, overseers of the press, and correspondents to London Yearly Meeting executed most of the meeting's business. Together they formed a kind of executive board that supervised book publication, collected funds, and took care of the Society's correspondence during the large part of the year that the Yearly Meeting was not in session. Overseers of the press had to meet quite frequently, so it was helpful if they lived close together.[39]

TABLE 2.6. DISTRIBUTION OF YEARLY MEETING OFFICERS

	1681-1705	1706-1730	1731-1753	1754-1780
Officers (No.)	16	32	35	28
% from each Quarterly Meeting:				
Philadelphia	62.5%	62.5%	71.4%	67.9%
Chester	12.5	12.5	2.9	14.3
Bucks	12.5	3.1	2.9	3.5
Burlington	12.5	21.9	22.8	14.3
Glou.-Salem	0	0	0	0
Shrewsbury	0	0	0	0
Total	100.0	100.0	100.0	100.0

SOURCE: PYM mins., 1681-1780
NOTE: Officers include clerks, treasurers, overseers of the press, correspondents to London Yearly Meeting, and representatives to the Meeting for Sufferings

rose to the highest level of leadership during the approximate period of Kinsey's tenure, from 1731 to 1753, than during the time before or after his clerkship. In the first, second, and fourth periods shown in Table 2.1, the number of men who served as officers or were appointed to four or more committees consistently equaled 21 percent of all representatives active during those years. In the third period, 1731-1753, the percentage dipped to about 18 percent.

[39] Philadelphia legislators also held a disproportionate share of leadership positions in the Pennsylvania Assembly throughout the period from 1732 until 1769. Ryerson, "Portrait of a Colonial Oligarchy"; Tully, *William Penn's Legacy*, 95-96.

The 1750s brought considerable change to the power structure of the Yearly Meeting. Philadelphia continued to hold the largest portion of the offices (as the members of the new executive committee formed in 1757, the Meeting for Sufferings, was composed almost entirely of city Friends), and Gloucester-Salem and Shrewsbury still had none, but Chester was able to pull some offices away from Burlington. More importantly, committee activity increased dramatically. The Yearly Meeting appointed committees to consider each new reform proposal, dealt with an increased number of disciplinary cases, and sent groups of Friends to supervise local meetings. This opened up many new leadership positions to Friends from throughout the Delaware Valley, as the Yearly Meeting scrupulously placed delegates from every quarter on each committee. Thus, in 1754-1780, the distribution of leadership among the quarterly meetings was much more even than it had been before (see Table 2.3).[40] The greatest loser in the Yearly Meeting power shifts of the 1750s was Burlington, which dropped from its elevated status to become a coequal of the rural meetings. In 1760, the central body stripped the West Jersey quarter of its last special honor in the Society of Friends, when it decided that it would no longer meet in Burlington every other year.[41]

IDENTIFICATION of the most active participants in Philadelphia Yearly Meeting and investigation of their personal involvements in slavery begins to shed some additional light on the development of abolitionism among Quakers of the Delaware Valley. It is now clear that opposition to slavery in the Yearly Meeting could be stifled prior to 1753 because many weighty Friends, including a large percentage of the overseers of the press, were slave owners; they

[40] The decline in the percentage of leading representatives from Philadelphia and Burlington was *not* compensated for by an increase in the average number of committee assignments given to their leading delegates. On the contrary, the average number of committee assignments per leader from the various quarterly meetings was more even in 1754-1780 than at any other time.

[41] PYM mins., 27/9M-2/10M/1760. Kenneth Carroll also found considerable differences on the issue of slavery between representatives to Maryland Yearly Meeting from the Eastern and Western Shores. Indeed, the Autumn 1759 session of the Yearly Meeting held at Third Haven (where Eastern Shore Friends were heavily represented) passed a rule against slave trading, which was rescinded by the subsequent meeting at West River (where a large majority of the representatives were Western Shore Quakers). Carroll attributed the Eastern Shore movement against slavery to the conversion from tobacco to wheat as their major crop. "Maryland Quakers and Slavery," *Quaker History* 72 (1983), 29-33.

primarily represented Philadelphia and Burlington quarterly meetings. Antislavery gained ascendancy in the 1750s only after the majority of Quaker leaders who owned slaves either died or left the meeting. Acceptance of abolitionism by the members of Philadelphia Monthly Meeting signaled the transition of power among influential city Friends. At last new leaders who did not own slaves rose to join longtime opponents of slavery and together they gained control of this crucial monthly meeting and the quarterly it dominated. At the same time an adjustment of power among the rural quarterly meetings left Burlington, ironically a bastion of slave owning in spite of the role of Woolman, with considerably less influence in the central meeting than it had had earlier. Both changes were necessary if the Yearly Meeting was to adopt a stance against slavery, and the timing of Philadelphia Yearly Meeting's action in the 1750s was determined largely because these alterations in power took place at that time.

Nevertheless, several important questions about what tipped the balance to antislavery reform remain unanswered. Most fundamental is the riddle of whether the decline of slave ownership among the Quaker elite resulted from socioeconomic considerations or whether the drop in the proportion of slaveholders in the Yearly Meeting occurred because religious concerns both induced leaders to avoid slaveholding by the 1750s—in spite of its continuing usefulness in their daily lives—and led to the exclusion from power of potentially weighty Friends who refused to give up their slaves. Although the ownership of slaves by at least one-third of the meeting leaders explains why the Yearly Meeting could not reach a sense of the meeting against slavery prior to 1753, the correlation between the decline in slaveholding and the rise of antislavery sentiment does not by itself demonstrate that Friends came to oppose slavery because they had little, perhaps less and less, personal interest in black labor. Later Quaker leaders may well have avoided slavery for reasons of conscience at considerable cost to their own worldly interests. It is therefore necessary to study in subsequent chapters the role slavery played in the economic lives of Friends in Pennsylvania and New Jersey. Did the "peculiar institution" become less tempting to them over the eighteenth century because other forms of additional labor were increasingly available, or because their economic activities changed, or because the size of their farms declined? Perhaps divergent policies toward slavery of several monthly meetings can be accounted for by varying local circumstances that influenced the relative importance of slavery to Friends in different socioeconomic contexts within the Delaware Valley.

The other significant issue left unresolved in this examination of the changing nature of Quaker leadership concerns whether the Yearly Meeting leaders had the support of rank-and-file Friends when they promulgated the new position against slavery. Had a consensus in favor of antislavery evolved among most Quakers by 1753, or did a new Yearly Meeting "oligarchy" make the decision on its own? Similarities and differences that can be observed between the actions of Yearly Meeting representatives from various quarterly meetings and the policies of their local meetings suggest that in the 1750s delegates from Philadelphia and Shrewsbury had the backing of their meetings for antislavery reform, while representatives from Burlington, and perhaps Chester, did not. In sum, closer study of the development of abolitionism in selected local meetings is needed to illuminate further the decisions more ordinary Quakers made on the issue of slavery and how their positions originated in their lives both as settlers of the Delaware Valley and as members of the Society of Friends.

· 3 ·

SLAVERY: TEMPTATION AND CHALLENGE

When James Claypoole, the wealthy Quaker merchant, prepared to move to Philadelphia from London in 1682, he asked his brother Edward in Barbados to send him two black laborers and a black boy and girl to serve in his house. Claypoole also planned to engage a number of English servants to work alongside the slaves in building his house, planting his crops, and doing carpentry, brickwork, and general labor. Probably, like his friend William Penn, Claypoole considered the purchase of blacks attractive because they could be held for life. The only concern he expressed to his brother was that they be "plyable and good natured: and ingenious;" he wanted to avoid "bad negroes" because his family included three young children.[1]

Claypoole was not an exception among the wealthy Quakers who founded and governed early Pennsylvania and New Jersey. As we saw in Chapter 2, most of the Quakers who controlled Philadelphia Yearly Meeting before 1730 brought black slaves from the West Indies and Africa to serve in their homes, shops, and fields. It was for this reason—that many Friends acquired blacks without thinking much about the inherent contradiction between slave ownership and their religious beliefs, and then thought they could not afford to give up their slaves when reforming Quakers pointed out the inconsistency—that slavery became such a controversial issue within the Yearly Meeting. The slaveholders had invested sizable sums to buy their bondsmen and bondswomen, or had received them as a large proportion of their inheritances. They had taken time to train them in specific jobs, and felt they needed their labor. The success of Quaker antislavery reformers in convincing masters to free their slaves varied considerably against this background, as members living in some parts of the Delaware Valley and those pursuing certain occupations manumitted their blacks much less readily than others.

Slavery played a substantial role in the economy of colonial Pennsylvania and New Jersey. While raising wheat and livestock required

[1] James Claypoole to Edward Claypoole, 23 September 1682, published in Jean R. Soderlund et al., eds., *William Penn and the Founding of Pennsylvania, 1680-1684: A Documentary History* (Philadelphia, 1983), 179-181; William Penn to James Harrison, 25 October 1685, published in Marianne S. Wokeck et al., eds., *The Papers of William Penn* (Philadelphia, forthcoming), 3: doc. 13.

significantly less labor than the sugar, rice, and tobacco crops produced in the West Indies, South Carolina, and the Chesapeake, middle colonists did often turn to slaves when they needed additional workers. The difference between the Delaware Valley and the plantation areas to the south was that in the latter, blacks quickly dominated the work force. In Barbados, for example, planters at first used white servants in the fields, but as production increased and the demand for labor dwarfed the supply of English and Irish workers, the sugar producers bought Africans. By 1660, only about twenty years after the Barbados planters moved into sugar, the labor force was almost entirely black. This same changeover occurred in the Chesapeake by 1700, as tobacco growers turned to Africans to fill their expanding need for labor.[2]

In Philadelphia and its surrounding rural areas, the work force remained predominantly white. For the majority of middle colonists, their own labor and that of their family and perhaps an indentured servant or two from England, Ireland, or Germany, filled their labor needs. Nevertheless, slavery played an active role in the region's economy as one form of labor available to producers. Merchants, urban craftsmen, and farmers who owned mills or carried on large operations had the year-round long-term demand for additional labor that black bondage could satisfy. And when white workers were scarce, middle colonists often turned to blacks. The main differences between mid-Atlantic slavery and the institution in the South were that few producers in the Delaware Valley required more than three or four servants or slaves, and white workers in Pennsylvania and New Jersey continued to do jobs like those filled by blacks.

THE first part of this chapter examines the role of slavery within the economy of the middle colonies, using new evidence from probate records and tax assessment lists in addition to data from importation statistics, census records, and tax lists that other historians have compiled. Four areas are studied—Philadelphia and Chester in Pennsylvania and Chesterfield and Shrewsbury in New Jersey—because the monthly meetings there adopted antislavery positions

---

[2] Richard S. Dunn, *Sugar and Slaves: The Rise of the Planter Class in the English West Indies, 1624-1713* (New York, 1972), 59-74; Philip D. Curtin, *The Atlantic Slave Trade: A Census* (Madison, Wis., 1969), 59; Russell R. Menard, "From Servants to Slaves: The Transformation of the Chesapeake Labor System," *Southern Studies* 16 (1977), 361, 374-375; P.M.G. Harris, "Integrating Interpretations of Local and Regionwide Change in the Study of Economic Development and Demographic Growth in the Colonial Chesapeake, 1630-1775," *Working Papers from the Regional Economic History Research Center*, 1, no. 3 (1978), 60-64.

at widely divergent times during the eighteenth century, stances that were representative of certain groups of local meetings within the Yearly Meeting. Furthermore, the local contexts of these four monthly meetings differed from each other in date of settlement, type of economic activity present, and distribution of land or wealth. The second part of the chapter looks at other aspects of slavery in the four localities, including density of the black population and the conditions under which blacks lived. To sensitive Friends, the "peculiar institution" threatened to undermine their society based on Quaker ideals, particularly in areas with relatively large numbers of blacks, in situations where Afro-American family life was most "unnatural," and at times when importation peaked. Slavery posed a complicated set of problems for Friends: though a tempting source of labor, blacks were potentially disruptive in family, shop, and society at large.

Of the four localities examined here, Philadelphia was distinguished by its city life and its direct link to the international Atlantic economy. Founded in 1682, the city's earliest inhabitants, among them James Claypoole, emigrated mostly from England and Ireland, though wealthy migrants came from the West Indies and other American colonies as well. These hopeful founders of the "holy experiment" established Philadelphia Monthly Meeting soon after their arrival.[3] The city grew quickly. By July 1683, William Penn reported that eighty houses were completed, many ships frequented the river, and merchants were busy setting up their trading networks.[4] Fifteen years later Gabriel Thomas reported that Philadelphia contained 2,000 houses, "curious wharfs," several timber yards, a yard where ships of "considerable Burthen" were built, several large ropewalks, three or four spacious malthouses, three or four breweries, and many bakeries.[5] Within the first decade, the city's merchants established the trade with the West Indies in provisions and lumber that became the backbone of the city's overseas commerce; and by 1700, Philadelphia's volume of trade nearly surpassed that of New York.[6]

[3] Frederick B. Tolles, *Meeting House and Counting House: The Quaker Merchants of Colonial Philadelphia 1682-1763* (Chapel Hill, N.C., 1948), 31-32; Phila. MM mins., 1682.

[4] William Penn to the Earl of Sunderland, 28 July 1683, published in Mary Maples Dunn et al., eds., *The Papers of William Penn* (Philadelphia, 1981–), 2:416-418.

[5] Albert Cook Myers, ed., *Narratives of Early Pennsylvania, West New Jersey, and Delaware, 1630-1707* (New York, 1912), 317, 330-331.

[6] Tolles, *Meeting House*, 86-87; Curtis Nettels, "The Economic Relations of Boston, Philadelphia, and New York, 1680-1715," *Journal of Economic and Business History* 3 (1931), 185-207.

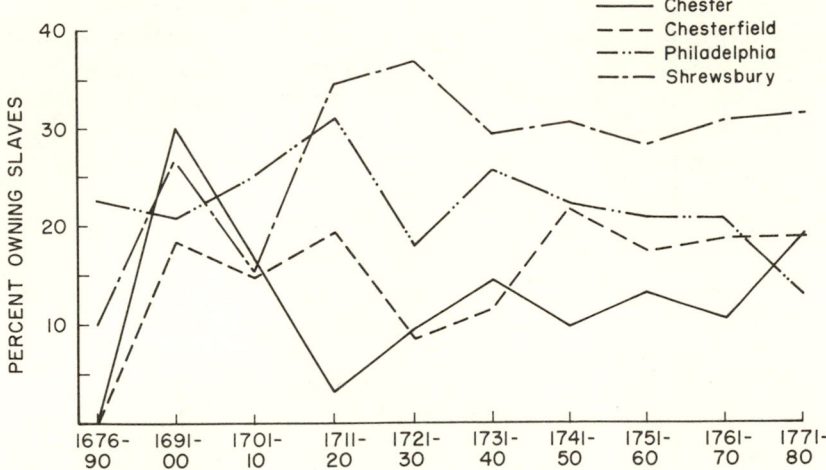

GRAPH 3.1. SLAVE OWNERSHIP AMONG ALL INVENTORIED DECEDENTS
SOURCE: Probate records

Through the colonial period, Philadelphia continued to serve as the primary trading center for southeastern Pennsylvania and West Jersey. Cycles of prosperity and depression notwithstanding, the city and region expanded steadily as immigrants continued to arrive and set up new homes, shops, and farms. Growth was strongest from the 1730s through the 1750s, as first the huge wave of German and Scots-Irish immigrants and then the Seven Years' War pumped new capital into the economy. After 1760, Philadelphia's expansion slowed as the rate of immigration declined and the Revolution caused disruption. An additional blow came when Baltimore began siphoning off much of Philadelphia's trade with western Pennsylvania.

Analysis of all Philadelphia probate inventories in the period 1682-1780, shown on Graph 3.1, outlines the history of slavery in the City of Brotherly Love. Among the Philadelphia population as a whole (to the extent it was represented in probate inventories) bondage was at its height during the first forty years of the city's growth.[7] The percentage of all urban decedents who owned slaves

[7] See Appendix B for a list of the probate records used in this study and the risks associated with these data. For additional evidence of this early peak, see population estimates in U.S. Bureau of the Census, *Historical Statistics of the United States, Colonial Times to 1970* (Washington, D.C., 1975), 2:1168; and the burial statistics cited by Gary B. Nash, "Slaves and Slaveowners in Colonial Philadelphia," *WMQ*, 3d ser., 30 (1973), 226-227, 230-231. Together these data show that, as a percentage of the total population, blacks were more numerous around 1720 than at any other time in the colonial period.

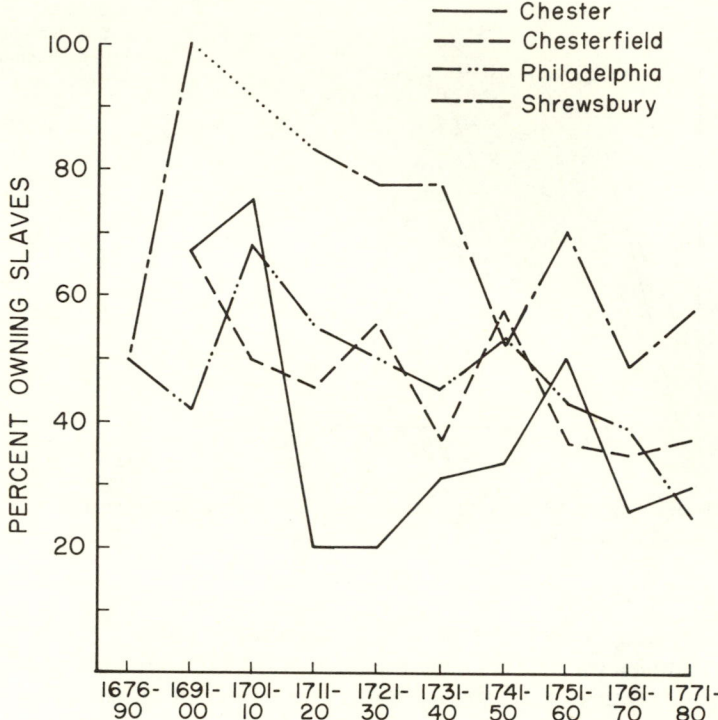

GRAPH 3.2. SLAVE OWNERSHIP AMONG INVENTORIED DECEDENTS
WITH OVER £200 STERLING
SOURCE: Probate records

reached a peak in the second decade of the eighteenth century and
then declined; slave ownership among the wealthiest decedents—
those with estates worth £200 sterling or more—actually peaked
earlier, during 1701-1710 (Graph 3.2). The number of slaves per
inventoried decedent was higher during these early decades than at
any other time.[8]

Increased importation of Africans and West Indian blacks also occurred in the Chesapeake
and New York in the period after 1700. *Historical Statistics*, 2:1172-1173; Paul G. E.
Clemens, *The Atlantic Economy and Colonial Maryland's Eastern Shore* (Ithaca, N.Y.,
1980), 60-61. Other evidence of a high rate of importation into Philadelphia during
these early decades was the imposition of revenue tariffs on slaves in the period 1700
through 1731 and the flurry of opposition to the slave trade in Philadelphia Yearly
Meeting in 1696 and 1711-1718. Darold D. Wax, "Negro Import Duties in Colonial
Pennsylvania," *PMHB* 97 (1973), 22-24; Chapter 1, above.

[8] Jean R. Soderlund, "Conscience, Interest, and Power: The Development of Quaker

After 1720, slave ownership in Philadelphia generally declined (Graph 3.1). An upswing in the 1730s in the proportion of all decedents who owned slaves resulted from a marked increase (to over 40 percent) in the percentage of less affluent decedents who owned slaves (Graph 3.3). Slave prices taken from inventories fell quite substantially after 1705 and were especially low in the mid-1730s (Graph 3.4). The supply of black labor apparently increased dramatically throughout mainland America and the West Indies during the 1710s, 1720s, and 1730s, creating lower prices and thereby making slaves more affordable to Philadelphians of moderate means.[9] From 1741 until 1780, slaveholding decreased fairly steadily in Philadelphia among all decedents, though the decline slowed considerably in the 1760s. In the 1770s, relatively few city dwellers still owned slaves at their deaths.

The rise and fall of slaveholding in Philadelphia was linked closely with the availability of white servants and free workers. For the most part, Philadelphians appear to have preferred using white labor. Servant ownership was highest in the first decade (Graph 3.5)

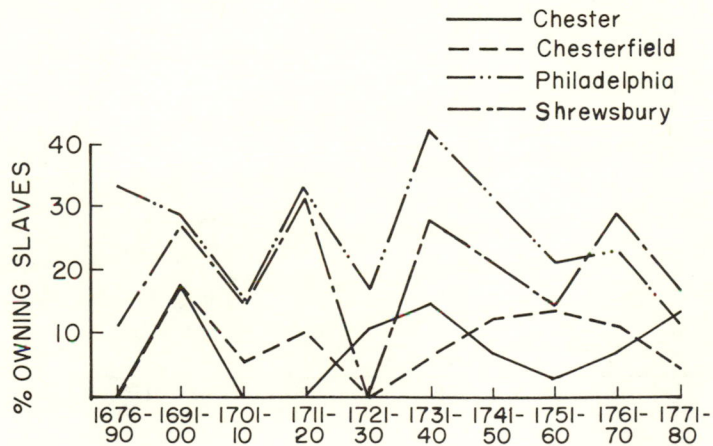

GRAPH 3.3. SLAVE OWNERSHIP AMONG INVENTORIED DECEDENTS WITH £50 TO £199.9 STERLING
SOURCE: Probate records

Opposition to Slavery in the Delaware Valley, 1688-1780" (Ph.D. diss., Temple University, 1982), 174.

[9] Using price series, P.M.G. Harris has found long-term deflation from 1700 to 1735 and inflation from 1735 to the end of the century. The prices shown on Graph 3.4 are adjusted for these changes, and it is significant that the prices of blacks declined after 1705 even when variations in the value of the £ sterling are taken into consideration. I am grateful to Professor Harris for sharing his findings with me.

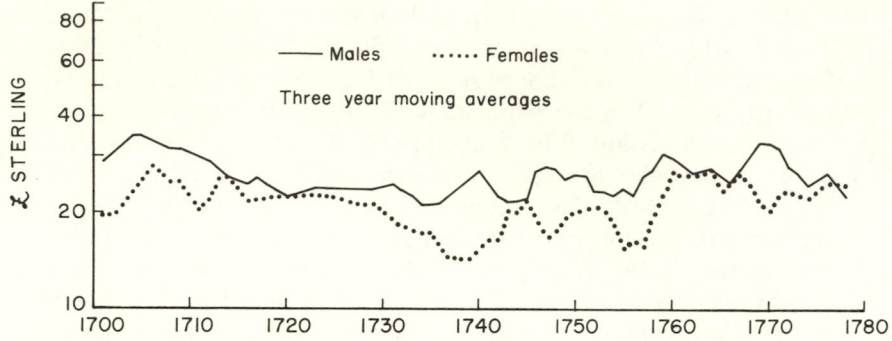

GRAPH 3.4. ADJUSTED PRICES OF ADULT SLAVES IN PHILADELPHIA
INVENTORIES
SOURCE: Probate records

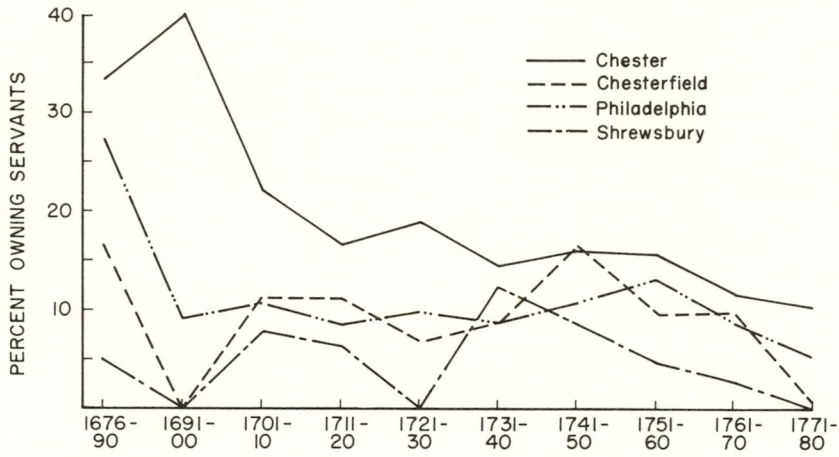

GRAPH 3.5. SERVANT OWNERSHIP AMONG ALL INVENTORIED DECEDENTS
SOURCE: Probate records

when the new settlers brought English servants to build houses,
shops, and farms. Penn's policy of granting fifty acres to each servant
when his or her service was completed encouraged many to come.[10]
The number of bound laborers (both black and white) per inven-

[10] William Penn, *A Brief Account of the Province of Pennsilvania in America* [London,
1681]; Gary B. Nash, *Quakers and Politics: Pennsylvania, 1681-1726* (Princeton, N.J.,
1968), 50.

toried decedent was highest during these first years;[11] thereafter it dropped as more children entered the labor force and the initial heavy work of settlement was completed. The interaction between the availability of white laborers and the importation of blacks was clearest during the 1740s through 1770s. In the 1740s and early 1750s when a huge number of German immigrants came and offered their labor, slave ownership declined and relatively few blacks were imported. With the Seven Years' War, however, European immigration was cut off and white servants ran off to enlist in the army; employers filled the gap by importing more black slaves.[12] After the war, slave importation slowed as white immigrants started to arrive again and a large number of free laborers filled the town. The postwar depression caused many craftsmen who had been looking for help in their shops to search instead for ways to supplement their incomes by working for others.[13] A restrictive duty of £10 per slave probably helped to discourage importation after 1761, though imports remained quite high until 1764. By the time the duty was raised to £20 in 1773, slave importation into Pennsylvania had nearly stopped.[14] In addition, the fairly high level of slaveholding among Philadelphians in comparison with Chester and Chesterfield decedents through most of the century (Graph 3.1) resulted partly from the fact that urban decedents were on average wealthier than the rural folk. Unsurprisingly, the mean value of the personal estates of slave owners was consistently higher than that of all probate inventories in the four localities studied.[15]

Afro-Americans performed a variety of jobs in Philadelphia's economy. Most worked as domestic servants and laborers, but some were skilled craftsmen. The occupations of slaves only occasionally

[11] Soderlund, "Conscience, Interest, and Power," 175.

[12] Marianne S. Wokeck, "A Tide of Alien Tongues: The Flow and Ebb of the German Immigration to Pennsylvania, 1683-1776" (Ph.D. diss., Temple University, 1983), ch. 3; Darold D. Wax, "The Negro Slave Trade in Colonial Pennsylvania" (Ph.D. diss., University at Washington, 1962), 46, 48. The numbers of blacks imported during the Seven Years' War were considerably higher than imports during the 1740s and early 1750s, but in proportion to the total population of Philadelphia, were probably no higher—and possibly somewhat lower—than peak periods of importation in the first two decades of the eighteenth century and in the 1730s. For Philadelphia population estimates, see Billy G. Smith, "Death and Life in a Colonial Immigrant City: A Demographic Analysis of Philadelphia," *The Journal of Economic History* 37 (1977), 865.

[13] Billy G. Smith, "The Material Lives of Laboring Philadelphians, 1750-1800," *WMQ*, 3d ser., 38 (1981), 163-202; Smith, " 'The Best Poor Man's Country': Living Standards of the 'Lower Sort' in Late Eighteenth-Century Philadelphia," *Working Papers from the Regional Economic History Research Center* 2 (1979).

[14] Wax, "Negro Import Duties," 24; Wax, "Negro Slave Trade," 46, 48.

[15] Soderlund, "Conscience, Interest, and Power," 199.

appear in the probate records, newspaper advertisements, and indentures. Thus it is difficult to know how most blacks served their masters. The adult male slave of a Philadelphia merchant could have worked in the shop or warehouse, performed domestic chores at home, driven the coach and four, or sailed on the merchant's ship. In fact, it is possible that he did all of these jobs at different times of the year or at different stages in his life. Some black men were listed with specific trades in probate inventories of Philadelphia decedents. John Parrock's man London was a sawyer, Mary Dicas's man Pompey was a tallowchandler, and David Caldwell held two skilled men, Pompey, a "tiner," and Cyrus, a "hammerman," who were valued at £115.6 sterling each, much higher than the average adult male slave.[16] Several men expected their slaves to carry on their trades after their deaths in order to support their families,[17] and others desired their young black boys to be bound out to trades.[18] Owners wishing to sell slaves often advertised their skills in the *Pennsylvania Gazette*. Black males listed in these advertisements included a miller, a man "brought up to the Distilling Business," and a tavern bar boy. Another advertisement sought to hire the labor of a white or black boy who would wait at table and do errands. The *Pennsylvanische Berichte* ran a sale notice for a black who could bake ship's bread and also reported that the current fashion among the middle and upper middle classes was for black boys to carry the trains of ladies' dresses.[19] In a survey of *Pennsylvania Gazette* advertisements of the late 1760s, Gary Nash found slaves "qualified as carpenters, millers, distillers, bakers, shipbuilders, blacksmiths, sailmakers, and manager of a bloomery."[20]

Evidence from the Philadelphia probate inventories and other records suggests that there was at least some differentiation by gender in the tasks assigned to slaves. While there are a few scattered references to black women working in shops, most slave women did domestic labor. They cooked and cleaned, washed and ironed laundry, kept fires, gardened, looked after children, and served as

[16] Phila. Co. Administrations, John Parrock, 1753, No. 141; Phila. Co. Wills, Mary Dicas, Bk. M, No. 211; David Caldwell, Bk. M, No. 209.

[17] Phila. Co. Wills, William Bevan, Bk. C, No. 38; William Chancellor, Bk. G, No. 12; Richard Standley, Bk. H, No. 222.

[18] Phila. Co. Wills, John Moll, Bk. B, No. 52; Joseph Pidgeon, Bk. C, No. 277; Austin Bartholomew, Bk. N, No. 132.

[19] *Pennsylvania Gazette*, 14 August 1766, 1 January 1767, 13 August 1767, 5 May 1773; *Pennsylvanische Berichte*, 16 May 1746, 16 May 1752. I am indebted to Marianne S. Wokeck for these references.

[20] Nash, "Slaves and Slaveowners," 250.

maids. Some also sewed and made cloth. For instance, one fourteen-year-old girl knew housewifery, knitting, and sewing, and had also learned to read.[21] Black women lived in their masters' houses and generally slept in garrets, kitchens, or rooms near kitchens. Merchants and professionals sometimes hired out women and girls by the year or by indenture;[22] and women could be lent or hired out for shorter periods to help tend the sick, plant gardens, preserve food, and wait on tables for special occasions. Girls were sometimes apprenticed to learn a trade, presumably housewifery or spinning.[23]

Although black men also worked as domestics in Philadelphia, the kinds of slaves owned by persons of various occupations suggest that the roles of men and women were dissimilar. Data from the Philadelphia inventories show that innkeepers and widows, whose slaves would do mostly domestic labor, owned more women than men when they died. Craftsmen, professionals, and merchants owned more men.[24] Husbands and fathers, in dividing their estates among heirs, often left a black woman or girl to their wives and daughters. If the woman married, her slave normally became the property of her husband under the law of coverture, but the black woman probably continued to work for the wife.

Changes in the level of slaveholding among occupational groups in Philadelphia over the eighteenth century provide valuable clues about why some Friends were more willing than others to give up their slaves. Early in the colonial period, before 1711, the majority of slave owners (as represented in the probate records) were merchants, professionals, and men who styled themselves gentlemen. Over three-quarters of all decedents in these occupational groups with estates over £200 sterling owned slaves (Table 3.1). It is likely that blacks were most valuable to these men as domestic servants.

[21] *Pennsylvania Gazette*, 22 January 1767; "Record of Indentures of Individuals Bound Out as Apprentices, Servants, Etc., and of German and Other Redemptioners in the Office of the Mayor of the City of Philadelphia, October 3, 1771, to October 5, 1773," *The Pennsylvania-German Society Proceedings and Addresses* 16 (1907), 70-71; Carole Shammas, "Mammy and Miss Ellen in Colonial Virginia?" (Paper presented at the Conference on Women in Early America, 5-7 November 1981, Williamsburg, Va.); Mary Beth Norton, *Liberty's Daughters: The Revolutionary Experience of American Women, 1750-1800* (Boston, 1980), 12-23.

[22] Phila. MM mans.; Phila. Co. Wills, Thomas Lloyd, Bk. A, No. 105; "Record of Indentures, 1771-1773."

[23] Phila. Co. Wills, Clement Plumstead, Bk. G, No. 163; William Coleman, Bk. O, No. 235-236.

[24] Jean R. Soderlund, "Black Women in Colonial Pennsylvania," *PMHB* 107 (1983), 60.

TABLE 3.1. OCCUPATION, WEALTH, AND SLAVEHOLDING AMONG
INVENTORIED DECEDENTS IN PHILADELPHIA

	Craftsmen			Merchants, professionals, and gentlemen			
	£100-199.9		£200+		£100-199.9		£200+	
No.	% Slave owners	No.	% Slave owners	No.	% Slave owners	No.	% Slave owners
1682-1690	0	—	0	—	0	—	4	75.0%
1691-1700	8	25.0%	5	20.0%	4	25.0%	8	62.5
1701-1710	13	23.1	9	44.4	6	16.7	17	82.4
1711-1720	18	33.3	14	57.1	13	23.1	26	50.0
1721-1730	6	33.3	10	40.0	16	25.0	24	58.3
1731-1740	12	50.0	5	80.0	16	50.0	28	39.3
1741-1750	20	50.0	9	77.8	18	33.3	39	56.4
1751-1760	20	35.0	24	62.5	17	11.8	55	47.3
1761-1770	25	40.0	35	51.4	17	35.3	83	42.2
1771-1780	13	7.7	27	29.6	20	25.0	63	28.6

SOURCE: Probate records

A staff of black servants clearly denoted the owner's power and wealth; their service left the master, mistress, and children free to engage in intellectual, religious, civic, and leisure activities. The percentage of wealthy merchants and professionals in Philadelphia who owned slaves when they died then declined after 1710. During the period from 1711 to 1750, fewer than 60 percent, and in 1751-1780, fewer than half, of these decedents held blacks. This trend was quite different from the pattern of slaveholding among craftsmen and among more ordinary shopkeepers and merchants. Before 1711, fewer than 36 percent of wealthy craftsmen held slaves, but in the 1730s through 1750s this proportion jumped to almost 70 percent. Slaveholding also became more common in this period among craftsmen and merchants of middling wealth. Part of the explanation for this increase must be the generally low price of slaves throughout the middle decades of the eighteenth century (see Graph 3.4). It seems likely that during prosperous times Philadelphia craftsmen could most effectively increase production by adding a laborer or two, who with minimal training could perform menial tasks without necessitating additional investment in expensive tools or work space.

In Philadelphia, then, Afro-Americans worked as laborers, craftsmen, and domestic servants. Blacks never replaced servants and freemen as they did in the plantation gangs of the West Indies, South Carolina, and the Chesapeake; but they did serve as one significant source of labor for the city's shops and homes. The importance of slaves in the economy declined generally after 1720. The immigration of large numbers of Germans and Scots-Irish from the mid-1720s to about 1755 and then again after the Seven Years' War lowered demand for blacks. In order to accumulate money to buy their own shops or farms, the Europeans, either as servants or as free laborers, willingly took jobs that African slaves might have filled. However, a somewhat greater proportion of urban producers turned to blacks in the 1730s and during the Seven Years' War when the number of white workers was inadequate for their needs.

THE patterns of slave ownership were different in rural Pennsylvania and New Jersey than in Philadelphia, but again the relative availability of indentured servants, freemen, and slaves, as well as the overall demand for labor and average local wealth, affected the proportion of residents who owned slaves. The three rural areas studied here, Shrewsbury, Chesterfield, and Chester, are chosen because the Friends meetings located in these places took varied stands on the issue of slavery. One of the reasons for these diverse positions, as we shall see, was the different way in which slavery developed in each region. These differences did not arise, however, from any dissimilarity among these places in the kind of agriculture practiced or in their proximity to market. In all three rural localities, most farmers raised a variety of products, of which wheat, Indian corn, cattle, and pigs were most important,[25] and the large majority of these farmers grew surpluses that they sold to merchants in Philadelphia or New York.[26] Instead, differences in slave ownership among the three areas were linked to variations in the availability of white laborers from place to place as well as over time and to local differences in the size of the segment of the rural population who were most likely to own slaves—wealthy farmers.

[25] These were the products normally listed in the probate inventories of farmers in Chester, Chesterfield, and Shrewsbury alike. See also the discussion of agricultural production on farms in southeastern Pennsylvania in James T. Lemon, *The Best Poor Man's Country: A Geographical Study of Early Southeastern Pennsylvania* (Baltimore, 1972), 150-167.

[26] Ibid., 179-183; Dennis P. Ryan, "Six Towns: Continuity and Change in Revolutionary New Jersey, 1770-1792" (Ph.D. diss., New York University, 1974), 27, 30-32; Peter O. Wacker, *The Musconetcong Valley of New Jersey: A Historical Geography* (New Brunswick, N.J., 1968), 133-134; Virginia Draper Harrington, *The New York Merchant on the Eve of Revolution* (New York, 1935), 166, 214-218.

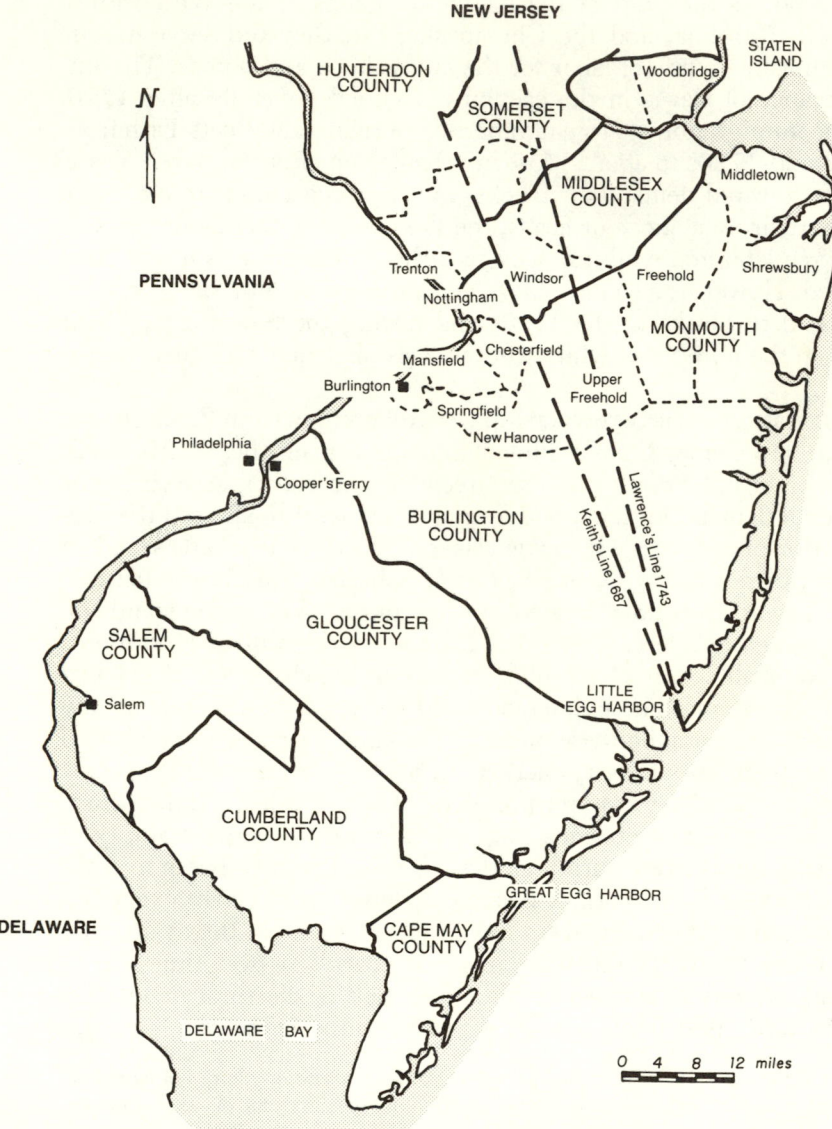

MAP 2. CENTRAL AND SOUTHERN NEW JERSEY, 1775

SOURCE: John P. Snyder, *The Story of New Jersey's Civil Boundaries 1606-1968* (Trenton, 1969), 20-21

Shrewsbury Friends lived primarily in Middletown and Shrewsbury townships in eastern Monmouth County (see Map 2). Unlike members of the other local meetings studied here, they were within the commercial orbit of New York. The first settlers of the Shrewsbury area were a group of Quakers and Baptists who in 1665 migrated from Long Island and Rhode Island. The original Monmouth patentees, among the earliest European settlers in New Jersey, bought a large triangle of land from the Lenni Lenape that extended from Sandy Hook to Barnegat Bay to a point on the Raritan River twenty-five miles west of its mouth. They obtained the Navesink Patent for this area from Governor Richard Nicolls on 4 April 1665. Additional settlers arrived from Rhode Island, Long Island, and Massachusetts during the next few years, and by 1673 the two New England-style towns, Shrewsbury and Middletown, had about 300 inhabitants each.[27] Most of the Baptist immigrants established their farms in Middletown, where they founded the first Baptist church in New Jersey in 1688. The Friends, who largely went to Shrewsbury though some stayed in Middletown, established their meeting soon after their arrival and built a meeting house in 1672.[28] Shrewsbury, then, was different from Philadelphia, Chesterfield, and Chester, because it was located close to New York City and preceded settlement by Friends in West Jersey and Pennsylvania by at least a decade, and because the founders of that East Jersey locality came mostly from elsewhere in America, not directly from the British Isles.

A small number of Swedes, Finns, and Dutch populated the Chester Monthly Meeting area in eastern Chester County (then called Upland) when the first Quakers arrived (see Map 3). Robert Wade and a few other Friends who had originally sailed with John Fenwick from England to Salem, New Jersey, came in 1675, and others who immigrated with the Burlington settlers arrived in 1677. Like the Swedes before them, these English Quakers established farms along the edge of the Delaware and its tributaries. European settlement west of the river's edge proceeded in earnest only after the arrival of William Penn. The earliest Chester Friends met together for religious services at the house of Robert Wade. The monthly meeting records date from 1681, and the first meeting

[27] John E. Pomfret, *The Province of East New Jersey, 1609-1702* (Princeton, N.J., 1962), 42-45; Peter O. Wacker, *Land and People: A Cultural Geography of Preindustrial New Jersey: Origins and Settlement Patterns* (New Brunswick, N.J., 1975), 130.

[28] Norman H. Maring, *Baptists in New Jersey* (Valley Forge, Pa., 1964), 13; Norman Penney, ed., *The Journal of George Fox*, 2 vols. (Cambridge, 1911), 2:226.

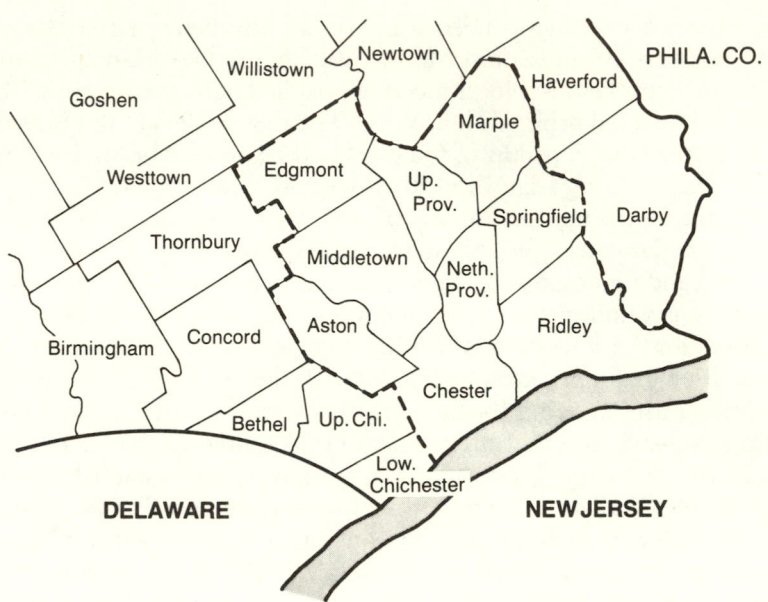

PHILA. CO.

Newtown
Willistown
Goshen
Haverford
Marple
Westtown
Edgmont
Up. Prov.
Springfield
Darby
Thornbury
Middletown
Neth. Prov.
Birmingham
Concord
Aston
Ridley
Bethel
Up. Chi.
Chester
Low. Chichester

DELAWARE
NEW JERSEY

– – – Boundaries of townships included in the Chester Monthly
Meeting area in this study.

MAP 3. EASTERN CHESTER COUNTY

house in Chester was completed in 1693. The Chester meeting area, like that of Shrewsbury, retained a predominantly rural economy throughout the colonial period, although the town of Chester developed as a small center for trading and governmental activities.[29]

The region of Chesterfield Monthly Meeting, where agriculture also prevailed, was settled after 1678 by Quaker immigrants primarily from northern England, but also from London and its vicinity. As increasing numbers of immigrants arrived in Burlington, lands were taken up in sections of West Jersey that became Chesterfield, Mansfield, Nottingham, and Trenton townships (see Map 2). Farnsworth's Landing, later named Bordentown, was established in 1682 and by 1683 settlement reached Crosswicks Creek, twelve miles north of the original colony at Burlington. Quakers founded Chesterfield Monthly Meeting in 1684 and set up subordinate meetings for worship as they spread out across the land. They

---

[29] George Smith, *History of Delaware County, Pennsylvania* (Philadelphia, 1862), 103-104, 115, 128, 188; Lemon, *Best Poor Man's Country*, 120-121.

established meetings at Crosswicks and "the Falls" (Nottingham-Trenton) first, and by 1696 they started a meeting for worship at Stony Brook (now Princeton) along a fork of the Millstone River. Friends in Upper Freehold Township set up meetings in the homes of Daniel Robins in 1736 and Joseph Arney in 1739, and a meeting house was built in Trenton in 1739.[30]

As should be expected, in all three of the rural monthly meeting areas, Chester, Chesterfield, and Shrewsbury, most slaves and their owners were agriculturalists. Over 96 percent of all slave owners whose estates were inventoried were active farmers at their deaths.[31] Even most slave-owning craftsmen, gentlemen, merchants, and professionals operated farms, and many of their blacks probably worked in the fields. Some bondsmen possibly engaged in trades, however, as over 30 percent of slave owners in Shrewsbury and about 20 percent in Chester and Chesterfield owned tools or implements used in milling and crafts such as weaving, carpentry, and coopering. Typical slave owners in rural Pennsylvania or New Jersey owned large farms and sometimes combined agriculture with a mercantile or milling operation, profession, or craft. Some examples include Ralph Fishbourn of Chester (d. ca. 1708) who owned four plantations, a bolting house, and a shop; Joseph Harvey of Ridley Township, Chester County (d. ca. 1756), who owned a plantation, a mill, and a malthouse; James Mather and Valentine Weaver, both innkeepers and farmers of Chester Borough who died ca. 1780; Capt. Daniel Hendricks of Middletown, Monmouth County (d. ca. 1728), "gentleman," who owned several plantations; Thomas Huitt of Shrewsbury (d. ca. 1711), owner of a plantation and cooper's tools; Joseph Eaton of Shrewsbury (d. ca. 1761), a surgeon and farmer; William Trent, of Burlington County (d. ca. 1726), a merchant and farmer who owned a large boat, gristmills, a sawmill, a fulling mill, and a bakehouse; and Thomas Lambert of Nottingham, Burlington County (d. ca. 1733), a wealthy farmer and tanner.[32]

[30] Wacker, *Land and People*, 126, 159, 178, 181; John E. Pomfret, "The Province of West New Jersey: A Quaker Commonwealth," *Proceedings of the New Jersey Historical Society* 67 (1950), 33-34; Franklin Ellis, *History of Monmouth County, New Jersey* (Philadelphia, 1885), 632-633.

[31] These "active farmers" may have been retired themselves, but all owned working farms when they died.

[32] Phila. Co. Wills, Ralph Fishbourn, Bk. C, No. 102. Chester Co. Wills, Joseph Harvey, No. 1603; James Mather, No. 3241; Valentine Weaver, No. 3288. Monmouth Co. Wills, Daniel Hendricks, 329, 675M; Joseph Eaton, 2627-2629M. N.J. Unrecorded Wills, Thomas Huitt, Vol. 11:211; Vol. 12:81-94. Burlington Co. Wills, William Trent, 1211-1216C, 1433-1448C; Thomas Lambert, 2373-2382C.

Affluent settlers who had large farms or diversified operations could keep slaves busy year-round. Though rural slave owners of the middle colonies held only about three blacks on average, on this small scale the institution of slavery could be as feasible economically for them as it was for planters in the tobacco, rice, and sugar regions to the south. As noted above, the mean value of personal estates of slaveholders in the country as well as in Philadelphia was higher than the average wealth of decedents who owned no blacks.

Comparison of data from Pennsylvania and New Jersey tax assessment lists (Tables 3.2 and 3.3) indicates further that, on average, slave owners had larger farm operations than their neighbors who had no blacks.[33] The similarities in the amount of land and livestock held by Shrewsbury and Chesterfield slaveholders were remarkable, considering the very different landholding patterns of the two areas. Landholding was much more concentrated in Chesterfield and the mean acreage was significantly larger than in Shrewsbury, but both groups of slave owners held on average approximately 300 acres of land, five horses aged two years or older and twelve cattle aged two years or older. The mean holdings of land and livestock (aged three years or older) of Chester slave owners were smaller than those of the New Jersey groups, but still were larger than those of non-slaveholders in Chester County.[34] Examination of slave ownership among farmers with different amounts of land (Table 3.4) also suggests that large farmers in each of the rural areas were more likely to own slaves than their neighbors with smaller plots. In Chester,

[33] See Appendix B for the tax assessment lists used in this study.

[34] The data on landholding obtained from tax assessment lists can only be considered approximations, as residents of one township sometimes held land in other places. This is true especially in Chester County where the townships were small. For the Chester tax lists, I attempted to eliminate obvious duplication of listings for taxpayers within the nine-township area, but I did not try to locate additional lands owned by Chester Monthly Meeting area residents in townships outside this locality. Determining exact landholdings would require extensive research of deeds in Chester County and New Jersey, and would probably be impossible in New Jersey where a large percentage of the deeds is lost.

One additional note of caution about the Chester tax assessment lists is that many of the persons taxed for land actually rented and did not own the land. Thus I have used the term "landholder" rather than "land owner" to describe all persons who paid tax on land whether they rented or owned the land. In her article, "Tenancy and Economic Development in Eighteenth-Century Chester County, Pennsylvania" (Paper presented to the Philadelphia Center for Early American Studies Seminar, 25 March 1983, Philadelphia), Lucy Simler shows that there were several types of tenants living in eastern Chester County in the period before the Revolution, including those who rented fairly large farms. These relatively affluent tenants chose to rent farms rather than buy their own and therefore do not fit the usual stereotype of poor tenants.

TABLE 3.2. SLAVE OWNERSHIP AND LANDHOLDINGS

	Chester 1775	Shrewsbury 1779	Chesterfield 1778-1779
No. of taxpayers	748	1,178	1,697
No. of slave owners	38[a]	84[b]	86[b]
No. of landholders[c]	400	784	782
(% of taxpayers)	(53.8%)	(66.6%)	(46.1%)
$\bar{X}$ acreage for all landholders	112.3	117.0	189.3
$\bar{X}$ acreage for landholding slave owners	148.1	297.8	309.2

SOURCE: Tax assessment lists
  [a] Owners of male and female slaves aged twelve to fifty years
  [b] Owners of male slaves aged sixteen years or more
  [c] All taxpayers who held land either as owners or tenants

TABLE 3.3. LIVESTOCK OWNERSHIP

	Chester 1775	Shrewsbury 1779	Chesterfield 1778-1779
No. horses per taxpayer	1.3[a]	1.5[b]	1.5[b]
No. horses per landholder	2.2	2.3	3.3
No. horses per slave owner	3.5	4.7	5.2
No. cattle per taxpayer	2.3	4.1	3.4
No. cattle per landholder	4.2	6.1	7.4
No. cattle per slave owner	6.4	12.1	12.0

SOURCE: Tax assessment lists
[a] Livestock aged three or more years
[b] Livestock aged two or more years

Chesterfield, and Shrewsbury, the percentage of landholders with 250 acres or more who owned slaves was twice the proportion among those who held only 150 to 249 acres, and was considerably higher still than the percentage of those who had fewer than 150 acres.[35]

[35] Six of the thirty-eight slave owners (15.8 percent) listed on the 1775 tax list for the nine Chester County townships held small acreages of land. Two owned mills, three

TABLE 3.4. SIZE OF LANDHOLDINGS AND SLAVE OWNERSHIP

% of landholders who owned slaves	Chester 1775	Shrewsbury 1779	Chesterfield 1778-1779
250+ acres	25.9%	43.5%	21.4%
150-249 acres	12.0	23.9	8.7
50-149 acres	7.3	4.1	6.6
0-49 acres	6.3	0.9	1.0

SOURCE: Tax assessment lists

From the probate records we can gain some information on the kinds of work slaves did for these generally well-to-do farmers. Most black males probably worked in the fields or in trades, while women and girls served in their masters' houses. However, workloads on a Pennsylvania or New Jersey plantation would vary by season and therefore flexibility was surely needed. Men could cut firewood, weave cloth, mend fences, construct or repair buildings, accompany their owners on trips to Philadelphia or New York, and perform any of a myriad of tasks during the approximate four-month off season of a mid-Atlantic farm. Women could help with the harvest and keep a garden during the summer, in addition to the domestic chores such as cleaning, cooking, food preservation, laundry, spinning, milking, raising poultry, and child care that continued throughout the year.

Bits of evidence from wills and inventories illustrate the kinds of jobs slaves performed. Thomas Potts of Mansfield Township spelled out in 1754 the services that his black woman should provide for the widow. Angelico was to wait on his wife, fetch her water, wash her clothes, make her bed, and make fires for her as long as she remained his widow. Matthew Covenhoven of Middletown stated that his slaves should continue to assist his wife in supporting his children. In 1757, William Evilman of Upper Freehold provided for the freedom of his black man Primus beginning nine months after his death, but specified that the slave must harvest, secure, and thrash the widow's grain if the nine months expired at harvest time. Several testators provided for their slaves in ways that suggest that

kept taverns, and one was a prominent government officeholder. Four of these slaveholders lived in Chester, the central market town of eastern Chester County. In contrast, only about 4 percent of slaveholders in both Chesterfield and Shrewsbury had primarily nonagricultural occupations.

the blacks were skilled farmers. For example, Elias Mestayer of Shrewsbury in 1731 expected two of his slaves, a husband and wife, to manage and make a profit from his plantation. Other owners gave their adult male slaves axes and livestock or small plots of land as freedom dues, evidently expecting them to earn livings as small farmers or farm laborers. No black women received these kinds of bequests by themselves in these wills.[36]

That rural owners, like those in Philadelphia, distinguished somewhat on the basis of gender between the kinds of jobs they assigned to their male and female slaves is also clear from the ways in which they divided up their blacks among their heirs. Dying slave owners apparently preferred to match slaves with heirs of the same sex and approximately the same age, thus fitting the type of slave service to the role in life of the heir as well as increasing the chance that the slave could serve for most of his or her new master's life. Joseph Pope, a Mansfield Township Quaker who died in 1767, left a black boy and girl to his wife Mary, a boy each to his underage sons, and a man, boy, and girl to his oldest son who also received the plantation. Edward Stevenson of Middletown, deceased in 1773, gave a black man and woman to his wife, a black man each to two sons, a girl to his daughter, and a "wench" to another son. Philip Evans of Aston Township, Chester County, bequeathed his black woman Dinah and her child Sylvia to the widow, a girl to his daughter, and a boy to his son.[37] These examples suggest that the usual pattern was to provide household help for the widow and daughters, and farm laborers (and/or craftsmen) for sons who inherited the plantation or were apprenticed to trades.

Thus we can generalize about slaveholding in the three rural areas studied in detail, Chesterfield, Chester, and Shrewsbury, to say that most blacks worked for wealthy farmers, of whom some were involved in diverse activities like milling, shopkeeping or innkeeping, and crafts. Yet it is clear, looking back at Graph 3.1, that a widely varying proportion of residents of these three localities purchased blacks to help them with their field work, trades, or domestic chores. Situated within the New York hinterland, Shrewsbury employed

[36] Burlington Co. Wills, Thomas Potts, 5491-5498C. Monmouth Co. Wills, Matthew Covenhoven, 3161-3165M; William Evilman, 2341-2347M; Elias Mestayer, 457M; William Woolley, 3753-3755M; Gershom Mott, 555M. N.J. Unrecorded Wills, Samuel Andrews, 1:337-346. Mott and Andrews granted plots of land to their slaves but did not free them. Chester Co. Wills, William Grantham, No. 2881.

[37] Burlington Co. Wills, Joseph Pope, 8228-8231C, 8568C. Monmouth Co. Wills, Edward Stevenson, 4037M. Chester Co. Wills, Philip Evans, No. 3270.

considerably more black labor after 1710 than the other rural localities. The percentage of inventoried decedents owning slaves swung upward to over 34 percent during the second and third decades of the eighteenth century and held close to this level for the remainder of the prerevolutionary era. This rise in slaveholding in Shrewsbury was part of a general surge in the New York area as a whole in the early 1700s.[38] The number of blacks imported through the port of New York swelled tremendously during the 1710s and remained high until the 1730s. Shrewsbury and Middletown, as part of the New York commercial area, apparently shared in this upswing in the slave trade. Some sparse import statistics, which generally follow the New York pattern, are extant for the port of Perth Amboy, but the numbers are exceedingly small, probably because most East Jerseyans purchased their blacks in New York or brought them as part of their households when they migrated from other colonies.[39]

Whatever the source of their black laborers, wealthy Shrewsbury residents owned slaves as early as 1676-1690 when the probate records begin.[40] Between 1711 and 1740, when the numbers of inventories are larger, over three-quarters of the decedents whose personal estates were valued at £200 sterling or more owned slaves, and the percentage remained above 47 percent for the rest of the colonial period (Graph 3.2). In Chester, on the other hand, slave ownership among inventoried decedents peaked very early, then plummeted after 1710. Unlike Philadelphia, the percentage of decedents owning slaves then rose gradually, reaching a second, though lower, peak in the 1770s.[41] Slave ownership among dece-

[38] Africans had been imported into New York as early as 1625 or 1626, and by 1703 that colony had a population of 2,386 blacks (11.5 percent of the total population). During the next twenty years, the number of blacks grew at an average annual rate of 4.8 percent, and thus in 1723 accounted for 15.2 percent of the total population of New York—the highest percentage of that colony's population constituted by Afro-Americans before the Revolution. Elizabeth Donnan, ed., *Documents Illustrative of the History of the Slave Trade to America*, 4 vols. (New York, 1969), 3:405; Evarts B. Greene and Virginia D. Harrington, *American Population before the Federal Census of 1790* (New York, 1932), 95-102.

[39] *Historical Statistics*, 2:1173; Donnan, ed., *Slave Trade*, 3:510-512.

[40] In the period 1676-1700, two of three decedents with estates worth more than £200 sterling owned slaves.

[41] Like the 1711-1730 probate records, the 1726 constables' return for a township immediately adjacent to the Chester Monthly Meeting area, Thornbury Township—the only such assessment list known to exist for a township in Chester County prior to 1759—also indicates that Chester County residents owned more servants than slaves. Of twenty-four taxed households, fourteen had bound or hired labor, including seventeen

dents in Chesterfield behaved rather as in Chester, though the early peak was lower. Here again, frequency of slaveholding did not decline among rural decedents after 1720 as it did among those in Philadelphia but instead increased after 1740.

In sum, there were several important differences among slaveholding patterns in these localities. After 1710 a much higher percentage of Shrewsbury decedents owned slaves at death than did residents of the other places. However, while the level of slave ownership in Shrewsbury was unsurpassed throughout the period before 1780, the percentage of decedents who owned slaves generally declined in that locality after 1730. The same pattern occurred in Philadelphia, where the level of slaveholding went down after 1720. At the same time, in Chester and Chesterfield, where a smaller proportion of decedents owned slaves than in Shrewsbury or Philadelphia for most of the eighteenth century, slave ownership did not decline after 1720, but rather continued to increase through the 1770s.[42]

As we will see later in this chapter and in subsequent chapters as well, economic advantage was not the only concern of mid-Atlantic colonists in deciding whether to buy, keep, sell, or manumit their slaves. Nevertheless, as in the case of the urban craftsmen, the availability of white servants or free laborers and the need for additional labor surely influenced large farmers in the three rural localities. That affluent planters turned to black slaves when they could not acquire white labor seems especially persuasive when we compare Shrewsbury to the other rural areas. East Jersey suffered from a dearth of white servants throughout the prerevolutionary period because few Europeans migrated to New York, the logical place for East Jersey planters to seek labor. New York was unattractive to prospective white immigrants who hoped eventually to set up their

---

bound servants, five blacks, and two hired servants. I am grateful to Lucy Simler for showing me this list, which is located in the Chester County Archives, West Chester.

[42] These differences in levels of slaveholding found in the probate inventories conform to evidence from censuses and tax lists. Enumeration of blacks in the three New Jersey censuses of 1726, 1738, and 1745 also indicates the wide margin between the two New Jersey localities—for example, 10.6 percent of the Monmouth County population and 6.5 percent of the Burlington County population in 1738 was black. In Pennsylvania, an analogous contrast is apparent from the tax lists. While 15.7 percent of Philadelphia taxpayers owned slaves in 1767, only 4.2 percent of Chester County taxpayers owned slaves in 1759. Greene and Harrington, *American Population*, 109-112; Nash, "Slaves and Slaveowners," 242-244. See also, Alan Tully, "Patterns of Slaveholding in Colonial Pennsylvania: Chester and Lancaster Counties 1729-1758," *Journal of Social History* 6 (1973), 284-305.

own farms, because just a few families controlled much of the land in huge tracts. This meant that residents of New York and its hinterland turned to blacks at an early date as a major source of labor.[43] Conversely, fewer residents owned slaves in Chesterfield and Chester, where servants were more plentiful than in Shrewsbury throughout the century.[44] Scots-Irish and German immigrants arrived in Philadelphia on their way to settle lands in western Pennsylvania, Virginia, and North Carolina even into the 1770s. Many offered their labor as servants or as free wage laborers in order to accumulate money to buy a farm or shop. Though they continued to migrate up to the Revolution, however, their numbers decreased after 1754 in relation to the total population, accounting for the decline of servant ownership in both rural West Jersey and Pennsylvania after 1750. Significantly, it was at this time that slaveholding tended to rise in farming areas on both sides of the Delaware.[45]

Thus, while the pattern of a changeover from servants to slaves found in the West Indies and the Chesapeake was not replicated in rural colonial Pennsylvania and New Jersey (just as it did not occur in Philadelphia), the supply of alternative forms of labor did affect the development of slavery in these areas. Shrewsbury residents found it difficult to obtain white workers as early as 1700 so they turned immediately to blacks. In Chester, a continuing supply of Europeans helped labor users avoid the "peculiar institution" after 1710. However, the diminished availability of white laborers on the Delaware after 1750 induced increased numbers of wealthy Chester and Chesterfield residents to purchase Africans and Afro-Americans to do their work.

The other economic factor helping to explain the varied slave-

[43] James G. Lydon, "New York and the Slave Trade, 1700 to 1774," *WMQ*, 3d ser., 35 (1978), 381; Sung Bok Kim, *Landlord and Tenant in Colonial New York: Manorial Society, 1664-1775* (Chapel Hill, N.C., 1978), 235-237.

[44] P.M.G. Harris has found that white servants were available into the 1720s on the nearby Eastern Shore of Maryland as well. Unpublished research funded by grants to the St. Mary's City Commission by the National Endowment for the Humanities (RO-10585-74-267 and RS-23687-76-41). That many residents of West Jersey bought servants in Philadelphia is evident from the "Record of Indentures, 1771-1773," 1-325.

[45] The tax records of Chester and Philadelphia counties indicate an increase in the number of indentured servants between the years 1766-1767 and 1774-1775. However, this rise was short-lived as the Revolution again cut off the flow of immigrants. Lucy Simler's analysis of 1766 and 1774 tax lists for all of Chester County; Sharon V. Salinger, "Colonial Labor in Transition: The Decline of Indentured Servitude in Late Eighteenth-Century Philadelphia," *Labor History* 22 (1981), 165-191.

holding patterns in rural New Jersey and Pennsylvania was demand for labor over and above what could be provided by the farmer's family or occasional day labor. Most mid-Atlantic planters chose to work without bound labor. For whatever reason—because they could not afford to expand or did not wish to—their farm operations were too small either to require the services of a year-round laborer or to support the bondsman and his or her family. Thus, in addition to the availability of white workers, the demand for slave labor in each locality depended on the number of large farm owners living there who could fully employ and support slaves. In Shrewsbury and Chesterfield Monthly Meeting areas, many taxpayers (7.8 percent and 11 percent respectively) held 250 acres or more; these were the farmers who, for strictly economic reasons, were most likely to own slaves. A somewhat smaller number of taxpayers (3.6 percent) held large acreages in the Chester area, which helps explain, along with the greater supply of indentured servants, why fewer Chester residents owned slaves.[46] It is also probable, however, that decreasing farm size among wealthy Shrewsbury farmers over the eighteenth century resulted in a lessening of their demand for slave labor after 1740 (Graph 3.2). East Jersey farmers were apparently more willing than their counterparts in Chesterfield to divide their lands among heirs, and so by 1779 a greater proportion of Shrewsbury area taxpayers owned farms, but the average acreage of the landholdings was much smaller than in West Jersey (Table 3.2). This perhaps meant that many Shrewsbury farmers—even those with large personal estates—had farms too small to employ slave labor efficiently, and so they were more easily convinced that they should free their slaves or avoid buying them at all.

These data from the probate records and tax lists add significantly to our knowledge of the role of Africans and Afro-Americans in the economy of the colonial North. Labor users turned to slaves in localities where, and during periods when, white servants and free laborers were scarce. The wide difference in slave ownership between Shrewsbury and Chester occurred to a large extent because Europeans chose to immigrate to Pennsylvania instead of New York. The decline in Philadelphia's interest in black workers after 1720 resulted in part from the increased immigration of Germans and Scots-Irish beginning in the 1720s, and the overabundance of free

[46] However, it is also likely that some Chester taxpayers held additional lands outside the nine-township area (see n. 34, above). Tax assessment lists for Shrewsbury (1779), Chesterfield (1778, 1779), and Chester (1775) Monthly Meeting areas. See Appendix B.

laborers in the city after the Seven Years' War. Conversely, Chesterfield and Chester increasingly turned to black workers after 1750 when the number of white workers in those rural areas could not fill their labor needs.

Wealth and the type of economic activity also affected labor users' demand for slaves. The higher mean wealth of decedents in Philadelphia accounted partially for the greater percentage of urban residents who owned slaves at death. Yet the fact that the city's shopkeepers, mariners, and craftsmen with middling estates were more likely than ordinary farmers in the countryside to purchase slaves also played a substantial role (Graph 3.3). In the rural areas, furthermore, affluent farmers with lands of over 250 acres invested most heavily in Afro-American labor. The relatively small number of substantial farm owners in Chester helped explain the rather low level of slaveholding in that locality for much of its prerevolutionary history, while the decline in the number of large landholdings in Shrewsbury was probably a major source of the decreased demand for black farm workers there after 1740—regardless of any abolition activity by local Quakers.

YET to examine the practical value of slavery to mid-Atlantic colonists is to gain only a partial insight into what the institution meant to Friends and their neighbors. As people who purchased blacks discovered very quickly, and indeed as James Claypoole knew even before he took the plunge, buying a slave entailed much more than acquiring a worker who would perform a certain set of tasks. Slaves were property—in economic terms they were both capital and labor. But they were also humans, who learned or refused to learn, loved and raised families, obeyed respectfully or rebelled, and socialized with other blacks and whites. They stole food and money, committed suicide, ran away to be with their families, learned to read, and preached religion. Many eighteenth-century Americans closed their eyes to the humanity of Afro-Americans and denied their equality with whites. For Friends, such denial was much harder, as individuals like John Hepburn, Benjamin Lay, John Woolman, and Anthony Benezet reminded them that all men and women were equal in the sight of God. Holding blacks as slaves was sinful because they were the spiritual equals of whites. Further, detaining men and women as slaves was potentially explosive because, as spiritual equals, they would certainly detest their condition and possibly disrupt the family and society in which they lived. And subjugation by violence or threat of violence, abhorred in theory by almost all eighteenth-century Quakers, was the only way blacks could be kept enslaved.

Thus it is important to look at how slavery developed in early Pennsylvania and New Jersey in more than just the economic realm. While much about their lives remains obscure, probate wills and inventories, tax lists, manumissions, church records, slave registration lists, personal papers, and other sources yield some information about the slaves' families, living conditions, and (regrettably very rarely) their attitudes toward these conditions. With the probate records specifically, we can trace how the circumstances of blacks changed over the century and varied from one place to another in the middle colonies.

The urban experience of slaves was fundamentally different from that of country blacks, perhaps not so much in the kinds of jobs they performed as in their opportunity to live with their families and to associate with other blacks. Especially after 1750, freed men and women and slaves in Philadelphia could go to school and church, and get married. Their numbers supported institutions that could never attract enough students or adherents in the rural districts. Consequently, Philadelphia blacks increasingly adopted Anglo-American culture. As slaves did so, they became less willing to put up with bondage, and many of their owners grew uncomfortable with keeping obviously talented and sophisticated blacks in chains.

Table 3.5 shows the percentage of Philadelphia, Shrewsbury, Chester, and Chesterfield slaves identified in the probate inventories by age and gender. In Philadelphia, the ratio of adult men to adult women was roughly equal throughout the century, and together the adults greatly outnumbered children. This pattern is somewhat dif-

TABLE 3.5. AGE AND GENDER OF BLACKS, 1681-1780

	Philadelphia	Chester	Shrewsbury	Chesterfield
Blacks (No.)	955	129	261	291
Men	34.0%	36.4%	28.0%	30.9%
Women	31.2	25.6	28.0	24.4
Boys	20.2	20.9	25.3	21.3
Girls	14.6	17.1	18.7	23.4
Total	100.0	100.0	100.0	100.0

SOURCE: Probate inventories
NOTE: Table includes only those blacks for whom gender and approximate age are known

ferent from that found in the three rural areas where the percentages of women, boys, and girls were more even, and is dissimilar also from the situation on the lower Western Shore of Maryland where there were approximately two children for every adult woman by the 1720s.[47] Two factors may explain why there were fewer children in Philadelphia than in the rural areas. One reason is that infant mortality in the city was very high. Susan E. Klepp found in her study of white families that almost one-half of the children born to mothers in colonial Philadelphia died before they reached age fifteen; one-fourth died during their first year. No one has done an equivalent study of infant mortality in Chester County or New Jersey, but evidence from elsewhere in colonial America suggests that mortality among the total population was lower in rural areas than in the cities.[48] The other reason is that urban owners sold black children to other families. Raising a child could be expensive, especially when food had to be purchased, and her or his service was possibly less useful to a city owner than to a rural family who owned a farm. Black girls and boys in Philadelphia were more likely to be the only slaves living in their households than were children in Chester, Shrewsbury, or Chesterfield. According to the probate inventories, 20.1 percent of girls and 27.5 percent of boys in Philadelphia were their owners' only slaves, while just 9.1 percent of girls and 22.2 percent of boys in Chester lived apart from other blacks. In Chesterfield 8.8 percent of the girls and 9.7 percent of the boys lived alone, and in Shrewsbury 16.3 percent of the girls and 15.2 percent of the boys were the only blacks in their households.

In Philadelphia, throughout the colonial period, owners held an average of only about 2.4 slaves.[49] This meant that entire black

[47] Russell R. Menard, "The Maryland Slave Population, 1658 to 1730: A Demographic Profile of Blacks in Four Counties," *WMQ*, 3d ser., 32 (1975), 29-54.

[48] Susan E. Klepp, "Social Class and Infant Mortality in Philadelphia, 1720-1830" (Paper presented to the Philadelphia Center for Early American Studies Seminar, 6 November 1981, Philadelphia), 17-18; Smith, "Death and Life," 887-889; Rodger Craige Henderson, "Comparative Mortality Rates and Trends: Eighteenth-Century Lancaster County, Pennsylvania, British North America, and the Caribbean" (Paper presented to the Philadelphia Center for Early American Studies Seminar, 15 April 1983, Philadelphia).

[49] This average includes blacks listed in the probate inventories of decedents who had lived in the city of Philadelphia (not including Southwark and the Northern Liberties) during the years from 1682 to 1780. I have not included blacks who are specifically noted as living outside the city. The actual mean number of blacks in each household was lower because some masters had more than one house and because they often hired out their slaves. According to the Philadelphia constables' returns of 1780 (Philadelphia City Archives, City Hall Annex), on average only 1.4 blacks lived in each slaveholding household.

families, including the mother, father, and several children, rarely lived under the same roof. While the sex ratio of adult blacks was fairly even in the city, according to the probate inventories, at most only two in five black women lived in the same household with an adult black man. Only 3 percent were listed in the probate records with men who were described specifically as their husbands. The relationship of the rest of the men to the women is unknown; they could have been husbands or mates, prospective mates or friends, men to whom the women had no attachment, or men whom they detested or feared. Records of black marriages in Christ Church and St. Peter's Church, Philadelphia, also indicate that relatively few slave married couples lived together. Between 1727 and 1780, sixty-four black couples were married at the Anglican churches (all but eight after 1765). In one-quarter of these marriages, both partners were free, and another 14 percent were marriages between a free black and a slave. Twenty-nine (45.3 percent) were marriages in which both the husband and wife were slaves; of these slave couples, fewer than one-fourth (seven of the twenty-nine) were owned by the same master.[50]

That so few of Philadelphia's black women lived in the same households with their husbands was perhaps less disruptive of family life than it seems, because most husbands probably lived close by. Philadelphia, which as late as the 1770s reached only as far back from the Delaware as 7th Street,[51] had a fairly large black population throughout the eighteenth century. For instance, in 1750 when the population of Philadelphia was about 15,000, as many as 1,500, or one-tenth, of the city's residents were black.[52] Evidence from other

---

Much of the evidence for the discussion that follows comes from my analysis of probate wills and inventories for Philadelphia and the three rural monthly meeting areas, 1676-1780. It is assumed that the slaves listed in the probate records, aggregated by decade, represent an approximate cross-section of the black population.

[50] Records of Christ Church, Philadelphia, Marriages, 1709-1800, Genealogical Society of Pennsylvania Collections, HSP.

[51] Sam Bass Warner, Jr., *The Private City: Philadelphia in Three Periods of Its Growth* (Philadelphia, 1968), 11.

[52] Billy G. Smith, "Death and Life," 863-889. Blacks probably comprised 8 to 10 percent of Philadelphia's population at mid-century. My estimate is based upon data from the bills of mortality analyzed by Gary Nash ("Slaves and Slaveowners," 226-227, 230-231), which show that 13.8 percent of the burials in Philadelphia in 1722 were of blacks, 19.2 percent in 1729-1732, 10.9 percent in 1738-1742, 11.3 percent in 1743-1748, 7.7 percent in 1750-1755, 9.2 percent in 1756-1760, 8.1 percent in 1761-1765, 9.2 percent in 1766-1770, and 7.4 percent in 1771-1775. My estimate would be wrong if blacks had a higher mortality rate than the total population. However, while the black death rate may have been somewhat above that of whites, especially during periods of high importation in the early eighteenth century, in the 1730s, and in the early 1760s,

sources suggests that the number of blacks living in the city was large enough to make white Philadelphians uneasy. The whites complained on a number of occasions about slaves and free blacks gathering in groups in the evenings and on Sundays. In 1696, Philadelphia Yearly Meeting urged its members to restrain their slaves "from Rambling abroad on First Days or other Times."[53] The Pennsylvania Assembly passed a law in 1706 prohibiting blacks from meeting together "in great companies," but this statute evidently had limited effect because a number of Philadelphians, seemingly unaware that this law was on the books, petitioned in 1723 for a similar ban. In 1750, another petition from inhabitants of Philadelphia County protested to the Assembly about the custom of shooting off guns at New Year's; they complained that such revelry was introduced into the country by immigrant Germans and was now practiced by servants and blacks. The behavior they found disagreeable included excessive drinking, firing guns into houses, and throwing lighted wadding into houses and barns.[54] And the historian Edward Turner claimed (albeit without giving the source of his information) that as many as a thousand blacks gathered for festivals on the outskirts of town.[55] Thus, although few black women lived in the same house with their husbands, there was a large slave population living in what we would now consider a small city, and hence there was a good chance that their mates lived nearby.

Of course, even this tenuous link between family members could be broken at any time by the owner. Slave-owning fathers sometimes gave young slaves to their children when they married,[56] and most testators either divided their blacks among the heirs or directed that the slaves be sold upon their deaths.[57] While the white family mem-

---

the difference was probably minimized by the fact that immigrants (who had higher than average death rates) made up a large segment of the white Philadelphia population. For example, the percentage of decedents who were black, according to the mortality statistics, in the period 1750-1755 (7.7 percent) probably represents a low figure because the early 1750s was a time when few slaves were imported, but was the peak period of German immigration; close to 35,000 Germans arrived in Philadelphia during the years 1749-1754. Wax, "Negro Slave Trade," 46; Marianne S. Wokeck, "The Flow and the Composition of German Immigration to Philadelphia, 1727-1775," *PMHB* 105 (1981), 267.

[53] PYM mins., 23/7M/1696.

[54] James T. Mitchell and Henry Flanders, comps., *The Statutes at Large of Pennsylvania from 1682 to 1801* (Harrisburg, 1896-1915), 2:236; *Pennsylvania Archives*, 8th ser. (Harrisburg, 1931), 2:1464; 4:3396-3397.

[55] Edward Raymond Turner, *Slavery in Pennsylvania* (Baltimore, 1911), 32-33, 42.

[56] For example, George Emlen gave the slave woman Dinah to his daughter Hannah Logan during his lifetime; Phila. Co. Wills, William Logan, Bk. Q, No. 324.

[57] For examples, see Phila. Co. Wills, George Claypoole, Bk. E, No. 175; Henry Dexter, Bk. I, No. 139.

bers who received the blacks might live fairly close together, an owner's demise could bring about a painful separation for slaves. No testators stipulated that their slaves be sold together.[58] Philadelphia newspaper advertisements also provide evidence that many owners sold husbands away from wives, and children away from their parents; most indicated no concern about the consequences for the slaves. Merle G. Brouwer found in a survey of newspaper advertisements of slaves for sale in Pennsylvania that masters rarely specified that a slave should be kept in the neighborhood of his or her kin. Indeed, runaway notices indicate that slave families were broken up, and husbands or wives taken to other colonies. The first place masters thought to look for their runaway slaves was in the vicinity of their former residence and with the family from whom they had been separated.[59]

While slave men and women throughout Pennsylvania and New Jersey faced the prospect of being cut off from their families by sale or by the death of the master, Philadelphia black women were even less likely to live with their children than were adult females in rural areas. According to the probate inventories, which show the slaves' lives at only one point in time, only 28.5 percent of slave women in Philadelphia had children described as their own living in the same household. In most cases a woman had only one child who was specifically described as hers. Another 18 percent (for a combined total of almost one-half) were listed on their owners' inventories with black children who *could* have been theirs but were not described as such. The number of city women who actually lived in the same household with their children was almost certainly lower than these percentages suggest. Some of the children listed on their owner's inventories, especially those over age five, were hired out to other families.[60]

[58] No wills were found in which the testators directed their executors to keep black families together when they were sold. Masters who cared that much about their slaves' needs either emancipated them or provided for their support by giving them small farms, houses, or tools. Some owners showed little concern about the consequences of separation for their blacks. Elizabeth Fishbourn of Chester, for example, directed that a young black boy be taken from his mother as soon as he was weaned (Phila. Co. Wills, Bk. C, No. 141), while others wanted their slaves sold to the highest bidders.

[59] Merle G. Brouwer, "Marriage and Family Life among Blacks in Colonial Pennsylvania," *PMHB* 99 (1975), 368-372.

[60] Though William Masters was hardly a typical Philadelphia slave owner—he held thirty-three blacks at his death—his inventory provides valuable information on the practice of binding out black children. Of seventeen children listed in his inventory, eleven were bound out, one as far away as Wilmington. Phila. Co. Wills, William Masters, Bk. M, No. 27.

Rural black women in Pennsylvania and New Jersey were much more likely to live with their families than were urban slaves. In eastern Chester County, 70 percent of the women were listed in inventories with black children who were theirs or who could have been, and as many as 48 percent lived with adult men.[61] Life was more difficult for Chester County women in another way, however, because many fewer blacks lived there and the distances between plantations on which other slaves lived were quite far. The situation for men in eastern Chester County was especially bad in the years from 1721 to 1740 and in the 1770s because, according to the inventories, men outnumbered women at those times by a considerable margin. Over the colonial period, at most only a third of the black men in Chester lived with a black woman, and even fewer lived with a black child.[62] By the 1760s and 1770s, another difference between slaves in Philadelphia and Chester was the percentage who were of mixed parentage. In those decades, 13.5 percent of the slaves listed in Chester area inventories were mulattos. By contrast, in Philadelphia, only 3.2 percent of the slaves listed in inventories during those decades had parents of different racial backgrounds. Data from Quaker manumissions show a similar pattern. Mulattos were 30 percent of the slaves freed by members of four Chester County meetings, but only 5.4 percent of those emancipated by Philadelphia Friends.[63] Almost 16 percent of the slaves registered by Chester County slaveholders in 1780 were mulattos.

Black women in Shrewsbury and Chesterfield lived with their

[61] Analysis of the Chester County Slave Register of 1780, which includes blacks registered in response to the gradual abolition act of 1780 by their owners from throughout Chester County, yielded somewhat similar results. Over 64 percent of the black women were listed with black children, and as many as 42 percent lived with a black man. Chester County Slave Register, 1780, Pennsylvania Abolition Society Papers, Reel 24, HSP. I am indebted to Gary Nash for this reference.

[62] The Chester County Slave Register of 1780 indicated an almost even adult sex ratio; thus 43 percent of the men were listed with a black woman, about the same as the percentage of women who were listed with men. The register also listed more men with children than did the inventories—as many as 44 percent—but still this percentage was considerably lower than the percentage of women living with black children. The discrepancy between data from the slave register and the probate inventories may have resulted from the fact that different geographic areas were covered, or because the Chester probate data for the 1770s are too small to represent the black population reliably.

[63] Chester MM manumissions (1776-1780); Concord MM manumissions (1777-1789); Goshen MM manumissions, recorded in the MM minutes (1775-1777); and Kennett MM manumissions (1776-1780); all located in Friends Historical Library, Swarthmore. Phila. MM mans. Only those emancipated blacks who lived in the vicinity of the monthly meeting are counted.

families approximately as often as the Chester women. Of adult females listed in Shrewsbury inventories, 67.1 percent lived with children who were either theirs or could have been theirs, and 53.4 percent lived with adult men. In Chesterfield, 66.1 percent of the adult women had children living in the same household, and 56.3 percent lived under the same roof as a black man. On their side, black men in Shrewsbury were better off than both their Pennsylvania and West Jersey brethren in that 53.4 percent lived with adult women, and almost one-half lived with children who might have been their own. Fewer Chesterfield men (44.4 percent) lived with black women, though fully 54.4 percent were listed on the same inventories with young slaves.

The circumstances in which Africans and Afro-Americans lived varied significantly from one region of the middle colonies to another. In Philadelphia, rather few lived in the same house with their families, but the city had a relatively large black population and it is likely that mothers, fathers, and children often lived fairly close to one another. In the three rural areas, slaves were more likely to live in the same household with their spouse and children. However, country blacks—especially those living in Chester—had fewer opportunities than those in Philadelphia to socialize with other slaves, as the black population was small and distances between plantations rather great.

It is clear, then, that slavery was far from homogeneous throughout the Delaware Valley. The level of slaveholding varied from one region to another according to both the availability of European bound and free labor and the overall demand for workers beyond those supplied by an employer's family and occasional day labor. The nature of slavery also differed in the four localities examined, as blacks in Philadelphia had greater access to social institutions than did slaves in the country. Density of the black population, the sex ratio of adult slaves, and the financial ability or willingness of masters to support growing black families all influenced the conditions of the slaves' lives in respect to whether they had daily contact with other blacks or were able to live in the same household with their families.

The important question that remains is what these variations meant to the growth of abolitionism in Philadelphia Yearly Meeting. How did a swell in importation such as occurred in East Jersey and Pennsylvania in the early eighteenth century affect the attitudes of Friends? Were Quaker religious beliefs responsible in part or in whole for the decline in slaveholding after 1710 among wealthy

Philadelphia merchants and professionals? In the next three chapters we will examine the diverse ways in which Quakers dealt with the issue of slavery in different parts of the Delaware Valley. First, we will pick up the story of the growth of antislavery reform in Philadelphia Yearly Meeting where we left it in 1758 and see what the local meetings did to enforce the ban on slave trading and to move toward prohibiting slaveholding itself. Then in Chapters 5 and 6 we will look closely at four monthly meetings, Shrewsbury and Chesterfield in New Jersey and Chester and Philadelphia in Pennsylvania, which decided to oppose slavery at divergent times during the eighteenth century. These meetings represent the range of positions taken by mid-Atlantic Friends, and investigation of their members' involvement in slavery as well as the particular interpretation of Quaker theology each meeting held will bring us much closer to understanding the dynamics of abolitionism within Philadelphia Yearly Meeting.

· 4 ·

THE LOCAL MEETINGS
DEBATE SLAVERY

Philadelphia Yearly Meeting's decision of 1758 to punish the buyers and sellers of slaves and to appoint a committee to visit slave owners went only part of the way toward eradicating slavery from the Society. It was a compromise, the most stringent policy Friends could agree upon at that time. Reformers drew hope from the decision that their final objective—an end to slaveholding in the Society— would soon be reached, while slave owners won time to ponder whether they should give up their blacks. As it happened, the Quaker slave masters had a considerable period in which to make up their minds, for a full sixteen years passed before the Yearly Meeting took another major step toward abolition.

The new policy of 1758 set up two mechanisms of change: one for eliminating from leadership all Friends who continued to buy or sell slaves and another for persuading owners to free the blacks they already owned. With the first of these measures the focus of abolitionist reform moved away from the Yearly Meeting and back to the local meeting houses. There Friends of all opinions and interests thought about how the new policy would affect their life styles, and debated the extent to which the ruling should be enforced. Some meetings, which had pushed for abolition in the first place, gladly adopted the 1758 mandate and even stretched the discipline on their own to include activities that had not been mentioned in the central meeting's directive (such as hiring the labor of slaves) and to secure manumissions for slaves whenever possible. Other meetings flatly refused to enforce the ban for a number of years. And still other meetings, originally uninterested in, though not opposed to, the antislavery thrust of the 1750s, dutifully implemented the Yearly Meeting's new rule. In doing so, gradually they helped to develop a momentum in the Yearly Meeting against slavery that would lead to the 1776 prohibition.

The ways in which monthly meetings handled disciplinary cases in the period from 1758 to 1774 varied widely, and some meetings substantially changed their practices over that time. Tables 4.1 and 4.2 include disciplinary cases related to slavery that came up in nineteen monthly meetings in Pennsylvania, New Jersey, Delaware, and Maryland between 1757 and 1776; the records of five other meetings (Exeter, Richland, Buckingham, Bradford, and Warrington) indicated that they dealt with no slave buyers or sellers at all. Most of these cases concerned importing, purchasing, and selling blacks; only a few meetings disciplined Friends for owning slaves before 1776. Table 4.1 shows how the number of breaches prose-

TABLE 4.1. THE TIMING OF DISCIPLINARY CASES CONCERNING SLAVERY

Meeting	Total	No. of Cases			
		1757-1759	1760-1764	1765-1770	1771-1776
Phila. QM					
Philadelphia[a]	56	13	28	5	10
Abington	9	0	5	0	4
Radnor	2	0	0	0	2
Gwynedd	8	2	2	4	0
Bucks QM					
Falls	7	0	4	2	1
Middletown	7	0	7	0	0
Wrightstown	2	0	0	1	1
Chester and Western QMs					
Chester	6	0	4	0	2
New Garden	4	0	3	0	1
Goshen	4	2	2	0	0
Concord	2	0	1	1	0
Darby	4	0	1	2	1
Sadsbury	7	0	3	1	3
Nottingham	7	0	4	2	1
Uwchlan[b]	1	—	0	0	1
Wilmington	13	0	8	3	2
New Jersey					
Chesterfield	2	0	0	0	2
Shrewsbury	14	1	5	4	4
Woodbridge	7	2	3	0	2
Total	162	20	80	25	37
	(100.0%)	(12.3%)	(49.4%)	(15.4%)	(22.9%)

SOURCES: The cases listed in this and the following table for Radnor, Gwynedd, Falls, and Wrightstown meetings are from a computer list entitled "Individuals Dealt With for Infractions of Quaker Discipline by Monthly Meetings in Pennsylvania, 1682-1776," compiled by Jack D. Marietta and on deposit at the Quaker Collection, Haverford College. Data for the rest of the meetings are my own.
[a] Includes Northern and Southern Districts, formed in 1772, in all tables in this chapter
[b] Meeting established 1763

cuted by the meetings changed over time. Of the meetings that disciplined slave buyers or sellers at all, most started hearing these cases in the early 1760s, when about half of the 162 cases considered during the entire twenty-year span came before the meetings.[1] The number of offenses then declined in the last half of the 1760s, but swung upward again in the 1770s as meetings that had previously disciplined no one for buying or selling slaves conformed with the rest, and as several meetings began dealing with Friends for practices not subject to discipline before, including owning or hiring the labor of slaves.

While Table 4.1 illustrates the general timing of the local meetings' implementation of the 1758 minute, it also shows a wide variation in the speed with which individual local meetings handled these cases. Only five of the nineteen meetings dealt with offenders before 1760; four of these were the same meetings—Philadelphia, Shrewsbury, Woodbridge, and Gwynedd—that raised the issue in the Yearly Meeting in 1757-1758. Philadelphia's record during these early years was especially outstanding as the city Friends prosecuted nearly twice as many cases as all the other eighteen meetings combined. On the other hand, Wrightstown heard no cases before 1765, and Radnor, Uwchlan, and Chesterfield heard none before 1771. Thus, while the total number of recorded slavery cases considered in these nineteen meetings peaked in the early 1760s and then decreased as fewer Friends bought and sold slaves after 1765, the local meetings and their membership differed widely in their enforcement of the rule and their obedience to it.

Beyond illustrating the general timing of implementation of the 1758 minute and the wide variation in how rapidly local meetings took action, these data tell us little about the development of antislavery policy in Philadelphia Yearly Meeting. This is because we cannot be sure what the numbers mean. Did Bradford and Richland treat no cases because none of their members bought or sold a slave, or because the meetings refused to enforce the discipline? Were there no offenses in Chester, Abington, and Nottingham before 1760, and in Chesterfield and Radnor before 1771, or did it take these Friends that long to develop a sense of the meeting in favor of enforcing the minute of 1758? Closer study of what happened in some of these

[1] A significant increase of slave importation into the Delaware Valley during these years partially accounts for this fact. Darold D. Wax, "The Negro Slave Trade in Colonial Pennsylvania" (Ph.D. diss., University of Washington, 1962), 46. Gloucester-Salem Quarterly Meeting reacted to the rise in the number of blacks imported into their locality in 1761 by requiring the monthly meetings to read the 1758 Yearly Meeting minute aloud in meetings. Gloucester-Salem QM mins., 25/9M/1761.

meetings is necessary in order to understand the extent and timing of their compliance to the Yearly Meeting discipline.

Table 4.2 offers some insight into the ways meetings *resolved* cases dealing with slavery. Here, too, though a wide variation existed among local meetings, we can generalize meaningfully about the entire group. These nineteen meetings heard a total of 162 cases involving slavery, which included twenty-three Friends who were disowned during the period 1757-1776 for other wrongdoings *in addition to* dealing in slaves. Of the 139 women and men who were brought before the meeting for slavery offenses alone, 37 percent (51) were either excluded under the dictates of the 1758 minute from participating in monthly meetings or contributing funds, or were disowned entirely (in cases that came up after 1774 when slave trading became a disownable offense). Close to half (63) of the 139 offenders were permitted to acknowledge their error and retain their right to participate fully in the Society, while the cases of 18 percent (25) were either dropped or their resolutions were not reported in the meeting minutes.

As in the speed with which they disciplined slave traders, meetings also varied from one to another in how severely they punished the accused Friends. The data in Table 4.2 suggest that some congregations were stricter than others in disciplining slave buyers, sellers, and owners, and some became either more or less rigorous as time went by. Concord Monthly Meeting barred both of its offenders from business meetings, while Radnor excluded none and Middletown (Bucks) expelled only one in seven. Wilmington, Goshen, Philadelphia, Abington, and Sadsbury all disowned or excluded from business meetings about one-half of their members who were accused solely of owning, buying, or selling slaves. One example of a meeting that became stricter over time was Philadelphia. In the years 1757 to 1764, over one-fifth of the cases brought before the city meeting had indeterminate resolutions or were dropped, while the remainder were evenly divided between exclusion from leadership and acceptance of acknowledgments. In the period 1765 to 1776, however, three-fourths of the Philadelphia slavery cases ended in expulsion from business meetings or from the Society itself. Shrewsbury, on the other hand, seems to have become more lenient, as it accepted a higher percentage of acknowledgments in 1765-1776 than it had received during the earlier period.

Unfortunately, the various categories of case resolution contained in Table 4.2 still tell us very little about the depth of commitment to abolitionism of individual meetings. A meeting that excluded a higher percentage of offenders was not necessarily "more abolitionist" than one that accepted acknowledgments from a greater proportion of its wrongdoers. Meetings truly concerned about the injustice of slaveholding could insistently pressure members to free the blacks they had bought and then accept their acknowledgments (these meetings thus appearing to be more lenient on a superficial level). At the same time, other meetings could strike swiftly against slave traders by excluding them all, and in this way seem relatively forceful against slavery but in reality having little concern for the fate of the slaves. We must get behind these data to find out how meetings actually disciplined their members. For instance, what did meetings require of accused Friends before accepting their acknowledgments? Did offenders have to free the slaves they had purchased

TABLE 4.2. RESOLUTION OF DISCIPLINARY CASES CONCERNING SLAVERY

| | | 1757-1764 | | |
Meeting	No. cases	Indeterm. or dropped	Acknowl- edged	Partial disown.
Phila. QM				
Phila. MM	37	21.6%	37.8%	40.6%
Abington	5	20.0	20.0	60.0
Radnor	0	—	—	—
Gwynedd	4	50.0	50.0	0.0
Bucks QM				
Falls	3	66.7	33.3	0.0
Middletown	7	0.0	85.7	14.3
Wrightstown	0	—	—	—
Chester and Western QMs				
Chester	4	0.0	75.0	25.0
New Garden	3	33.3	33.3	33.3
Goshen	4	0.0	50.0	50.0
Concord	1	0.0	0.0	100.0
Darby	1	0.0	100.0	0.0
Sadsbury	3	0.0	33.3	66.7
Nottingham	3	33.3	33.3	33.3
Uwchlan[b]	0	—	—	—
Wilmington	7	0.0	57.1	42.9
New Jersey				
Chesterfield	0	—	—	—
Shrewsbury	6	0.0	50.0	50.0
Woodbridge	5	40.0	40.0	20.0
Total	93	18.3	45.2	36.5

TABLE 4.2 (*cont.*)

Meeting	No. cases	1765-1776 Indeterm. or dropped	Acknowl- edged	Partial disown.[a]
Phila. QM				
Phila. MM	8	12.5%	12.5%	75.0%
Abington	4	0.0	50.0	50.0
Radnor	2	50.0	50.0	0.0
Gwynedd	3	0.0	100.0	0.0
Bucks QM				
Falls	3	33.3	33.3	33.3
Middletown	0	—	—	—
Wrightstown	1	0.0	0.0	100.0
Chester and Western QMs				
Chester	2	0.0	50.0	50.0
New Garden	1	0.0	100.0	0.0
Goshen	0	—	—	—
Concord	1	0.0	0.0	100.0
Darby	2	0.0	50.0	50.0
Sadsbury	4	50.0	25.0	25.0
Nottingham	1	0.0	100.0	0.0
Uwchlan[b]	0	—	—	—
Wilmington	5	40.0	20.0	40.0
New Jersey				
Chesterfield	1	0.0	100.0	0.0
Shrewsbury	7	14.3	71.4	14.3
Woodbridge	1	0.0	100.0	0.0
Total	46	17.4	45.6	37.0

SOURCES: Table 4.1
[a] Also includes persons disowned for slavery offenses during 1775-1776
[b] No cases involving slavery only

or sold? Further, it is imperative to find out how meetings dealt with the buyers and sellers of slaves in comparison with other offenders. A meeting that was firmly committed to antislavery may have disowned few slave purchasers or sellers simply because the leadership hesitated to exclude members for *any* offense. Some of these questions can be answered only through a close examination of the dynamics of leadership and the enforcement of discipline within local meetings. Subsequent chapters on four local meetings present the results of such a study. Before doing that, however, evidence from the meeting minutes presented here can demonstrate effectively the range of ways in which monthly and quarterly meetings enforced the 1758 decision.

As suggested by Tables 4.1 and 4.2, some meetings firmly rejected the 1758 minute. For example, even though Chesterfield Friends freely admitted in their quarterly reports throughout the 1750s and 1760s that members continued to buy and sell slaves, this West Jersey meeting took no action during these decades against the offenders.[2] Burlington Quarter, of which Chesterfield Friends formed an influential part, did not push them to enforce the ban.[3] Deer Creek Monthly Meeting, located west of the Susquehanna River in Maryland, also refused to deal with slave buyers and sellers as they were required to do under the 1758 discipline. This meeting was small, however, and had much less sway in its quarterly meeting than Chesterfield had. Thus Western Quarter (which was created in 1758 when Chester Quarterly Meeting split in half) consistently reminded Deer Creek Friends to discipline all offenders. But Deer Creek's weightiest members were slave owners; and some were among the slave purchasers and sellers as well. They took no action in response to the quarter's urgings. The number of antislavery adherents at Deer Creek did increase during the 1770s, but as late as 1781 Western Quarterly Meeting continued to report that it kept close watch over these Maryland Quakers and expressed hope that they would overcome their "weakness."[4] The same quarterly meeting also had to remind Duck Creek (Delaware) and Bradford (Chester County) monthly meetings in 1761 to implement the 1758 decision,[5] but these meetings required less pressure than Deer Creek. Indeed, Duck Creek Friends, who later manumitted hundreds of slaves,[6] began treating with slave purchasers within six months of the quarterly meeting's reminder.[7] In contrast, Bradford Friends did not discipline their slave traders during the 1760s, and appointed a committee to visit slaveholders only in 1770, later than other meetings in Western Quarter. The Bradford meeting nearly broke apart during the early 1760s over punishing members who

[2] Chesterfield MM mins., 4/5M/1758, 2/11M/1758, 1/2M/1759, 7/8M/1760, 6/8M/1761, 4/2M/1762, 5/8M/1762, 3/2M/1763, 2/8M/1764, 7/8M/1766, 6/8M/1767. See Chapter 5 for a more complete discussion.

[3] Burlington QM mins., 1755-1780.

[4] Deer Creek MM mins., 1761-1780; Western QM mins., 1761-1783.

[5] Western QM mins., 16/2M/1761.

[6] Book of Manumissions of Duck Creek (Camden), Delaware, Monthly Meeting, 1774-1792, MS, Genealogical Society of Pennsylvania Collections, HSP.

[7] Western QM mins., 7/8M/1761.

stayed in government offices during the Seven Years' War, persons who did not attend meetings, and perhaps slave traders as well.[8]

While other meetings did not actually refuse to deal with slave purchasers, their visible foot-dragging in the late 1750s and early 1760s suggests that they were not in total agreement with the Yearly Meeting's decision of 1758. Burlington Monthly Meeting is a good example of this kind of meeting, even though we would have expected the home meeting of John Woolman to take an active part in the fight against slavery. In point of fact, however, Burlington meeting did not participate in the preliminary maneuvers that brought the issue before the Yearly Meeting during the 1750s, and in May 1759, Woolman's fellow members even suggested that the central meeting had gone too far and too fast in making disciplinary changes at the 1758 session. In the minutes the clerk wrote, "this meeting recommends it to be considered by the Quarterly Meeting, whether it may not be adviseable to request the Yearly Meeting that before any New Rules of Discipline are concluded, notice of such being under consideration may be sent down to the Quarterly & Monthly Meetings."[9] Burlington Friends may have been opposing another discipline change made in 1758 concerning the taking of oaths, or may have simply disliked the method by which the two changes were made; but their subsequent record on dealing with slave buyers suggests that the minute concerning slavery was at least one source of their unhappiness. Of six cases brought before the meeting between 1759 and 1765, two were dropped without resolution—including one in which the offender promised to free the black he had purchased but sold the person instead. Another man received a certificate of removal when he promised to buy no more slaves, and a fourth said he would abide by the Golden Rule in the future. The fifth offender, Benjamin Swett, was permitted to return the man he had bought to the seller without further penalty, and John Folwell, the sixth, was disowned in 1765, but his errors included excessive drinking as well as buying a slave.[10]

Many meetings, such as Darby, Goshen, Concord, and Middletown (Bucks), consistently dealt with offenders by the early 1760s, but did not make new policies on their own. These Friends treated with slave purchasers by the same methods employed in dealing with other kinds of offenses. Overseers reported the wrongdoers to

[8] Western QM mins., 1761-1765; Bradford MM mins., 1761-1770.
[9] Burlington MM mins., 7/5M/1759.
[10] Burlington MM mins., 1759-1765.

the meeting who then assigned Friends to visit and attempt to convince them of the evil of slave buying and selling. The offenders were expected to admit their mistake and promise not to repeat it. They often explained in their condemnations (acknowledgments) that they had been unaware of the change in discipline, but promised to use the blacks well and to educate them in the Christian religion. Slave buyers and sellers who refused to offer acknowledgments were usually excluded from business meetings (or partially disowned).[11]

The most stringent meetings believed, however, that condemnations were not sufficient in slavery cases, because unlike acts such as fornication or simple assault which could be righted by the sincere confession and apology of the transgressor, slavery-related offenses could be eradicated only when the fundamental wrong, the bondage of the slave, was removed. These meetings included Wilmington and Shrewsbury, who used the 1758 minute against buying and selling slaves to secure manumissions even in their earliest cases. Several additional meetings adopted this strategy later in the 1760s, and the Yearly Meeting agreed to it in 1774.

Wilmington, for example, required the first slave purchaser brought before the meeting in 1760 to educate the young boy he had bought, teach him a trade so that he could earn a comfortable living, and free him at age twenty-one. The offender refused and was partially disowned even though he acknowledged his error. Wilmington Friends expected all other members who subsequently bought or sold slaves to secure freedom for the blacks involved. If they did not, they too were excluded from meetings of business. In 1767, Wilmington even tried to disown outright someone who sold a slave; but Chester Quarterly Meeting overturned that decision.[12] The efforts of Wilmington Quakers to obtain freedom for slaves were evidently quite successful, though, because by 1761 they were recording manumissions in a book designated specifically for that purpose (fifteen years before the Yearly Meeting suggested this action); and in 1766 the meeting reported that few members still owned slaves.[13]

---

[11] Darby MM mins., 1757-1780; Goshen MM mins., 1757-1780; Concord MM mins., 1757-1780; and Middletown (Bucks) MM mins., 1757-1780.

[12] Wilmington MM mins., 15/10M/1760, 11/3M/1767, 16/12M/1767, and 15/9M/1768.

[13] Wilmington MM mins., 16/9M/1761 and 16/7M/1766. David Ferris, a very weighty member of this meeting and an ardent abolitionist, recorded the manumissions. He attempted to convince members of other meetings to do the same, arguing that otherwise the freed blacks might lose their manumission papers and be re-enslaved. Wilmington

A few other meetings also demanded that offenders provide in some way for the liberty of their slaves. Woodbridge Monthly Meeting in 1763 instructed one of its slave sellers to give the money he received in the sale to the meeting for the black woman's future use. Beginning in 1764, Abington Monthly Meeting compelled members to free the slaves they bought or sold. Chester adopted the same policy in 1773. Philadelphia Monthly Meeting accepted simple acknowledgments at first, but during the 1760s began to require promises that slaves would be freed after a term of years in the owners' wills.[14]

This wide range of responses in enforcing the Yearly Meeting's decision of 1758 not only suggests the various ways in which Friends reacted to the new ruling, but also indicates which meetings supported, opposed, and were indifferent to the policy change. Clearly, some meetings had been more active than others in supporting the new discipline back in 1758. A lively debate had taken place not only in the central meeting, as Woolman described, but also in quarterly and monthly meetings.[15] Study of the development of antislavery opinion, or its lack of development, in several meetings whose stances were quite different during the 1750s and 1760s will substantially expand our understanding of how abolition grew in the Yearly Meeting as a whole.

Explaining why the local meetings had such a diversity of attitudes toward slavery is feasible only after the history of several meetings is looked at in detail—a major endeavor of this study. Already it is clear, however, that the differences among meetings over the institution did not divide neatly according to geographic region, economic activity, or density of the black population. Chesterfield

MM mins., 11/1M/1764; David Ferris to James Rigby, 7 April 1766, and Ferris to Samuel Hansom, 2 June 1766, Ferris Collection, FHL. The letter from Ferris to Rigby is published in J. William Frost, ed., *The Quaker Origins of Antislavery* (Norwood, Pa., 1980), 182-186.

[14] Woodbridge MM mins., 17/3M/1763; Abington MM mins., 1757-1780; Chester MM mins., 1757-1780; Phila. MM mins., 1757-1780.

[15] Chester Quarter, from which Western Quarter was divided in September 1758, was probably the scene of an animated discussion when the representatives of Wilmington and Deer Creek, Goshen and Bradford, converged. Indeed, John Churchman informed John Pemberton in August 1758 (before the start of the Yearly Meeting) that Chester Quarterly Meeting had discussed the issue of slavery. "Something of contention shew itself in various matters, particularly about Negroes and contributing towards furnishing wagons and horses in the present expedition," he wrote, "but at length 'twas concluded to give hints of each to the Yearly Meeting, 'tho some would have had both [passed?] over as things not worthy of noting." Churchman to Pemberton, 17 August 1758, Pemberton Papers, 12:142, HSP.

Monthly Meeting—among the last in the Delaware Valley to accept antislavery—was located to the north of most other meetings in the Philadelphia area, away from contamination by the planters of Maryland and Virginia, while Wilmington Friends, who were ardent abolitionists, lived near the tobacco colonies with their numerous slaves. Though Deer Creek (Maryland) Friends behaved as one might expect a meeting made up of unyielding plantation owners would, the Duck Creek (Delaware) meeting displayed remarkably little resistance to antislavery ideals considering its many and influential slaveholders. The number of blacks living in a locality also seems to have had little influence on meeting decisions. Philadelphia had a higher percentage of blacks in its population than any other place in Pennsylvania during the 1760s,[16] but after 1753 Friends there were leading activists in the abolitionist campaign. Bradford Monthly Meeting in central Chester County, on the other hand, had a very small black population but required considerable prodding by Western Quarter before it would deal with slave buyers and sellers.

A more careful study of the influences at work on the attitudes of local meetings in this period before 1774, during which monthly meetings devised their own strategies on slave trading and slavery itself, is therefore necessary. Why did Shrewsbury, like Wilmington, jump at the chance to use the 1758 minute, which banned only buying and selling slaves, as a way to *manumit* blacks? For what reasons was Burlington Quarter, John Woolman's home base, so resistant to abolitionist reform? What changes occurred in the region comprising Chester and Western quarterly meetings to cause bitter disagreements over slavery in the 1750s and 1760s among local meetings that had in fact spearheaded the thrust against buying imported slaves earlier in the century? And why did Philadelphia Friends change their meeting's earlier policy so drastically as to become the protagonists of antislavery reform? And we need to understand as best we can the attitudes toward slavery of Quakers in the quiet meetings. Were they silent because they opposed the measures taken by the Yearly Meeting but believed themselves too weak vis-à-vis the Philadelphia elite to win their case? Were they simply uninterested in the question because few or no members owned slaves? Or were they hopelessly divided on the issue? Finally, and perhaps most difficult, how did the changing configuration of attitudes, interests, and actions in local meetings contribute to the

[16] See Chapter 3, above.

development of antislavery reform in the Yearly Meeting as a whole? This is the business of chapters that follow.

In the years between 1758 and 1774, the Yearly Meeting did not completely abdicate to local meetings its role in encouraging the elimination of slavery. For although it made no additional rules of discipline concerning slave trading or slaveholding during that time, it carefully monitored implementation of the 1758 decision, and after 1765 required meetings to appoint committees to visit slave owners. The central meeting also maintained its now considerable concern about the education of slaves and free blacks.

The Yearly Meeting's first efforts against slaveholding were extended through John Woolman, John Sykes, John Scarborough, John Churchman, and Daniel Stanton, who in 1758 had volunteered to visit slave owners in order to convince them to give up their slaves. These men reported on their progress at each Yearly Meeting for the four years following their appointment. Woolman recorded in his journal that he and other members of the committee visited slave owners in each of the quarterly meetings between November 1758 and August 1761. In 1762, however, they asked to be released from their duty because they believed that concern had now spread among Friends to the extent that leaders of the various local meetings could henceforth carry on the work.[17]

Other Friends also treated with slave owners on their own initiative, or at the suggestion of their local meetings. They had widely varying experiences among those they visited. William Cox of Deer Creek wrote to Israel Pemberton II in 1758 that John Churchman, accompanied by other members of Nottingham Monthly Meeting (the meeting to which Deer Creek Friends belonged at that time), "had very close alarming testimonies" in his neighborhood. Cox, a slave master, hoped that their labors "may excite to more diligence in us," but he was evidently not convinced of the evils of slave trading, for he later considered selling his five slaves in order to raise money to alleviate his financial difficulties.[18] On the other side of the Delaware, Joshua Evans, a minister of Haddonfield meeting, met with slaveholders in his locality in 1761. He found that his efforts "went hard with some who held slaves, and who thought it would cause uneasiness between them and their black servants; and

---

[17] PYM mins., 1759-1762; Phillips P. Moulton, ed., *The Journal and Major Essays of John Woolman* (New York, 1971), 94-97, 102, 106, and 117.

[18] William Cox to Israel Pemberton II, 4 December 1758, Pemberton Papers, 13:15, HSP; Cox to Pemberton, 10 September 1765, Pemberton Papers, 18:47, HSP.

so would scarcely permit us to perform the visit." He spoke to the slave owners alone after a family worship session in order to avoid the charge that he was inciting a slave rebellion. At the same time Evans also decided to stop using products made by slaves in the West Indies. He found that "many supposed that in this respect I was going too far, they thinking we might use what we bought and paid for; and some were not clear of casting reflections on me for my singular conduct."[19]

John Woolman continued to focus his ministry among Friends, from New England to Maryland, on the subject of slavery.[20] He was so affected by the protests of Quaker slave owners similar to those Joshua Evans heard that he did not want Philadelphia Yearly Meeting to pay for the printing of his *Considerations on Keeping Negroes, Part Second* (1762). Woolman thought slaveholders who contributed to the Yearly Meeting stock were "not likely to be satisfied with those books being spread amongst a people where many of the slaves are learned to read, and especially not at their expense." In visiting the owners, he was saddened because so many obstacles, such as their style of life and scale of annual expenses, kept them from manumitting their slaves. Woolman's second essay on slaveholding acknowledged that a master might hold a slave for purely unselfish reasons (such as supporting a black who could not take care of himself). But he clearly argued that slavery was oppression and that persons who exploited the labor of native-born slaves were just as guilty as those who kidnapped Africans and sent them to America.[21]

Another fervent abolitionist was intimidated—at least on one occasion—by the opposition of slaveholders. David Ferris, almost certainly an initiator of Wilmington Monthly Meeting's front-rank stance against slavery, felt an "inclination" to speak against slavery when he visited Friends at Deer Creek in 1766. He held his tongue, however, and instead wrote to James Rigby, one of the leaders of the Maryland meeting, on his return home. In the letter, Ferris warned the Quaker slaveholders in Deer Creek that "those who will not quit their beloved gain of oppression, will loose their hold of the Truth; and the Society will bear a Testimony against such, who withstand the deliverance of Captives, and will not let the oppressed go free." Ferris argued further that male slaves should be freed at

[19] "Joshua Evans's Journal," *Friends' Miscellany* 10 (1837), 16-18.
[20] Moulton, ed., *Journal . . . of John Woolman*, 106-162.
[21] Ibid., 117-118, 141, 210-237.

age twenty-one and females somewhat earlier, and that black children should receive the same education as whites in reading, writing, and religion.[22]

While these individuals tried to convince slave owners of their error, Philadelphia Yearly Meeting encouraged local meetings to carry on the service of the five-man committee of 1758. In 1763, the central meeting appointed a group of twenty-five men and women to visit all quarterly and monthly meetings and assess their adherence to the discipline. The committee reported in 1764

> that a relapse from the Pure Watchful, and timely restoring Spirit of true Christian Discipline hath overtaken individuals, whereby weakness sometimes sorrowfully appears in Quarterly & Monthly meetings, and we apprehend the neglect of Friends in some places in not putting in practice the Yearly meeting advice in some important matters, & in particular with respect to our Testimony relating to Slaves, & holding Offices in Civil Government, and continuing some such in high Stations in the Church, & employing others in Services therein, have contributed much to the weakness which is apparent in many places.

In response, the Yearly Meeting instructed local meetings to take more care in dealing with offenders and warned that if they did not, the Yearly Meeting would send representatives to supervise their meetings.[23]

In the following year, 1765, the central meeting focused its attention specifically on slavery and directed local leaders to visit slave owners in their meetings, "that all may acquit themselves with Justice and Equity towards a People who by an unwarrantable Custom, are unjustly deprived of the common Priviledges of mankind."[24] The Yearly Meeting enforced this directive by requiring local meetings to send in reports concerning visits to slaveholders along with their written answers to the queries about purchasing and selling slaves and the treatment of blacks. Abolitionists from most monthly meetings visited slaveholders every few years, although several meetings (notably Chesterfield and Deer Creek) did not even appoint visiting committees until 1774.[25] Quarterly meetings generally re-

[22] David Ferris to James Rigby, 7 April 1766, Ferris Collection, FHL; published in Frost, ed., *Quaker Origins*, 182-186.

[23] PYM mins., 22-29/9M/1764.

[24] PYM mins., 21-27/9M/1765.

[25] PYM mins., 1766-1781; Chesterfield MM mins., 1765-1780; Western QM mins., 1765-1780.

ported in their annual answers to the queries that a few members of their quarter had bought or sold slaves in the past year, and that while Friends generally neglected the religious education of their blacks, they did not mistreat them physically. The language of these answers varied little from one meeting to another, and from one year to the next. In 1767 Chester Quarter exhibited a bit more individuality, and perhaps a bit more abolitionist fervor as well, by noting "we are under a difficulty in saying Negro's grown to full age are used well, & yet kept in perpetual Bondage without any hopes of Liberty."[26]

By 1773, the abolitionists' visits to slave owners began to bear fruit. Throughout the 1760s and early 1770s Friends visited slave-owning families, gently (or perhaps sometimes not so gently) trying to persuade them of their wrong. Many of the Quaker masters were recalcitrant, but the visitors did not give up. By 1773 the Yearly Meeting could report that "by the Accounts receiv'd from our several Quarters, and Epistles from our neighbouring Provinces, it appears that there is a pious, and we hope a growing Concern to support the Testimony of Truth in its several Branches, & more especially against that antichristian and oppressive Practice of depriving our fellow Men of that Share of christian and civil Liberty due to all Men."[27]

The next year, 1774, brought the issue to a head. Several quarterly meetings raised questions about the decision of 1758, starting a discussion that ended with another major revision of the discipline. Bucks Quarter asked two technical questions about the limits of the 1758 minute. They wanted to know whether Friends who had been disciplined for buying or selling slaves should still be considered members and therefore subject to punishment for other offenses. And they further questioned if members who transferred ownership of their slaves to others without exchange of money but in order to clear "their Estates of any future Incumbrance" had violated the discipline. This probably applied to Friends who foresaw a ban on ownership and had given their slaves to non-Friends in order to avoid manumitting their blacks and having to post the £30 (in Pennsylvania) or £200 (in New Jersey) bond required for manumission. Philadelphia Quarterly Meeting more straightforwardly requested a reconsideration of the minute of 1758 "in order for the

---

[26] Chester QM mins., 10/8M/1767.
[27] PYM mins., 27-30/9M/1773.

further Advancement of our Testimony" against the practice of keeping slaves.[28]

The Yearly Meeting directed these questions to a committee headed by Hugh Roberts (ca. 1706-1786), a wealthy Philadelphia merchant.[29] This committee found that a "general Concern [prevailed] that our Christian Testimony may be more extensively held forth against the unrighteous Practice of enslaving our fellow Creatures," and suggested several changes in the discipline which the Yearly Meeting accepted. From that time on, slave buyers and sellers would be disowned outright if, beyond just condemning their actions, they refused to free or (in the case of slaves they had sold) obtain freedom for the injured blacks. In addition, the Yearly Meeting instructed quarterly and monthly meetings to join "in a speedy & close Labour" with members who owned slaves. Local meetings should turn in the names of slave owners who refused to free their blacks to the next Yearly Meeting, and should not employ these die-hards "in the Service of Truth." This rule, if followed, would effectively exclude all slaveholders from positions of leadership in the Society. The central meeting also admonished members to avoid hiring the labor of slaves or acting as executors or administrators of estates "where Slaves [were] bequeathed or likely to be detain'd in Bondage." These last matters, however, did not become a part of the discipline.[30]

The response to this Yearly Meeting directive was promising, for by early 1775 every monthly meeting in which members owned slaves appointed visiting committees. Nevertheless, some meetings were more ardent and successful than others in their efforts to obtain manumissions in the years before 1776. Chesterfield and Radnor monthly meetings, for example, showed no enthusiasm for the task, but Buckingham Monthly Meeting reported in August 1776 that all of its slaves were manumitted and Burlington Monthly Meeting announced in the same month that a "considerable" number were freed.[31] Several small meetings with just a few slaves could soon report that only one or two cases remained.[32] By 1776 the Yearly

[28] PYM mins., 26/9M-1/10M/1774.

[29] William Wade Hinshaw, *Encyclopedia of American Quaker Genealogy* (Baltimore, 1969), 2:414.

[30] PYM mins., 26/9M-1/10M/1774.

[31] Chesterfield MM mins., 1774-1776; Phila. QM mins., 6/11M/1775; Bucks QM mins., 29/8M/1776; Burlington MM mins., 26/8M/1776.

[32] Egg Harbor and Kingwood monthly meetings of Burlington Quarterly Meeting, Burlington QM mins., 26/8M/1776; Sadsbury MM mins., 1775-1778; Richland Monthly Meeting of the Philadelphia Quarter, Phila. QM mins., 6/2M/1775.

Meeting was ready to take the final step. Though they found that the 1774 minute had achieved emancipation for a large number of slaves in the past two years, they appointed a committee to "report to this Meeting their Sense & Judgement on the most effectual religious Means for perfecting a Work which has long been the occasion of heavy Labour to the faithful Members of the Church." The committee decided, and the meeting agreed, that the local meetings should disown all slaveholders who, after much advice and time had been spent on them, still refused to manumit their slaves. The Yearly Meeting wanted blacks of all ages to be freed, and directed monthly meetings to record their manumissions for future reference.[33]

Every monthly meeting in Philadelphia Yearly Meeting followed the directions of the minute of 1776, although some acted sooner than others. According to data from Quaker manumission records (see Table 4.3), slave-owning Friends freed about 65 percent of

TABLE 4.3. THE TIMING OF MANUMISSIONS

Meeting[a]	No.	1763-1774	1775-1777	1778-1779	1780-1796
Phila. QM					
Phila. MM[b]	189	2.1%	62.5%	15.3%	20.1%
Abington MM	33	6.1	75.7	6.1	12.1
Exeter MM	6	0.0	33.3	0.0	66.7
Bucks QM	60	0.0	61.7	10.0	28.3
Chester &					
Western QMs					
Chester MM	25	8.0	44.0	28.0	20.0[c]
Concord MM	15	0.0	80.0	6.6	13.4
Kennett MM	3	0.0	33.3	33.3	33.3
Goshen MM	8	0.0	100.0	0.0	0.0
Burlington QM					
Burlington MM	35	2.9	82.8	5.7	8.6
Chesterfield MM	69	2.9	46.4	24.6	26.1
Total	443	2.5	62.0	14.7	20.8

SOURCE: Manumissions
[a] Salem MM is excluded because the number of slaves freed after 4M/1777 is unknown
[b] Includes slaves living within the Philadelphia, Northern District, and Southern District MMs only
[c] One owner released five slaves

[33] PYM mins., 23-28/9M/1776.

their slaves before 1778, and 80 percent before 1780.[34] As with enforcement of the minute of 1758, however, there was considerable variation among meetings in the speed with which they secured freedom for blacks. Substantial differences are shown graphically in the records of even two monthly meetings that were both within Burlington Quarter: Burlington obtained 85.7 percent of its manumissions before 1778 while Chesterfield secured only 49.3 percent by that year. Burlington, it appears, had become more convinced of the iniquity of slavekeeping since the 1760s when it got off to a slow start in disciplining members who bought and sold slaves. As we see here, however, Chesterfield remained backward in its position on slavery even into the 1770s. (See also Tables 4.1, 4.2.) Chester and Gloucester-Salem quarters reported by early 1778 that their meetings were mostly clear of slaveholders.[35] But Table 4.3 suggests that only some meetings in Chester Quarter had secured manumissions for most of their blacks by that time. Goshen and Concord were free or almost free of slavery by 1778,[36] but Chester Monthly Meeting had manumitted only 52 percent by that year. While not quite as slow as Chesterfield, Chester—unlike its position earlier in the eighteenth century when it opposed the slave trade— was hardly in the forefront of the abolitionist movement after 1750. Philadelphia Quarterly Meeting announced in August 1776 that its members had freed 115 blacks and mulattoes and reported an additional 37 manumissions during the next year. In August 1778, most of that quarter's meetings were nearly clear.[37] Abington Friends, who had moved quite forcefully against slave traders in the 1760s and early 1770s, secured liberty for over 80 percent of their blacks by 1778. The city Friends, who had been in the vanguard in enforcing the minute of 1758, were about average in obtaining manumissions; by 1778 they had freed about 65 percent.

Little evidence is available about the period of soul-searching that Quaker slave owners went through while committees from their monthly meetings paid repeated visits to convince them to manumit their slaves. The committee reports, summarized in the minutes, sometimes indicated how the service was going. The slave-owning

[34] The quality of these data is limited by the fact that the manumissions for about half of the meetings in New Jersey and Pennsylvania no longer exist—or have not yet been located. See Appendix B for further comment on these records.

[35] Chester QM mins., 11/8M/1777; Gloucester-Salem QM mins., 20/3M/1778.

[36] These same meetings had disciplined slave buyers and sellers strictly in the 1750s and 1760s. See Tables 4.1 and 4.2.

[37] Phila. QM mins., 5/8M/1776, 4/8M/1777, and 3/8M/1778.

Friend might have purposefully absented himself from home, or have received the committee with courtesy and respect. He or she often pleaded economic necessity, promised to free the black in a short while, or simply asked for more time to consider manumission.

The experience of a Virginia Quaker in the early 1780s shows graphically the dilemma of a slaveholding Friend. Clark Moorman of Caroline County owned two slaves whom he refused to free for over a year, despite frequent visits by members of his monthly meeting. When the Friends were close to giving up on him, but agreed to pay him one last visit, he refused to come out of the field to meet them. The committee waited for him until he did come home for dinner, when they "met him pleasantly and enquired after his health etc. After dinner was over [committee member] Caleb Jones observed, 'Well Clark, we have come to pay thee a little visit, and wish to have a private opportunity with thee if thou hast no objection,' he replied he had none, so they all sat down together, as he said with his mind braced against anything they might offer. They sat in silence about an hour when Caleb Jones observed 'Well Friends I reckon we had as well ride,' they said Farewell without saying one word on the subject of their visit, to his surprise and mortification." Moorman was troubled by the visit, and soon after had a dream in which a black boy controlled the gate to heaven and refused to let Moorman enter. The slave owner took that as a sign, and manumitted his blacks the next day.[38] The dream sequence makes this story unique, but still we are able to appreciate the strain under which visiting committees could place members who owned slaves.

In the chapters that follow we will look closely at the very different patterns in which abolitionism grew in four localities in New Jersey and Pennsylvania—the areas that comprised Shrewsbury, Chesterfield, Philadelphia, and Chester monthly meetings. As we have already seen, each of these meetings approached the issue of slavery in a different manner. Investigation of the varying careers of the institution in the four areas will help us understand why some Quakers opposed slavery and others did not. This analysis will incorporate data from probate inventories and tax lists in order to learn everything we can about slaves owned by non-Quakers as well as by Friends, and those who were retained as well as those who were freed. That way we can find out whether Friends were truly different

<hr />

[38] Moorman's "conversion" is described in a letter from his grandson Thomas H. Tyrell [Terrell] to Benjamin Seebohm, 25/12M/1848, Library of the Society of Friends, London, published in Philip J. Schwarz, "Clark T. Moorman, Quaker Emancipator," *Quaker History* 69 (1980), 27-35.

than their neighbors in their attitudes about slavery, and why some Quakers came to oppose slavery before other members of their religion.

Before doing this, however, we can learn something more about the variety of Quaker attitudes and obtain hints about the sources of that variation, from the manumissions. It must be remembered that these data reveal nothing about Afro-Americans who were *not* freed by Quaker owners, and do not include slaves owned by non-Friends. In Table 4.4, the meetings for which manumissions are available are grouped by how quickly they obtained freedom for their blacks: "early" meetings (Abington, Concord, Goshen, and Burlington) gained at least 80 percent of their manumissions by 1778; "average" meetings (Philadelphia and Bucks) obtained 60 percent by that year; and "late" meetings (Exeter, Chester, Kennett, and Chesterfield) recorded from only one-third to about one-half by 1778.

TABLE 4.4. AGE AND GENDER OF BLACKS LISTED
IN MANUMISSIONS, 1763-1796

Meeting	No.	Males		Females	
		21+	Under 21	18+	Under 18
"Early"					
Abington	33	7	7	8	11
Concord	15	5	2	6	2
Goshen	8	3	2	2	1
Burlington	35	9	11	8	7
Total		24	22	24	21
"Average"					
Phila.	189	52	52	56	29
Bucks QM	60	23	9	15	13
Total		75	61	71	42
"Late"					
Exeter	6	1	3	1	1
Chester	25	4	7	7	7
Kennett	3	2	0	0	1
Chesterfield	69	12	27	16	14
Total		19	37	24	23
Salem	40[a]	10	10	8	11
Grand Total	483[a]	128	130	127	97
	(100.0%)	(26.6%)	(27.0%)	(26.3%)	(20.1%)

SOURCE: Manumissions
[a] Including one whose gender is unknown

In Table 4.4, for all of the meetings together, the numbers of emancipated men, women, boys, and girls are about equal (though there are somewhat fewer girls). The same holds true for slaves manumitted by "early" and "average" meetings. Among the meetings in which a large proportion of members freed their slaves *late*, however, a higher percentage of the manumitted blacks were males under age twenty-one. Chesterfield and Exeter are especially noteworthy in this respect. The preponderance of boys in those two meetings (39 percent and 50 percent of all freed blacks respectively) possibly occurred because many of the emancipating slave owners had invested recently in blacks; people buying slaves for the first time often bought adolescents and women who cost less than adult men and posed less challenging problems of control to inexperienced owners.[39] In addition, a large percentage (31.2 percent) of the blacks who were freed *late* in the meetings that obtained manumissions more *quickly* were boys, suggesting that Friends owning young males were among the most resistant to the abolitionists' demands. At the same time, however, the low proportion of *adult* males (18.4 percent) in the "late" meetings may have come about because slaveholders in those meetings found men particularly useful on their farms, refused to free them, and were disowned—thus leaving no manumission record. Viewed in this way, the manumission data raise the possibility that the die-hard members of the "late" meetings relied more on black labor to run their farms or trades and were therefore less willing to give up their slaves than were Friends who employed blacks for less directly utilitarian purposes such as in domestic service or as symbols of conspicuous consumption where women and young people might be expected to be more frequent.[40] Analysis of evidence from probate records and tax lists in the following chapters will provide a fuller examination of the validity of this proposition.

Besides these variations among local meetings in the age and gender of slaves freed early and late, the manumissions also show

[39] P.M.G. Harris has found that planters in a number of areas of the Chesapeake invested first in black women and teenagers and only later bought adult men; "Further Perspectives on the Spread of Slavery in the Chesapeake" (Paper presented at the Third Conference on Maryland History, May 1984, St. Mary's City, Md.).

[40] It is also possible that a higher percentage of the slaves freed after 1779 were minors in part because antislavery Friends recognized that most of the children would serve their present masters until maturity whether or not the owner quickly submitted a written manumission. Thus some meetings may have moved slowly before disowning Friends who owned minors in the hope that the children would be freed by the time they reached adulthood.

considerable differences both in the speed with which men and women *owners* freed their slaves and in the kinds of blacks they possessed. According to the evidence in Table 4.5, women formed a substantial proportion of the Quaker slaveholders who freed their slaves at the latest dates. Fewer than one-fifth of all manumitting slaveholders were women, but they were over one-third of the owners who emancipated their blacks after 1779. The reason for this divergence was not that women were more hard-hearted toward their slaves than men. Though some of these females were simply holding out, quite a few ended up in the "late" column because they could free their slaves only after the deaths of spouses who had rejected manumission. Under eighteenth-century law, married women could normally own no property. Even if she had owned slaves before marriage, they became her husband's property on their wedding day.[41] Chester Quarter raised the question in 1778 about how a meeting should deal with slavery cases in which the mistress of a slave, but not the master, was a member of the Society. The Yearly Meeting decided that the local meetings should determine whether each woman would free her slaves if she had the power. If the woman rejected the advice of 1776, then she should be disowned, but a wife who was willing to free the slaves but could not obtain her husband's agreement was permitted to remain within the church.[42]

TABLE 4.5. TYPES OF SLAVE OWNERS LISTED IN MANUMISSIONS

	1763-1779		1780-1796		Total 1763-1796	
	No.	%	No.	%	No.	%
Males	150	71.8%	24	49.0%	174	67.4%
Females	32	15.3	18	36.7	50	19.4
Husband/wife[a]	14	6.7	4	8.2	18	7.0
Group[a]	13	6.2	3	6.1	16	6.2
Total	209	100.0	49	100.0	258	100.0

SOURCE: Manumissions
[a] Each husband/wife couple and group is counted as one owner

[41] Marylynn Salmon, "Trust Estates and Marriage Settlements" (Paper presented at the Philadelphia Center for Early American Studies Seminar, November 1979, Philadelphia).
[42] PYM mins., 26/9M-5/10M/1778.

In addition, Table 4.6 shows clear differences in the kinds of slaves that men and women owned and in the kinds they manumitted late. For the entire period 1763-1796, women freed considerably more adult women, while men emancipated many more boys. Female owners tended to hold on to girls the latest, however, while after 1779 boys again formed the majority of the blacks whom men freed.[43] Not conforming to these general patterns, however, are slaveholding women in Philadelphia who manumitted their slaves after 1779: over 45 percent (5 of 11) of these owners in fact held adult men. Though not convincing in itself, this evidence suggests that some urban widows and spinsters relied on black men to earn wages or to help carry on the businesses of their deceased husbands or fathers.[44] Women who relied on these men at least in part for their support were undoubtedly less willing to free their blacks than were other mistresses whose slaves were simply domestics.

THE records of the local meetings—as well as of the central meeting—of the Society of Friends in the Delaware Valley thus reveal considerable variety in the attitudes of Quakers toward slavery.

TABLE 4.6. AGE AND GENDER OF BLACKS FREED
BY WOMEN AND MEN IN MANUMISSIONS

| | 1763-1779 | | 1780-1796 | |
	Female owners	Male owners	Female owners	Male owners
Blacks (No.)	76	271	34	49
Males 21 +	25.0%	30.3%	26.5%	16.3%
Males under 21	15.8	28.4	11.8	51.0
Females 18 +	40.8	23.2	32.3	12.3
Females under 18	18.4	18.1	29.4	20.4
Total	100.0	100.0	100.0	100.0

SOURCE: Manumissions

[43] This tendency of males to own a greater proportion of male slaves and females to hold more women and girls is similar to patterns of inheritance. See Chapter 3.

[44] A number of testators in Philadelphia left male slaves to their wives or daughters, with instructions that the men should be hired out or should continue in their present occupations to support the widow and children (if any). For examples, see Phila. Co. Wills, John Jennings, Bk. A, No. 121; William Bevan, Bk. C, No. 38; John Jones, Bk. C, No. 83; Richard Preston, Bk. E, No. 136.

Though Philadelphia Yearly Meeting moved gradually toward its abolitionist stance of the 1750s, each step required a careful balancing of the beliefs and interests of different groups of Friends. Quaker theology contained the seeds of abolitionist thought from the very start. Nevertheless, in the first half of the eighteenth century just a few outspoken individuals and the Chester Friends, supported by Shrewsbury and Gloucester-Salem quarters in 1730, called for a ban on slavery or the slave trade. As late as 1750, abolitionists had managed to obtain support for no more than a toothless admonition against buying imported blacks. The chief opposition to antislavery reform came from Quakers in Burlington and Philadelphia quarters.

In the 1750s, however, the city leadership accepted the antislavery position. The abolitionists in the Yearly Meeting then had enough backing to impose penalties against the purchasers and sellers of slaves and to begin a program to eradicate slaveholding among Friends. Monthly meetings reacted in different ways to these new rulings; their divergent behavior both indicates the sources of support for and opposition to antislavery reform and shows why the Yearly Meeting did not ban slavery entirely for fully eighteen years after the decision of 1758. Some meetings like Wilmington and Shrewsbury vigorously disciplined slave buyers and sellers and used the power they held over errant Friends who wanted to remain members to secure freedom for the blacks involved. Other meetings adhered conscientiously to the discipline but went no further against slaveholding on their own. And another group—including Chesterfield and Deer Creek—insistently refused to implement the Yearly Meeting's directive to punish members who bought and sold slaves.

The Friends of the Delaware Valley did finally come together in the mid-1770s to wipe out slaveholding within their ranks. Yet some meetings still took longer than others to secure manumissions and to excommunicate die-hard slave owners. As with disciplining slave purchasers, meetings did not divide over the issue of slavery strictly on the basis of their proximity to the plantation colonies of the Chesapeake. Nor does density of the black population or economic activity alone account for differences among the meetings. This survey of Quaker records has shown, rather, that such superficial and one-sided explanations do not hold up. But the minutes and manumission records cannot alone explain the variations, either. It is necessary to tap other materials to discover how Friends in diverse parts of Pennsylvania and New Jersey came to oppose slavery at widely varying times during the eighteenth century.

The following chapters investigate the range of circumstances of slave ownership among ordinary Friends, Quaker leaders, and their neighbors, with sources that more precisely reflect how much slavery there was and how it first spread and then faded. Were the Friends who took so long to manumit their slaves and those who were disciplined for buying and selling slaves the only members who owned slaves during the critical decades from 1750 to 1780, or had other Quakers freed their blacks before regular manumission records begin in the 1770s? Were these remaining slave-owning members powerless holdouts in local meetings that had for a long time accepted antislavery reform, or were they substantial leaders who were finally forced to give up their slaves if they wished to maintain control? Did slavery mean the same thing for Friends as it did for their non-Quaker neighbors, or were they less likely to yield to economic motives in exploiting forced labor of their fellow women and men? And in what ways did the slave owning patterns of Friends and their neighbors, and Quaker anticipations of the place the ex-slaves should hold in society, affect the stances of local meetings on antislavery? These are questions that require intensive study of probate records, tax assessment lists, and church records that goes well beyond the preliminary survey of meeting minutes and manumissions presented here. Patterns and issues noted so far, however, give us some idea of what we might find, what that might tell us, and what methods of search are necessary to put together the required answer.

· 5 ·

SHREWSBURY AND CHESTERFIELD
MEETINGS

When Delaware Valley Friends gathered for the 1758 Philadelphia Yearly Meeting they were prepared for a clash over slavery. At the previous meeting, representatives from the small coastal quarterly meeting at Shrewsbury had supported a stronger rule against buying and selling blacks. Now the powerful Philadelphia Quarter, controlled for the last several years by reformers, would do the same. The influence of the Philadelphians in the central meeting was so great that opponents of abolition would be hard pressed to prevent the meeting from making a change. Wealthy slave owners, who led a number of monthly meetings in Chester and Burlington quarters, believed that they needed blacks to run their plantations and wanted no religious bars to prevent them from holding, buying, and selling slaves at will. As it happened, the Friends in 1758 reached a sense of the meeting to stop trading in slaves, but could not reach agreement to ban slave owning.

This chapter and the next take a look at four local meetings that played pivotal roles in this drama over whether Friends should be allowed to own, buy, and sell blacks. The two New Jersey meetings examined in this chapter took vastly different stances on slavery. Shrewsbury opposed the institution much earlier than most other local meetings in New Jersey and Pennsylvania and was in the forefront of the attack on slavery, while Chesterfield purposefully lagged behind and helped postpone the final decision to ban slaveholding in the Yearly Meeting for over twenty years. Chester and Philadelphia, investigated in detail in Chapter 6, followed divergent paths as Chester first fought against the slave trade in the early eighteenth century and then by the 1750s lost its abolitionist zeal. Philadelphia brushed off early efforts to prohibit slave trading but at mid-century—controlled by Friends who interpreted Quaker ideas in a fresh way—made an about-face and pushed the Yearly Meeting toward antislavery reform. As we learned in Chapter 3, slavery developed differently in each of the four areas where these meetings were located. The purpose now is to trace the growth (or lack thereof) of abolitionist sentiment in Shrewsbury, Chesterfield, Chester, and Philadelphia within their local socioeconomic settings in order to identify common influences that led Friends to oppose the enslavement of blacks.

In this chapter, comparison of Shrewsbury and Chesterfield meetings enables us to evaluate a number of hypotheses concerning the source of antislavery commitment. Several possibilities are discounted. Neither Quaker group was a persecuted minority in the locality where they lived; both had members who belonged to the socioeconomic and political elite. A considerable number in both meetings owned slaves. Shrewsbury meeting, however, was established almost twenty years before its counterpart in West Jersey; the East Jersey Friends formed a smaller proportion of the population in their locale; and slavery became entrenched at an earlier date and to a much greater extent in eastern Monmouth County than in the Chesterfield area. In addition, the founders of Shrewsbury meeting immigrated to New Jersey from Long Island and Rhode Island while most early Chesterfield Friends came directly from England. By 1750, Shrewsbury and Chesterfield meetings arrived at opposite conclusions about slavery primarily because slave labor was of less importance to members of one meeting than the other, yet also because the groups interpreted Quaker thought in different ways. Careful examination of the meetings' proceedings on slavery will help elucidate these points.

In 1665, a group of Long Island Quakers and Baptists arrived in eastern Monmouth County and established two New England-style towns, Shrewsbury and Middletown. Most of the Friends settled in Shrewsbury, where they established their meeting soon after their arrival and built a meeting house in 1672. George Fox, the founder of the Society of Friends, described in his journal his 1672 visit to the settlement. He and his companions arrived at Middletown harbor from Long Island and then traveled "about 30: miles in the new Country through the woods very bad boggs, one worse then all, where wee and our horses was faine to slither downe a steepe place, & lett them to lie & breath themselves, & they call this purgatory; And soe wee came to Shrewsberry, & on the first day of the weeke we had a pretious Meettinge."[1]

The Quakers migrated to East Jersey at least in part to escape persecution in New England and New York. As founders of Shrewsbury, they participated in the provincial government from the very beginning. Fox marveled that in Shrewsbury "a friende is made A

[1] Norman Penney, ed., *The Journal of George Fox*, 2 vols. (Cambridge, 1911), 2:226.

Justice."[2] Eliakim Wardell, a Quaker minister whose wife Lydia had appeared almost naked as a "sign" in the Newbury, Massachusetts, church, was elected one of three deputies from Shrewsbury to the Monmouth "assembly" in 1667.[3] Several early Shrewsbury Friends were members of the Provincial Assembly, including Jedidiah Allen who was elected in 1703 to the first assembly convened under the royal government and Richard Hartshorne who served from 1703 to 1707.[4] And though the immigration to Monmouth County of Dutch settlers from Long Island and of Scottish ex-servants from Amboy circa 1700 quickly reduced the percentage of Quakers in the population, Friends remained part of the political elite of Monmouth County until the Revolution. John Eaton (1727-1751), Richard Lawrence (1761-1769 and 1772-1776), and Robert Hartshorne (1769-1772), all Shrewsbury Friends, represented the Monmouth County constituency in the New Jersey Assembly for much of the colonial period.[5]

Quakers were also well represented among the socioeconomic elite of eastern Monmouth County, as indicated by analysis of all surviving probate records for Middletown and Shrewsbury townships in the periods 1715-1739 and 1764-1780.[6] In the early period,

---

[2] Ibid.

[3] Rufus M. Jones, *The Quakers in the American Colonies* (London, 1911), 108, 372; Thomas Jefferson Wertenbaker, *The Founding of American Civilization: The Middle Colonies* (New York, 1963), 124; John E. Pomfret, *The Province of East New Jersey, 1609-1702* (Princeton, N.J., 1962), 46.

[4] "Tables of the Sittings of the Provincial Assemblies, with the Names of the Members," *Proceedings of the New Jersey Historical Society* 5 (1850), 19-33; Donald L. Kemmerer, *Path to Freedom: The Struggle for Self-Government in Colonial New Jersey, 1703-1776* (Cos Cob, Conn., 1968), 358.

[5] Peter O. Wacker, *Land and People: A Cultural Geography of Preindustrial New Jersey: Origins and Settlement Patterns* (New Brunswick, N.J., 1975), 168; Ned Landsman, "Scottish Communities in the Old and New Worlds, 1680-1760" (Ph.D. diss., University of Pennsylvania, 1979), ch. 5; "Tables of the Sittings of the Provincial Assemblies," 19-33; Kemmerer, *Path to Freedom*, 358.

[6] The information in Tables 5.1, 5.3, 5.5, and 5.6 originated from the analysis of *all* extant probate records for the New Jersey areas in which most Shrewsbury and Chesterfield monthly meeting members lived. The samples used in these tables are selected by time and bounded by geographic area. Two periods—1730-1739 and approximately 1765 to 1780—are studied because they yield information concerning the economic activities and slaveholding of Friends and their neighbors during or immediately following the times when the positions on slavery of the two monthly meetings are known (1730 and 1756-1780).

The probate records and tax lists of Shrewsbury and Middletown townships were chosen for study because almost all Shrewsbury Monthly Meeting members lived in those two townships. In fact, most lived in Shrewsbury. In the Chesterfield area, the

almost one-half of decedents in the wealthiest 30 percent of these inventoried estates, whose religion could be identified, were Friends; later, in the 1760s and 1770s, one-third of this elite group still was Quaker.[7] Like their affluent neighbors of other religions, Friends employed slaves on their plantations. During the period 1715-1739 over 85 percent of the Quaker decedents in the wealthiest 30 percent owned slaves—slightly higher even than the percentage of *all* decedents in the same wealth category (see Table 5.1).

Some Shrewsbury Friends had probably brought black slaves with them when they came to New Jersey. In any event, many owned them by the time they died in the early eighteenth century. For example, Sarah Reape, widow of William Reape who was once deputy governor of Rhode Island and who with John Tilton of Gravesend, Long Island, had negotiated the Navesink purchase, owned eight slaves when she died in 1715.[8] One-half of the most active members of Shrewsbury Monthly Meeting who died before 1741 owned slaves at death (see Table 5.2).[9] As part of the New

inclusion of all townships where Friends lived was difficult because, although most lived in Burlington County, a few lived in four other counties as well. The small number of Friends living in Somerset, western Middlesex, and Hunterdon counties did not seem to warrant extensive analysis of these localities. Therefore, the samples of all extant probate records for Chesterfield Monthly Meeting include only the five townships in Burlington County where most Chesterfield Friends lived (Chesterfield, Nottingham, Mansfield, New Hanover, and Springfield townships) and Upper Freehold Township in Monmouth County.

[7] Sources of church records for both the Shrewsbury and Chesterfield monthly meeting areas include: Shrewsbury MM mins., 1732-1780; Shrewsbury QM mins., 1705-1780; Shrewsbury MM Birth, Death, and Marriage records, 1657-1780; PYM mins., 1681-1780; Chesterfield MM mins., 1684-1783; Chesterfield MM Birth, Death, and Marriage records, 1659-1780; Burlington MM mins., 1681-1780; Burlington MM Birth, Death, and Marriage records, 1678-1780; all located in Friends Historical Library. First Reformed Church of Freehold and Middletown (Marlboro, N.J.), Book of Baptisms, Marriages, Officers, and Communicants, 1709-1780, trans. and published in *Genealogical Magazine of New Jersey*, 22-26, 31-32, 35 (1947-1951, 1956-1957, 1960). Old Tennent Presbyterian Church, Freehold, N.J., Records of Pastors, Officers, Subscribers, Communicants, Baptisms, and Burials, 1706-1780, published in Frank R. Symmes, *History of the Old Tennent Church*, 2d ed. (Cranbury, N.J., 1904), 175-359. Christ Church, Shrewsbury, Parish Register, 1733-1780, published in John E. Stillwell, *Historical and Genealogical Miscellany*, 5 vols. (New York, 1903), 1:157-219. Baptist Church, Middletown, N.J., Records, 1712-1780, published in Stillwell, *Miscellany*, 2:256-262. James Mott's Journal (Book of Church Discipline, Middletown Baptist Church), 1748-1777, published in Stillwell, *Miscellany*, 2:263-275. St. Mary's Church, Burlington, N.J., Parish Register, 1703-1780, published in Stillwell, *Miscellany*, 2:49-133.

[8] Wertenbaker, *Founding*, 124; Pomfret, *East New Jersey*, 44; Monmouth Co. Wills, Sarah Reape, 58-63M.

[9] Participants in the monthly meetings, whom I also refer to as "leaders," were all

TABLE 5.1. SLAVE OWNERSHIP AND RELIGION AMONG
WEALTHIEST 30 PERCENT OF INVENTORIED DECEDENTS IN
SHREWSBURY MONTHLY MEETING AREA

| | 1715-1739 | | 1764-1780 | |
	No.	Slave owners	No.	Slave owners
Quakers	7	85.7%	6	16.7%
Anglicans	2	100.0	3	100.0
Presbyterians	0	—	2	100.0
Baptists	4	75.0	3	100.0
Dutch Reformed	2	50.0	4	75.0
Religion unknown	6	83.3	5	40.0
Total	21	81.0	23	60.9

SOURCES: Probate and church records (see nn. 6, 7)

York hinterland, the Shrewsbury area had greater access to blacks than most other local monthly meeting areas in New Jersey and Pennsylvania. Beginning particularly in the second decade of the eighteenth century, substantial numbers of slaves were imported into New York. Residents of the Shrewsbury area took advantage of this supply of labor, especially because relatively few white indentured servants were available for work. Data from the probate inventories for Shrewsbury and Middletown townships indicate a substantial increase in the percentage of decedents who owned blacks when they died in the decade 1711-1720; at that time the proportion owning slaves soared to almost 35 percent (see Graph 3.1). The percentage of inventoried decedents owning slaves surpassed 36 percent in the 1720s and then declined to about 30 percent

---

Friends who were appointed to offices (such as clerk of meeting or treasurer), or committees (to investigate the behavior of Friends, etc.). In the sample of early Shrewsbury Monthly Meeting participants (those active before 1732), all were important leaders because only the representatives to the Yearly and Shrewsbury Quarterly meetings are known. There are no extant minutes of the monthly meeting before 1732.

The sample of probate records used for tables dealing with meeting leadership is different from those of all extant probate records for the periods 1715-1739 and 1764-1780. The wills and inventories of *all* Shrewsbury and Chesterfield monthly meeting participants who died before 1781 and who lived in any township in the meeting areas have been analyzed regardless of year of death. For those participants who did not die by 1780, the tax lists of 1774 and 1778-1779 for the entire meeting areas have been utilized.

TABLE 5.2. SLAVE OWNERSHIP AMONG
SHREWSBURY MONTHLY MEETING PARTICIPANTS

Date of death	No. participants	Slave owners
1681-1700	0	—
1701-1720	6	50.0%
1721-1740	6	50.0
1741-1760	22	27.3
1761-1780	20	0.0
Total	54	22.2

SOURCES: Probate records; Shrewsbury MM mins., 1732-1780; Shrewsbury QM mins., 1705-1780; PYM mins., 1681-1780

for the rest of the colonial period, but in comparison with other parts of New Jersey and Pennsylvania, blacks remained quite numerous in Monmouth County. For example, the New Jersey census of 1738 showed that blacks were 10.6 percent of the population of Monmouth County, compared with 6.5 percent of the population in Burlington County.[10]

The huge upsurge in slave imports in the 1710s and the widespread purchase of black labor by Friends and non-Friends alike prompted a quick reaction from at least one abolitionist, John Hepburn, a Scot living near Freehold, Monmouth County, who considered himself a Quaker but whose standing among Friends is unclear. In 1714 Hepburn wrote one of the earliest abolitionist tracts published in America, *The American Defence of the Christian Golden Rule, or an Essay to Prove the Unlawfulness of Making Slaves of Men.* In this essay, he argued that slavery was inconsistent with Christianity and violated the Golden Rule to do unto others as you wish others to do unto you. He indicted Presbyterian, Anabaptist, and Anglican preachers and laymen in his locality for owning slaves. As for the Quakers, Hepburn charged that while no Christian sect was stricter in other principles and practices, "no group of people [were] more forward in making slaves of men."[11]

Hepburn's tract, though possibly exaggerated on some points,

---

[10] See Chapter 3, above, and Evarts B. Greene and Virginia D. Harrington, *American Population before the Federal Census of 1790* (New York, 1932), 110.

[11] John Hepburn, *The American Defence of the Christian Golden Rule, or an Essay to Prove the Unlawfulness of Making Slaves of Men* ([New York?], 1715), 1-2, 12-25.

presents an enlightening portrait of slavery in early eighteenth-century East Jersey.[12] In addition it sheds light on the ways in which the institution offended sensitive Friends. Slave owners, according to Hepburn, could enrich themselves without physical labor, and keep their hands clean except when blood-spattered from beating their slaves. These masters could afford to wear fine-powdered wigs and greatcoats, and their wives had time to paint their faces and puff and powder their hair. Their children grew up in idleness. In contrast, according to Hepburn, slaveholders clothed their slaves with rags, or with no clothes or shoes even in the winter. Some slaves were forced either to lie in the ashes of the fire or to live in huts outside. Slaves were given names like those of dogs or horses— Toby, Jack, and Hector—and some were forced to punish or hang fellow blacks. Hepburn believed that the separation of husbands from wives, and children from parents, was an especially bad aspect of slavery that forced adult blacks to commit adultery and made children unable to honor their parents. He attributed the 1712 suicide of a black in his neighborhood to the poor treatment generally afforded slaves in East Jersey.[13]

Although it is uncertain that John Hepburn convinced weighty members of Shrewsbury Monthly Meeting that slavery was inconsistent with Quaker ideals, East Jersey Friends were becoming concerned about the growth of slavery in their locality by the 1720s. The minutes of the meeting are missing before 1732, and are silent on the subject of slavery and the slave trade until 1757; but there is evidence that the meeting developed an antislavery position independently of Philadelphia Yearly Meeting prior to the 1750s. The meeting sent no official petitions to the Yearly Meeting and no abolitionist pamphlets written by confirmed meeting members exist. Quaker records do reveal, however, that Shrewsbury Friends opposed the slave trade by 1730, for in that year Shrewsbury Quarterly Meeting agreed with the petition put forward by Chester Quarterly Meeting to prohibit members from buying imported blacks.[14] Because only one other meeting (Woodbridge) belonged to Shrewsbury Quarter, the agreement of Shrewsbury Friends was almost certainly necessary for the quarterly meeting to reach this decision.

Other evidence of an early antislavery movement among Shrewsbury Quakers comes from the wills of deceased Friends. Simeon

[12] There is no evidence that Hepburn traveled to Maryland, Virginia, or the West Indies.

[13] Hepburn, *American Defence*, 3-6.

[14] PYM mins., 19-28/7M/1730.

Moss found in his analysis of the abstracts of New Jersey wills that Shrewsbury residents led the colony in emancipation by will.[15] Indeed, a study of the probate records themselves reveals that in 1720, John Lippincott, a weighty Shrewsbury Friend and slave owner, was the first in his meeting to make provision to free his "Negro man Oliver" in his will. He was followed with increasing frequency by other Quaker slave owners. In the 1715-1739 sample of all Middletown and Shrewsbury probate records (see Table 5.3), 30 (26.5 percent) of the 113 decedents who left wills and/or inventories owned slaves. Ten, or one-third, of these slave owners can be identified as Quakers; and four of these Friends freed all their slaves in their wills while one freed a single man who was among the several slaves he owned. More specifically, of the four slave-owning Quakers in this sample who died in the 1730s only one failed to manumit his slaves. In contrast to the Friends, only one local slave owner who was *not* a Quaker made freedom possible for his slaves in his will. Elias Mestayer, a French Protestant who had no wife or children when he died in 1731, provided that the black husband and

TABLE 5.3. SLAVE OWNERSHIP AND RELIGION AMONG ALL DECEDENTS IN SHREWSBURY MONTHLY MEETING AREA

	1715-1730		1731-1739		1764-1780	
	No.	Slave owners	No.	Slave owners	No.	Slave owners
Quakers	23	26.1%	15	26.7%	32	6.2%
Anglicans	2	0.0	7	28.6	26	26.9
Presbyterians	1	100.0	2	100.0	6	50.0
Baptists	4	50.0	5	40.0	13	30.8
Dutch Reformed	4	50.0	6	33.3	15	53.3
French Protestant	0	—	1	100.0	0	—
Religion unknown	23	13.0	20	15.0	53	18.9
Total	57	24.6	56	28.6	145	23.4

SOURCES: Probate and church records

[15] Simeon F. Moss, "The Persistence of Slavery and Involuntary Servitude in a Free State (1685-1866)," *JNH* 35 (1950), 300. The value of his analysis is limited because blacks mentioned in wills and inventories themselves were not always listed in the abstracts printed in the *New Jersey Archives*. Moss did not investigate the religion of the emancipators.

wife he owned should operate his plantation for five years and then be freed.[16] The Quaker emancipationist movement in Shrewsbury was even stronger among the Friends who took an active role in their monthly meeting. No fewer than seven of eight slave-owning leaders who died after 1725 but before 1761 freed their slaves in their wills.

However, several questions arise concerning the depth and scope of antislavery sentiment among these Friends. Most of the decedents, for example, deferred the freedom of their blacks, or required the freed persons to make yearly payments to the deceased's heirs. John Lippincott, the first emancipator, gave the use of his black man to his wife during her life and then to his two sons for one and one-half years each. The sons, John and Preserve, were then directed to sell Oliver in either New York or Pennsylvania for ten days, after which he was to be free for the rest of his life. Joseph Wardell, who died in 1735, also freed his slaves Jack and Joany only after his wife's death. Other Friends deferred emancipation until the blacks reached age thirty or thirty-five years. George Williams I, deceased in 1744, freed his mulatto man James McCarty at age thirty. McCarty would receive freedom dues of a horse under seven years old and two suits of clothes (one new); but if he were to "take bad ways" and bring charges against the estate, the executors were free to sell him. John Lippincott II freed his black woman Hesther immediately upon his death (which occurred in 1747), but her five children aged sixteen to twenty-nine were each required to serve until age thirty-five. They were also warned to behave themselves if they expected to be freed. Two other Friends, Thomas White I (d. 1747) and Dr. Walter Harbert (d. 1755), freed their black men immediately, but required James and Sesar to pay an annual sum (£5 and £2 respectively) which would be used if they became unable to support themselves.[17]

One might reasonably ask if Shrewsbury Friends were in the forefront of the Quaker antislavery movement if manumitting owners deferred freedom and required annual payments. A 1769 entry from the diary of the premier Quaker abolitionist John Woolman explains

[16] Monmouth Co. Wills, Elias Mestayer, 457M. That a fairly small percentage of decedents for whom religion is unknown held slaves at death (see Table 5.3) can probably be attributed to the fact that they were less wealthy on average than those decedents whose religion can be identified.

[17] Monmouth Co. Wills, John Lippincott, 111M; Joseph Wardell, 649-651M; George Williams I, 1193-1197M, 1853-1859M; John Lippincott, 1413-1414M, 1537M; Thomas White I, 1457-1462M; Walter Harbert, 2075-2080M.

the Friends' reasons for such restrictions, and even suggests that Woolman found the reasons acceptable, at least until that year.

> As persons setting Negroes free in our province are bound by law to maintain them in case they have need of relief, some who scrupled keeping slaves term of life (in the time of my youth) were wont to detain their young Negroes in their service till thirty years of age, without wages, on that account. And with this custom I so far agreed that I, as companion to another Friend in executing the will of a deceased Friend, once sold a Negro lad till he might attain the age of thirty years and applied the money to the use of the estate.[18]

The 1714 New Jersey law to which Woolman referred required that a "Master or Mistress manumitting and setting at Liberty any Negro or Mulatto Slave, shall enter into sufficient Security unto her Majesty, her Heirs and Successors, with two Sureties, in the Sum of Two Hundred Pounds" in order to prevent the freed blacks from becoming "a Charge to the Place where they are." The executors of wills made by testators who desired to free their slaves were required to post bonds for the ex-slaves' support.[19] Thus, in demanding deferred freedom or annual payments from their slaves, the manumitting Friends were attempting to ensure that the support of freed blacks would not become a burden on their estates. That New Jersey Friends emancipated their slaves in spite of this extremely high surety bond is compelling evidence of the strength of their opposition to slavery. The bond required of manumitting owners in Pennsylvania was only £30.

Another question concerning the intensity of antislavery fervor among Shrewsbury Friends arises from the fact that these slave-owning Quakers freed their slaves only after their deaths, thus reaping the benefits of slavery themselves and depriving only their heirs. It is unknown how many Quakers may have freed their slaves during their lives, but analysis of probate inventories indicates that slaveholding itself declined markedly among Quakers after 1740. Friends in the Shrewsbury area stopped buying slaves and freed those they owned before their deaths. Of the six Quakers whose estates ranked in the wealthiest 30 percent of all inventories for Shrewsbury and Middletown during 1764-1780, only one, William Woolley, owned

[18] Phillips P. Moulton, ed., *The Journal and Major Essays of John Woolman* (New York, 1971), 152.

[19] Samuel Nevill, ed., *The Acts of the General Assembly of the Province of New Jersey 1703-1752* (1752), 23-24.

slaves, and he freed them in his will probated in 1769 (see Table 5.1). Catherine Hartshorne, whose estate did not rank in the top 30 percent, owned a black girl Dinah, whom she freed when she died in 1767 (Table 5.3).[20] During 1741-1760, fewer than one-third of the probated Quaker participants in the monthly meeting owned slaves at their deaths, and none who died during the years 1761-1780 owned slaves at death (see Table 5.2).[21] By the 1760s, the difference between wealthy Shrewsbury Friends and their upper-class neighbors is striking, in that eleven of the twelve non-Quaker decedents in the top 30 percent of inventoried estates owned slaves at death. Only one of these non-Quaker slave owners, an Anglican, freed her black man William in her will.[22]

The monthly meeting minutes reveal that some Shrewsbury Friends continued to own slaves into the 1770s. By the 1750s, however, the meeting had adopted an antislavery position. And when Philadelphia Yearly Meeting decided that slave importing and buying, and then slaveholding itself, should be banned among its members, Shrewsbury Monthly Meeting proceeded quickly, but judiciously, against its nonconforming members. Shrewsbury Friends pressed in the Yearly Meeting for increasing strictness in the discipline concerning slavery, and many of their discipline cases involved Friends who held blacks only for a term.

In 1757, when John Wardell bought a slave, Shrewsbury Monthly Meeting requested the quarterly meeting's opinion on whether a Friend who bought a slave, and refused to make satisfaction by condemning the crime, could be disowned. The quarterly meeting (made up of Friends from Shrewsbury and Woodbridge monthly meetings) decided he could be disowned, and in doing this went considerably farther than the Yearly Meeting was willing to go. Indeed, the next year the Yearly Meeting decided only to bar slave buyers from participating in monthly meetings or contributing funds.[23]

---

[20] Monmouth Co. Wills, William Woolley, 3753-3755M; Catherine Hartshorne, 3329-3331M.

[21] The Philadelphia Yearly Meeting and Shrewsbury Quarterly Meeting decisions of 1755-1757 to discipline slave buyers and sellers had little immediate effect on slave owning among deceased Shrewsbury Monthly Meeting participants who died during 1757-1760. Two of eight decedents (25 percent) in this group owned slaves—only slightly less than the percentage for the entire period 1741-1760.

[22] Monmouth Co. Wills, Joanna Eaton, 3666-3667M. The man had to pay Eaton's daughter 40 shillings per year.

[23] Shrewsbury QM mins., 25/7M/1757; PYM mins., 23-29/9M/1758; minutes of all quarterly meetings of the Yearly Meeting.

During the 1760s, several Shrewsbury Friends bought and sold slaves. In each case, the meeting required the offending member to provide for or obtain the freedom of the black. Although some of the slaves had to serve for a number of years—Thomas Wooley stated to the satisfaction of the meeting that he and the black man he bought had agreed before the purchase that the slave would be free after sixteen years—the meeting even expected members who sold slaves to obtain their freedom. Stephen Cook sold two blacks for term of life in 1764. When he was unable to buy them back and free them, the meeting testified against him.[24] Before 1770, few other monthly meetings in the Yearly Meeting expected more than that their offending members apologize and promise not to deal in slaves again.[25]

In 1770, the meeting extended the Yearly Meeting's position even further when it learned that several Friends, Brittain Corlies, Samuel Parker, William Parker, and William Jackson, had bought slaves for a term of years that went past age twenty-one. A committee was appointed in 1772 to decide whether they had disobeyed the Yearly Meeting minute of 1758. This committee decided they had, the quarterly meeting agreed, and the erring members were required to obtain freedom for the blacks after their terms expired and to acknowledge their wrongdoing. In January 1774, the meeting continued its role in the antislavery vanguard by prohibiting Amos White of Deal from even hiring the labor of a slave.[26]

When Philadelphia Yearly Meeting in 1774 instructed monthly meetings to appoint committees to treat with slave owners, Shrewsbury Friends selected a group of weighty Friends, who with the help of the quarterly meeting committee, visited slave-owning members. In their 1775 report, they found that nine members owned a total of twenty-four blacks. Of these slaves, thirteen were above the age that the Yearly Meeting specified for freedom (eighteen years for females, twenty-one years for males). Four of the slave owners, who held a total of twelve slaves (six above age), showed no disposition to give them education or freedom at any age. Four other Friends promised to free their slave children when of age. The ninth owner had hired a man from a non-Quaker, and had already made arrangements for the man to earn money to buy his freedom. The

[24] Shrewsbury MM mins., 7/6M/1762, 5/11M/1764, 4/3M/1765.

[25] See Chapter 4. From the early 1760s, Wilmington Monthly Meeting also required freedom for blacks who were bought and sold.

[26] Shrewsbury MM mins., 2/7M/1770, 6/8M/1770, 1M to 4M/1772, 1M/1773 to 2M/1774.

report also indicated that at least five of the slaves, including two adults and three children, had been taught to read.[27]

The committee reported again in 1776. By that time only Josiah Parker, and Zilpha and John Corlies, the widow and son of the one monthly meeting leader who died after 1725 without freeing his slaves,[28] refused to manumit or educate their slaves. John Stevenson was willing to free his two adult women, but could not "see his way clear to do it" because one was old and very infirm and the other had four young children. Robert, John, and Esek Hartshorne had freed or promised to free all their adult slaves by 1 January 1777, and the young ones were to be educated and freed at suitable ages. Richard Lawrence's black man had served his time and was now free. The appointed meeting members continued to treat with slave owners. By April 1778, only John Corlies refused to manumit his slaves, although John Stevenson had died leaving his black women and children in such a situation that they could not legally be freed. In December 1778, Corlies was disowned, and by 1780 the meeting had procured (though with considerable effort) written manumissions for all slaves, over and under age, owned by meeting members.[29]

Whenever a group embarks on a policy change that forces its leaders to alter their behavior or be removed from office, the possibility arises that the issue is being used in an opportunistic manner by an "outgroup" to take power. For instance, Samuel P. Hays hypothesized that early twentieth-century progressive reformers took up the anticorruption standard in order to control municipal government, not out of any true commitment to democratic ideals.[30] In the case of Shrewsbury meeting, there is no evidence that a group of less affluent Friends used abolitionism to undermine the power of a slaveholding elite. In the period before 1750, when the struggle in the meeting over slavery would have taken place, Friends disciplined no member for a slavery offense (of course slave trading and keeping were not considered matters of discipline by the Yearly

[27] Shrewsbury MM mins., 7/8M/1775.

[28] Monmouth Co. Wills, John Corlies, 2443-2446M. Corlies died in 1760.

[29] Shrewsbury MM mins., 1/7M/1776, 6/4M/1778, 7/12M/1778, 2/10M/1780. The task of obtaining manumissions was certainly made more difficult by the fact that owners were required under New Jersey law to post a £200 bond for each manumitted black in case he or she became incapacitated and needed financial support. This requirement probably encouraged Shrewsbury meeting to be more patient in treating with reluctant slave owners.

[30] Samuel P. Hays, "The Politics of Reform in Municipal Government in the Progressive Era," *Pacific Northwest Quarterly* 55 (1964), 157-169.

Meeting at that time) and some leaders (though a diminishing number) continued to hold blacks. During the period from the 1750s through the 1770s all of the evidence suggests that Shrewsbury's antislavery drive was a sincere effort to remove the last vestiges of slaveholding from the meeting. While the only member disowned for holding slaves was the richest man on the Shrewsbury Township tax list in 1779, and Table 5.4 shows a considerable difference

TABLE 5.4. WEALTH AND LANDHOLDING OF SHREWSBURY AND CHESTERFIELD MONTHLY MEETING PARTICIPANTS AND SLAVE OWNERS

	No. on tax lists	Land-holders	Land-holdings (mean acreage)	Mean assessment[a]
Shrewsbury MM (1779)				
All participants	59	83.0%	154.8	£ 42.3
Antislavery participants	21	95.2	177.6	£ 53.3
Slave owners, buyers, and sellers	18	100.0	249.2	£ 83.8
Chesterfield MM				
All participants On 1774, 1778, and 1779 tax lists[b]	107	81.3	229.0	
On 1778-1779 tax lists	102			£ 91.8
Antislavery participants On 1774, 1778, and 1779 tax lists[b]	27	85.2	187.5	
On 1778-1779 tax lists	25			£ 96.2
Slave owners, buyers, and sellers (1778-1779)	35	88.6	222.5	£ 112.8

SOURCES: Shrewsbury MM mins., 1732-1780; Chesterfield MM mins., 1684-1780; Tax assessment lists, 1774, 1778, and 1779
[a] In New Jersey currency (adjusted; see n. 31)
[b] Some Chesterfield participants were on the 1774 tax lists but not on the 1778 and 1779 tax lists. Their landholdings are included here but not their assessments

between the assessed wealth and number of acres of land held by those who violated the discipline and those who dealt with the violators, one faction in the meeting was not wielding the slave issue to oust a wealthier group from power.[31] The antislavery activists included those who were the most important meeting leaders of the 1750s, 1760s, and 1770s: twenty-four of the thirty-one men (77.4 percent) who treated with people who disobeyed the antislavery discipline were officers of the meeting during those years.[32]

The absence of factional infighting in the meeting is further illustrated by the fact that the antislavery group even included three slave owners, Robert and John Hartshorne and Richard Lawrence, who dealt with cases concerning slavery either before or after their particular offenses were brought before the meeting. John Hartshorne and Lawrence both treated with a slave buyer in 1769, and John Hartshorne was a member of the committee that in 1773 treated with the four men who had hired the labor of slaves. Shrewsbury meeting evidently had no aversion to appointing slave owners to visit slave buyers or sellers or those who hired the labor of slaves before slave ownership itself was prohibited by the Yearly Meeting.

[31] The economic variations do describe differences between the groups that may have influenced their attitudes toward slavery, however, as we will see later in this chapter.

The tax ratables lists are located in the Division of Archives and Records Management, Trenton, New Jersey. Few exist for the years prior to 1774. The first year for which lists survive for most townships in the Shrewsbury and Chesterfield meeting areas is 1779. The lists used were: for Shrewsbury Monthly Meeting, Shrewsbury Township 1779 and Middletown Township 1779; for Chesterfield Monthly Meeting, Chesterfield Township 1779, Mansfield Township 1779, New Hanover Township 1779, Nottingham Township 1779, and Springfield Township 1779 in Burlington County, and Upper Freehold Township 1778 (none exists for 1779) in Monmouth County.

The value that took into account the total assessed wealth of taxpayers varied from one tax list to another. Some listed the amount of tax to be paid, while others indicated a "rate" from which the actual tax was calculated. In order to compare mean wealth in these different townships, I have computed the value of assessed property by determining the ratio of tax or rates on each tax list to the value of assessed property. Upper Freehold is not included in the computation of mean assessment because different assessment methods and rates were used in the two years. The wide gap between mean assessments in East and West Jersey that is evident in Table 5.4 suggests that different methods might have been used in the two areas. The tax assessments in both places were governed by the same provincial laws, however, and the same rates were assigned to livestock. Therefore, the variation probably arose from real differences in wealth based on the differences in landholdings.

I have not converted these assessment values from provincial currency into £ sterling because John J. McCusker's tables end in 1775 and I have no idea by how much these rates may be inflated. McCusker, *Money and Exchange in Europe and America, 1600-1775: A Handbook* (Chapel Hill, N.C., 1978), 314-317.

[32] Officers included clerks, treasurers, overseers, ministers, and elders.

After the ruling against owning blacks was initiated in 1774, Shrewsbury Friends made some changes in the committee appointments. Lawrence was no longer given any committee assignments even though he had played a very active role in the meeting since 1763, and John Hartshorne participated on only one committee (to keep order at the quarterly meeting) between 1774 and November 1776, by which time he had freed or agreed to free his slaves. Both men returned to active duty in 1777, and Robert Hartshorne became a leader of the meeting in the late 1770s, after he had freed his slaves. Robert Hartshorne dealt with John Corlies, the meeting's one recalcitrant slave owner, in 1778. Thus, while Shrewsbury meeting followed the Yearly Meeting's advice of 1774 by not employing slave owners "in the service of Truth," it did not use the slavery issue as a means of removing slaveholders from power permanently.[33]

The movement to eradicate slave trading and slave ownership in Shrewsbury Monthly Meeting after 1756 therefore involved no upheavals nor even a change of policy. The large majority of the meeting elite simply used, and even stretched a bit, the new power given them by the Yearly Meeting to pull the last holdouts belonging to their meeting into the antislavery fold. The aim of the meeting was to end slaveholding among its members in any form. Its leaders did not use the issue as a front for a power struggle during the period from the 1750s to the 1770s. There is no evidence, because of the loss of records before 1732 and the silence of the minutes after that date on the issue of slavery, whether such a struggle had occurred earlier.

Shrewsbury Friends, then, developed a straightforward stand against slavery before Philadelphia Yearly Meeting as a whole. Almost all meeting leaders who died owning slaves after 1725 freed them in their wills, and most Quakers who did not participate in meeting business followed their example. Slave ownership among Shrewsbury Friends declined to the extent that after 1760 no deceased leaders owned slaves at death, and only two Quaker decedents (nonparticipants) owned slaves at death. The meeting opposed slave trading in 1730, supported disownment for slave buyers and sellers in 1757 (before the Yearly Meeting), and required those who sold

[33] Shrewsbury MM mins., 1732-1780. Robert Hartshorne and Richard Lawrence were members of the New Jersey Assembly. Lawrence in 1761 and 1762 supported bills laying importation duties on slaves, including one bill that would have been prohibitive had it passed. In 1775 he supported an easier manumission law that did not pass. I am indebted to Thomas Purvis for this information.

slaves to buy them back and free them. Shrewsbury Friends con-scientiously disciplined errant members according to the meeting's interpretation of the Yearly Meeting rules, but did so in a fashion that suggests that little strife and no change of policy took place after 1756. These East Jersey Quakers initiated their antislavery program well before 1750 by freeing their own slaves rather than by telling others to free theirs, and even after 1756 Shrewsbury Friends were more interested in obtaining eventual freedom for blacks than in punishing offending Friends. All members who bought, sold, or hired the labor of slaves were required to provide for their freedom (even when non-Quakers actually owned the slaves), and the meeting patiently tried to obtain manumissions for every black man, woman, and child on whom meeting members had any claim. Only one obstinate member was disowned for holding slaves.

In contrast, the members of Chesterfield Monthly Meeting in West Jersey steadfastly resisted antislavery reform. Despite several official visits of the abolitionist John Woolman to families of that meeting and his friendship and acquaintance with many of its members,[34] Chesterfield meeting refused to discipline persons who bought or sold slaves until after 1770. One possible explanation for their refusal lay in the fact that many Chesterfield leaders of the 1750s and 1760s owned slaves. However, since weighty Shrewsbury Friends had also held slaves while at the same time opposing the purchase of imported blacks in 1730 and manumitting their own slaves, a more satisfying explanation must be sought.

Chesterfield Monthly Meeting was founded in 1684 primarily by Friends who migrated to Burlington County from England in the late 1670s and early 1680s. The population of the area remained largely Quaker well into the eighteenth century, and Friends were influential in the provincial government throughout the colonial period, even though they were politically dominant in West Jersey for only a short time under the proprietors. In 1705 Lord Cornbury "complained of the political machinations of the Quaker members of the Assembly who held all but two of the seats for West Jersey," and Lewis Morris attributed the difficulty of forming a militia in West Jersey to the cohesive resistance of Friends.[35] Active members of Chesterfield Monthly Meeting who were representatives to the

---

[34] Moulton, ed., *Journal . . . of John Woolman*, 27, and 23-192 *passim*.
[35] Wacker, *Land and People*, 184.

Assembly included Thomas Lambert (1703-1707, 1709-1716, 1721-1730), William Biddle (1703-1704), Joshua Wright (1704-1707, 1730-1738), Jacob Doughty (1716-1721), William Cooke (1738-1754), Daniel Doughty (1743-1746, 1761-1769), Samuel Wright (1745-1749), Barzillai Newbold (1751-1757), Joseph Bullock (1769-1772), and Anthony Sykes (1772-1776). Francis Davenport was a member of the Provincial Council from August 1702 until his death in 1708.[36] Many Friends were active as township and county officials as well.[37] Thus, members of Chesterfield meeting, like those in Shrewsbury, took an active role in provincial politics. The contrasting attitudes toward slavery of these meetings therefore cannot be linked to any differences in their ability to influence governmental policy.

Quakers also dominated the socioeconomic elite in the townships in Burlington County and in Upper Freehold Township in Monmouth County that made up the Chesterfield Monthly Meeting area. During the 1730s, all of the wealthiest 30 percent of decedents whose estates were inventoried, and who can be identified by religion, were Quakers. This preponderance was reduced somewhat by the 1760s and 1770s as members of other religions moved into the Chesterfield Monthly Meeting area and as former Friends joined other churches.

Slavery was considerably less extensive in Chesterfield than in Shrewsbury for most of the colonial period. Except during the 1740s, fewer than 20 percent of all inventoried decedents in the Chesterfield area townships owned slaves, while over 29 percent of Middletown and Shrewsbury decedents owned blacks during most of the eighteenth century. Part of the explanation for this difference probably lies in the fact that many of the Friends who formed a great proportion of the inhabitants of Burlington County avoided slaveholding; but a more abundant supply of indentured servants in West Jersey compared with the number available in eastern Monmouth County also played a role.[38]

Even though slavery was less important in West Jersey society as a whole, the leaders and members of Chesterfield Monthly Meeting did own slaves. Unlike most of their co-religionists in Shrews-

---

[36] "Table of the Sittings of the Provincial Assemblies," 19-33; Kemmerer, *Path to Freedom*, 358.

[37] Ewan M. Woodward and John F. Hageman, *History of Burlington and Mercer Counties, N.J.* (Philadelphia, 1883) includes civil lists for townships in Burlington County.

[38] See Chapter 3, above.

bury, they held on to them into the 1770s. Few Chesterfield Quakers freed their slaves in their wills. Whereas in Shrewsbury three-fourths in the 1730s—and all in the 1760s and 1770s—of Quaker slave owners freed their slaves in their wills, no Chesterfield Quaker decedents freed their blacks during 1730-1739 and only two of six Quaker owners did so in the later period. In addition, Table 5.5 shows that as late as the 1760s and 1770s, almost one-fourth of the deceased Quakers in Chesterfield whose estates were inventoried and ranked in the top 30 percent of local wealth owned slaves at death. And Table 5.6 indicates that 14.3 percent of all eighty-four Quaker decedents whose estates were probated during the 1760s and 1770s owned slaves. Table 5.5 also suggests that slaveholding was not as pervasive among members of other religions in the Chesterfield area as it was among non-Friends in the Shrewsbury Monthly Meeting locality. Only one of five Anglicans whose estates were inventoried and ranked in the top 30 percent during 1766-1780 and one-half of the Presbyterians in the same wealth category in the Burlington townships and Upper Freehold owned slaves, although all of the Baptists and Dutch Reformed in the top 30 percent were slave owners. Thus, there is some evidence that reasons other than the opposition of Friends to slavery, including perhaps

TABLE 5.5. SLAVE OWNERSHIP AND RELIGION AMONG WEALTHIEST
30 PERCENT OF INVENTORIED DECEDENTS IN CHESTERFIELD
MONTHLY MEETING AREA

| | 1730-1739 | | 1766(64)-1780[a] | |
	No.	Slave owners	No.	Slave owners
Quakers	16	37.5%	25	24.0%
Disowned Quakers	0	—	2	50.0
Anglicans	0	—	5	20.0
Presbyterians	0	—	4	50.0
Baptists	0	—	3	100.0
Dutch Reformed	0	—	2	100.0
Religion unknown	4	0	16	31.2
Total	20	30.0	57	35.1

SOURCES: Probate and church records
[a] Includes all inventories from the Burlington County townships for 1766-1780 and from Upper Freehold Township, Monmouth County, for 1764-1780

TABLE 5.6. SLAVE OWNERSHIP AND RELIGION AMONG ALL DECEDENTS IN
CHESTERFIELD MONTHLY MEETING AREA

| | 1730-1739 | | 1766(64)-1780[a] | |
	No.	Slave owners	No.	Slave owners
Quakers	40	22.5%	84	14.3%
Disowned Quakers	0	—	9	22.2
Anglicans	2	50.0	19	26.3
Presbyterians	0	—	14	35.7
Baptists	0	—	12	58.3
Dutch Reformed	0	—	4	75.0
Religion unknown	40	5.0	82	8.5
Total	82	14.6	224	18.3

SOURCES: Probate and church records
[a] Includes all inventories from the Burlington County townships for 1766-1780 and from Upper Freehold Township, Monmouth County, for 1764-1780

the availability of indentured servants, contributed to the relatively low incidence of slaveholding in West Jersey.

In addition, the pattern of slaveholding at death among partici-pants of Chesterfield Monthly Meeting was much different from that found in Shrewsbury.[39] The percentage of decedent participants who owned slaves at death was similar in the two meetings through 1760, although a smaller proportion of Chesterfield Friends who died during 1721-1740 owned slaves (Table 5.7). The chief dif-ference lay in the fact that 15.2 percent of the Chesterfield partic-ipants who died after *1760* owned slaves, while *none* of the Shrews-bury leaders dying during those years was a slave owner. Furthermore, *no* slave-owning Chesterfield leader manumitted his slaves before 1746, and even after that year only five (27.8 percent) of the eighteen decedent slave owning participants freed their slaves—in their wills or before death—compared with 75 percent after 1745 in Shrewsbury. Two of these five freed their blacks only after 1776, and the slaves of one were freed by the agreement of the majority of his heirs rather than by the testator himself.[40]

[39] The sample of meeting participants is different in Chesterfield than in Shrewsbury during the period before 1732 because all of the minutes survive in Chesterfield; thus men who played smaller roles in this meeting are also included.
[40] Burlington Co. Wills, William Cooke, 6613-6616C (man freed in 1760 by heirs);

TABLE 5.7. SLAVE OWNERSHIP AMONG CHESTERFIELD
MONTHLY MEETING PARTICIPANTS

Date of death	No. participants	Slave owners
1681-1700	9	22.2%
1701-1720	8	50.0
1721-1740	20	25.0
1741-1760	46	30.4
1761-1780	46	15.2
Total	129	24.8

SOURCES: Probate records; Chesterfield MM mins., 1684-1780

The reluctance of Chesterfield Friends to oppose slavery is also apparent in the monthly meeting minutes. They steadfastly rejected abolitionist reform until the 1770s. In May 1730, the meeting "calmly" considered the petition of Chester Friends to ban the purchase of imported blacks and appointed a committee of weighty Friends, including clerk of meeting Thomas Lambert, Benjamin Clark, Abraham Farrington, and Isaac Horner, to draw up the sense of the meeting.[41] These Friends, who included two slave owners,[42] reported to Burlington Quarterly Meeting "that as Friends both here and elsewhere have been in the Practice of it [purchasing imported blacks] for time past & many Friends differing in their Opinions from others in that matter: we think restricting Friends at this time & bringing Such as fall into the same thing under dealing as Offenders will not be convenient lest it create contention & uneasiness among them which Should be carefully avoided."[43]

Chesterfield continued to oppose antislavery reform through 1770. While the meeting often reported to the quarterly meeting

Benjamin Shreve, 4861-4866C (man freed in 1751 but was to pay 40 shillings per year for five years for old age); Daniel Doughty, 10569C (freed old man at death in 1778); William Wood, 10729C and Chesterfield MM mans., 1777 (manumitted slave children before his death in 1778); Matthew Watson freed slaves before his death in 1750 (Burlington Co. Abolition Society Papers, Burlington Co. Historical Society [BCHS], Burlington, N.J.).

[41] Chesterfield MM mins., 3M/1730.

[42] Thomas Lambert owned five slaves when he died in 1733, and Isaac Horner owned at least two in 1760. Burlington Co. Wills, Thomas Lambert, 2373-2382C; Isaac Horner, 7081-7084C.

[43] Chesterfield MM mins., 6/6M/1730.

that members had in fact bought or sold slaves, the meeting disciplined no such offenders before 1771. In response to the Yearly Meeting's query of whether any Friends had imported or bought slaves, Chesterfield Friends wrote in 1758 "mostly clear" (5th month) and "We dont know but what we are clear in them respects except one" (11th month). In February 1759, the clerk wrote "Clear as far as we know except one but care is on the minds of friends to treat with him as soon as opportunity will admit." Friends apparently never found the "opportunity" to deal with the anonymous offender in this case or any other that came up during the 1750s and 1760s, although the meeting repeatedly reported it was "not all clear of purchasing negroes" through the 1760s. Then in 1771, Chesterfield Quakers disciplined one member for a long list of offenses including marrying out, fornication, fighting, and buying blacks, but he acknowledged his guilt and remained a Friend. The next year, the meeting again reported the sale of a slave but did not discipline the offender.[44] However, the policy of the meeting was now starting to change. It appointed a committee to visit slaveholders in 1775 at the urging of Philadelphia Yearly Meeting and Burlington Quarterly Meeting, but the committee found the service difficult. They reported after visiting members for about six months that they found "several friends disposed to set their Negroes free but most of those are discouraged from the apprehension of incumbrance which it might occasion to their outward Estates and some few refuse at present."[45] The "incumbrance" was probably the £200 security bond required in New Jersey for manumission, and Chesterfield slave owners were using it as an excuse—justifiable or not—to hold on to their slaves. Though one Trenton Friend, Mary Dury, had already emancipated two black men in 1774,[46] before 1777 the committee convinced few slave owners to manumit their slaves. In that year fifteen Chesterfield Friends freed thirty-two slaves, and in 1778 five more owners emancipated seven blacks.[47] The committee also reported the names of seven members who refused to free their slaves by 1778. The meeting quickly disowned six of these Friends along with one other man who sold a black. Josiah Appleton, the

[44] Chesterfield MM mins., 4/5M/1758, 2/11M/1758, 1/2M/1759, 7/8M/1760, 6/8M/1761, 4/2M/1762, 5/8M/1762, 3/2M/1763, 2/8M/1764, 7/8M/1766, 6/8M/1767, 3M/1771 to 5M/1771, and 6/8M/1772.

[45] Chesterfield MM mins., 3/8M/1775.

[46] Chesterfield MM mans., 1774. She left her personal property (£26.9 sterling) to four other blacks when she died in 1783. Hunterdon Co. Wills, Mary Dury, 1201J.

[47] Chesterfield MM mins., 1/8M/1776; Chesterfield MM mans., 1777-1778.

seventh owner in the 1778 report, died before he was disowned; but his son John, who evidently inherited the slave, was disowned when he, too, rejected manumission. Ten owners freed ten more slaves in 1779 (one woman was jointly held by seven Friends from Stony Brook who probably acquired her by inheritance), and the meeting testified against four more recalcitrant members in 1779-1780.[48] But still the duties of the committee on slavery were not ended, for in the years 1779-1782, the committee reported that a few blacks were not yet freed, and six Friends signed manumissions for seven blacks in the years 1781 through 1783. Then at last, in the latter year, the slavery committee could report that members held no blacks in bondage except for two cases that were not under the meeting's control. These blacks were probably among the eleven manumitted during 1786-1797 by widows and children after the deaths of slaveholders who had been disowned by the meeting for slavery or other offenses and had refused to give up their blacks.[49]

Thus in Chesterfield meeting the eradication of slavery was not an easy task. A major policy shift was necessary in the 1770s before the meeting would comply with the Yearly Meeting discipline. This change was accomplished only after substantial resistance among leaders and members was overcome. It is uncertain whether some leaders specifically used the slavery issue to gain control of the meeting from its slaveholding elite. But it is clear that some turnover in leadership, whether caused by death, change of residence, or exclusion from power of the slave-owning leaders, accompanied the policy change. While many slave owners served on Chesterfield committees during the 1760s and early 1770s, very few held positions of power in 1777, when the meeting finally moved against Friends who held blacks.

Between 1760 and 1777 eight participants in the monthly meeting, including Isaac Horner and Eliakim Hedger who held offices, died owning slaves; none of these men freed his blacks.[50] Daniel Doughty, a Chesterfield representative at the quarterly meeting from 1748 until 1776, moved to Burlington Monthly Meeting in 1776

[48] Chesterfield MM mins., 10/9M/1778, 3/12M/1778, 4/3M/1779, 6/5M/1779, 5/8M/1779, 11M/1779, 5M/1780, 10M/1780; Chesterfield MM mans., 1779-1780.

[49] Chesterfield MM mins., 5/8M/1779, 8M/1780, 8M/1781, 8M/1782, 5M/1783; Chesterfield MM mans., 1781-1797.

[50] Burlington Co. Wills, Isaac Horner, 7081-7084C; John Newbold, 8555C; William Pancoast, 7517-7524C; Timothy Abbott, 10062-10075C; William Cooke, 6613-6616C; Isaac Forman, 9654C. Hunterdon Co. Wills, Gideon Bickerdike, 557J. Somerset Co. Wills, Eliakim Hedger, Bk. 12, 470.

and died two years later owning a slave. Another long-term leader, William Morris, freed a black woman and her child as late as 1774.[51] The loss of these men as leaders and the dropping out or exclusion by 1776 of seven of nine other slave owners who had participated in the monthly meeting before 1770 changed the balance of opinion in the meeting and permitted Friends who were more inclined to accept antislavery to take control. Each of the two slave owners who remained active in the meeting after 1776 manumitted his slave in 1777.[52] Of the four slave owners who participated in the monthly meeting only after 1770, Thomas Thorn alone was assigned duties between 1775 and 1779, before he had manumitted his two young blacks. Two others of these four slave owners did not become active until after they freed their slaves.[53] As might be expected from this turnover, almost no slave owners participated on antislavery committees. The lone exception was Robert White who, with six other people from Stony Brook, manumitted a black woman, Susannah, in 1779. White became a participant in the monthly meeting and was assigned to treat with slaveholders only after her manumission was secured.[54]

Even though Chesterfield meeting could reach agreement to discipline slave buyers, sellers, and owners only after many slave-owning leaders had died or stopped participating in the meeting's affairs, there is still little evidence that an "outgroup" used the issue to take control of the meeting from a wealthy elite. Just 51.8 percent (fourteen of twenty-seven) of the Chesterfield men assigned to committees that treated with slaveholders were officers of the meeting whereas 77.4 percent (twenty-four of thirty-one) were officers in Shrewsbury. But at least part of the reason for this difference was that the Shrewsbury committees served over a longer period and so more officers could be involved. Chesterfield meeting recruited almost one-half (thirteen of twenty-seven) of the antislavery committee members from among men who had begun performing tasks for the monthly meeting only since 1770, but still the meeting leadership of the late 1770s included older officers who started serving the monthly meeting in the era from the late 1740s to the early 1760s

---

[51] Chesterfield MM mins., 1730-1776; Burlington Co. Wills, Daniel Doughty, 10569C. Doughty freed his old black man Syrah in his will. For Morris, see Phila. MM mans., 1774.

[52] The two were Samuel Worth and Joseph Horner. Chesterfield MM mans., 1777.

[53] Chesterfield MM mans., Thomas Thorn 1779, Samuel Olden 1777, Robert White and William Clarke, 1779; Chesterfield MM mins., 1770-1783.

[54] Chesterfield MM mins., 1770-1783; Chesterfield MM mans., 1779.

such as Stacy Potts (who became clerk of meeting in 1776), John Bullock, Anthony Sykes, Benjamin Field, Samuel Satterthwaite II, and Abraham Skirm. They were joined by less experienced men who started participating in the meeting between 1767 and the early 1780s, including Fretwell Wright, Jacob Middleton, Barzillai Forman, Isaac Wright, Benjamin Linton, and Benjamin Clarke. Thus, the policy of the monthly meeting on slavery was reversed by a coalition of men who had served under the old regime and new men who took the places of slaveholders (and nonslaveholders) who died or otherwise left their leadership positions by the early 1770s. Given this continuity, it seems unlikely that the issue of slavery was used by the antislavery group as a way to gain power in the meeting, even though most slave owners were in some way removed from influence. As in Shrewsbury, some slaveholders either returned to or took new places of leadership in the meeting after they manumitted their slaves, and many of the antislavery proponents already had influential positions before 1776.

Chesterfield Monthly Meeting members, like their co-religionists in Shrewsbury, thus debated antislavery on its own merits, as a question involving the issue of how Quakers should relate their religious ideals to their daily lives. Several Chesterfield leaders active throughout the eighteenth century had strong antislavery views. John Sykes, a well-respected Friend whose career in the meeting began in 1709 and who with John Woolman and three others served on the committee appointed in 1758 by Philadelphia Yearly Meeting to visit slave owners,[55] was almost certainly a constant source of irritation to proslavery apologists in his meeting. As executor of the will of Mathew Champion of the town of Burlington in 1735, Sykes secured freedom for a black man, Jo, who had belonged to the deceased. Sykes's own will set aside money to take care of Jo in case he should become chargeable to Sykes's estate, and appointed his son, Anthony Sykes, to support the freed man if necessary. The younger Sykes himself possibly helped to obtain the agreement of William Cooke's heirs in 1760 for the manumission of that deceased man's slave, and in 1770 he served with other prominent antislavery Friends on the Yearly Meeting committee appointed to administer the estate of James McCarty, an ex-slave from Shrewsbury.[56]

In sum, Chesterfield Monthly Meeting, like Shrewsbury, did

[55] PYM mins., 23-29/9M/1758.

[56] Burlington Co. Wills, Mathew Champion, Lib. 4, 38; John Sykes, 9059C; William Cooke, 6613-6616C. Report of the Committee on James McCarty's Estate, 17/9M/1770, Burlington Co. Abolition Society Papers, BCHS.

genuinely oppose slavery when it finally started disciplining slave purchasers, sellers, and owners. However, unlike the Quakers of eastern Monmouth County, who had voiced their opposition to the importation of blacks as early as 1730 and were systematically manumitting their slaves in their wills before 1750, Chesterfield meeting could decide to oppose the institution only in the late 1770s. What accounts for the wide difference in timing between these two meetings? Why was one moving earlier, the other later, than the Yearly Meeting as a whole? In each meeting, the success of the drive against slavery depended on two factors: the socioeconomic circumstances in which Friends made choices concerning slavery and the members' beliefs about how Quaker teachings related to these practical concerns.

In their efforts to convince slave masters to release their blacks, antislavery reformers never contended that slavery was economically unsound. Their arguments emphasized instead that owning slaves was inconsistent with Christianity. Nevertheless, socioeconomic considerations did influence the debate over slavery within the meetings, because slave owners (and potential slave owners) could not avoid weighing the benefits of the Afro-Americans' labor, the value of their invested or inherited capital in slaves, and the cost or risk of manumission bonds, against the force of the reformers' ideals. The strength and effectiveness of the proslavery faction in each local meeting depended on the number and influence of slave owners, and the steadfastness with which they held on to their slaves.

The differences in slave ownership patterns between Shrewsbury and Chesterfield have already been discussed. The eastern Monmouth County Quakers were heavily involved in slavery by the 1720s, but from that decade on, many leaders and members manumitted their slaves in their wills and others avoided buying any blacks at all. By 1757, Shrewsbury meeting had developed a clearcut antislavery policy, and it used the Yearly Meeting decisions of 1758 and 1774 to force the few holdout slave owners to comply. Chesterfield Friends, on the other hand, do not appear to have enmeshed themselves in slavery as completely as early Shrewsbury leaders. Subsequently, however, they held on to their slaves much later and even refused to accept the Yearly Meeting proscription against slave trading until after 1776. A relatively large band of influential slaveholding Quakers kept Chesterfield meeting out of the abolitionist camp.

The timing of the development of slavery in East and West Jersey helps explain why the behavior of these two meetings was so different. As discussed in Chapter 3, residents of East Jersey invested most heavily in slave labor before 1730. In the Chesterfield Monthly Meeting area, some early settlers owned slaves, but an increase in their dependence on slavery turns up in the probate records only after 1740. West Jersey Friends and their neighbors bought slaves as indentured servants grew scarce—especially during the Seven Years' War. The development of large farms and increased average wealth among decedents in the Chesterfield area by the 1750s created greater demand for slave labor.

Table 5.4 suggests that socioeconomic concerns affected the stances on antislavery of participants in both local meetings. For instance, in Shrewsbury, the amount of land held by monthly meeting participants who were listed on the Shrewsbury and Middletown tax lists was significantly less than the acreage owned by Friends who held or traded in slaves. The slaveholders also owned on average much more land than the antislavery group (who included most of the meeting leadership). The mean acreage for the eighteen Quaker slave owners, buyers, and sellers was 249.2 acres—close to the average of all eastern Monmouth County slave owners of 283.7 acres. Thus Shrewsbury Friends who bought and held on to their slaves into the 1760s were large landholders who, like other slave owners of the locality, employed extra labor to work their farms.[57] Although the average amount of land owned by Shrewsbury Quakers who had manumitted their slaves earlier is not known, it seems significant that such a wide gap existed between the average acreages owned by the antislavery and slave-owning groups of the late 1750s through 1780s. That many leading as well as ordinary Friends simply did not need additional labor probably facilitated their decision to oppose slavery.

In Chesterfield Monthly Meeting, on the other hand, the size of their landholdings did not make the acceptance of antislavery reform easier for the 107 participants who were listed on the 1774 and 1779 tax lists. Those meeting members who owned slaves held only an average of 5.8 percent more land than the meeting participants as a whole. If the average holdings of just the land owners among each group are compared, the meeting participants on average actually possessed slightly more than the slave owners. Thus, many

---

[57] For some the large landholdings merely denoted substantial wealth which the slaveholders invested in diversified operations. In that case, at least some of their blacks would have worked in mills, crafts, mines, or shops.

of the meeting participants of the 1740s through 1770s who were still household heads in 1774 and 1779 were large farm owners, and their awareness of possible labor needs must have entered into their decision on whether to oppose slavery among their fellow Friends.

In short, in both Shrewsbury and Chesterfield, slave-owning Quakers—like most slaveholders in the two areas—owned large farms. The determination of many to hold on to their slaves surely stemmed from their need for additional labor. The significant difference between the two meetings in the average size of landholdings of all meeting participants thus accounts in part for their disagreement on antislavery. Most Shrewsbury Quakers owned lands too small to require or support slave labor, but the majority of Chesterfield participants continued to own farms large enough to require extra labor as late as 1779.

In these ways, then, economic considerations affected the Quaker debate over slavery. Quaker farmers who continued to find slave labor useful resisted abolitionist reform. As long as these slave owners held influence in the meeting, as they did in Chesterfield until the mid-1770s, a sense of the meeting in favor of antislavery could not be reached. The rapid growth of slavery in Shrewsbury in the early eighteenth century had soon illuminated for Friends living there the inconsistency of the institution with Quaker ideals. Robert Barclay's instructions to avoid violence were familiar to all Friends, and many came to believe that his injunction should be interpreted to proscribe the force required to enslave blacks and keep them subordinated.[58] Rumors of real and imagined slave rebellions in New York, South Carolina, and the West Indies certainly concerned pacifist Friends.[59] And the daily struggle to force unpaid laborers and their children to work and behave, without using violence, must have taxed the imaginations of conscientious Quakers.[60] Thus, in

[58] Robert Barclay, *An Apology for the True Christian Divinity* ([Aberdeen?], 1678), 399-407.

[59] Herbert Aptheker, *American Negro Slave Revolts* (New York, 1974), 162-208. Aptheker has been criticized for including many rumored conspiracies and individual or small group acts of violence that cannot be considered actual slave revolts. However, his examination in his second chapter of how rumors of rebellion—both real and imaginary— aroused fears among whites is very important.

[60] Several Friends who manumitted their slaves in their wills, as mentioned above, used freedom as a reward for correct behavior by including the restriction that the slaves would be freed in the future only if they behaved themselves in the meantime. For example, see Monmouth Co. Wills, George Williams I, 1193-1197M, 1853-1859M; John Lippincott (II), 1413-1414M, 1537M.

Shrewsbury, the startling growth of slavery by the 1720s stirred the consciences of Friends to oppose the institution. In Chesterfield, to the contrary, since the black population remained small before 1750, few Friends were moved to oppose further development of slavery—especially because the need for labor from rapid economic development in the third quarter of the eighteenth century occurred just as alternative sources of free and bound immigrant labor shrank.

THIS concern of reform-minded Friends in Shrewsbury about the upsurge in slaveholding early in the eighteenth century, and contrasts by 1760 in the degree of involvement in slavery between leading Friends in Shrewsbury and Chesterfield, explain adequately the wide interval in the *timing* of the two meetings' acceptance of antislavery. But there is also evident a difference in the *manner* in which these two groups of Quakers enforced other items of the discipline in addition to slavery that provokes further investigation. Their divergent views about what kind of a relationship Friends should have with people of other religions suggest that the leaders of the two meetings interpreted Quaker theology in different ways— one that stressed humanitarianism and another that emphasized group cohesiveness. Both of these tendencies were consistent with and securely rooted in the traditions of the Society of Friends.

In this vein, J. William Frost has suggested that there were two kinds of reformers in Philadelphia Yearly Meeting in the 1750s: those who supported more stringent enforcement of the rules of marriage, and others who advocated antislavery and similar philanthropic concerns. He hypothesizes that the 1755 Philadelphia Yearly Meeting decision to tighten the discipline against marrying members of other religions—which has been seen as evidence that Friends became more tribalistic in the wake of their loss of power in the Pennsylvania government—was advanced by Friends like John Churchman and Israel II, James, and John Pemberton who had less interest in abolitionism than Friends like John Woolman and Anthony Benezet.[61]

The behavior of Shrewsbury and Chesterfield meetings supports Frost's conjecture about different threads behind reform in the Society. Shrewsbury Monthly Meeting adopted a stance against slavery earlier than most other local meetings in the Delaware Valley and was concerned greatly about the welfare of blacks. But before

[61] J. William Frost, "The Origins of the Quaker Crusade against Slavery: A Review of Recent Literature," *Quaker History* 67 (1978), 56-58; Tolles, *Meeting House*, ch. 10.

1755 these Friends showed limited interest in disciplining members who married outside the meeting. In contrast, Chesterfield stalled on abolitionism until the 1770s and cared little about whether slaves actually obtained liberty; at the same time these Quakers consistently punished members who married out even before the Yearly Meeting directive of 1755.

Tables 5.8 and 5.9 clearly illustrate these dissimilarities between the two groups of New Jersey Friends. In the period before 1755— when meetings were not under the watchful eye of the Yearly Meeting on this issue—Shrewsbury was very lenient toward those marrying out. Although the Shrewsbury overseers reported six cases of irregular marriages between 1732 and 1742, none was disowned, and from 1743 until 1754 the meeting disciplined only one woman for wrong marriage—she married a man too nearly related (see Table 5.8). That the absence of cases was not the result of the obedient behavior of the Shrewsbury children became clear in 1755 when Philadelphia Yearly Meeting reminded local meetings to enforce the marriage discipline. Shrewsbury meeting then expressed concern that it was "remiss" in disciplining members who married out and so in 1755 and 1756 the overseers called in twenty-seven Friends who had married out during previous years and requested their acknowledgments. Eighteen of the offenders expressed sorrow for their errors, and their membership was continued. Furthermore, in 1758, Shrewsbury leaders explained to the Yearly Meeting that they had not visited families because they were "under a sence of [their] Innabillities" to dispense advice to other families when their

TABLE 5.8. ENFORCEMENT OF MARRIAGE DISCIPLINE IN SHREWSBURY AND CHESTERFIELD MONTHLY MEETINGS

	Shrewsbury MM			Chesterfield MM		
	1732-1742	1743-1754	Total	1732-1742	1743-1754	Total
Total discipline cases	9	13	22	22	70	92
Marriage cases (No.)	6	1	7	10	45	55
Marriage cases (%)	66.7	7.7	31.8	45.4	64.3	59.8

SOURCES: Shrewsbury and Chesterfield MM mins., 1732-1754

TABLE 5.9. DISCIPLINARY CASES IN SHREWSBURY AND CHESTERFIELD
MONTHLY MEETINGS

	Total cases		Marriage cases[a]		Slavery cases[b]	
	No.	% Disowned	No.	% Disowned	No.	% Disowned
Shrewsbury MM						
1732-1740	6	16.7%	4	0.0%	0	—
1741-1750	10	0.0	2	0.0	0	—
1751-1760	97	25.8	40	37.5	1	0.0%
1761-1770	110	40.9	58	53.4	9	55.6
1771-1780	128	39.8	51	39.2	5	20.0
Total	351	34.8	155	42.6	15	40.0
Chesterfield MM						
1732-1740	18	55.5%	7	57.1%	0	—
1741-1750	37	37.8	28	28.6	0	—
1751-1760	153	45.8	69	46.4	0	—
1761-1770	124	37.1	91	36.3	0	—
1771-1780	245	59.2	117	55.6	15	86.7%
Total	577	49.4	312	45.5	15	86.7

SOURCES: Shrewsbury MM mins., 1732-1780; Chesterfield MM mins., 1732-1780
[a] All cases dealing with marriage including those involving other offenses
[b] All cases dealing with slavery including those involving other offenses

own were not in order.[62] Shrewsbury Friends generally indicated only a mild interest in the enforcement of discipline throughout the period 1732 to 1780. Although the proportion grew to about 40 percent after 1761—largely because Shrewsbury Friends were now enforcing the marriage discipline more strictly—only 34.8 percent of the disciplinary cases brought into the monthly meeting ended in disownment during the entire period 1732-1780 (Table 5.9). In contrast, Chesterfield enforced the rules much more rigidly during the entire period than did Shrewsbury, and disowned offenders at a relatively high rate especially during the 1730s and 1770s. As Table 5.8 shows, Chesterfield Monthly Meeting consistently disciplined Friends who married out even before the 1755 directive of the Yearly Meeting.

It appears, then, that in their views on both slavery and enforcement of the marriage discipline, Friends from Shrewsbury and Chesterfield drew guidance in interpreting Quaker theology from two

[62] Shrewsbury MM mins., 3/7M/1758.

different traditions. Shrewsbury Quakers showed little concern in maintaining group coherence by establishing and enforcing rules that drew boundaries between themselves and members of other religions. Instead, they demonstrated several of the characteristics of what Max Weber called "exemplary prophecy," which emphasizes "the possession of the deity or the inward and contemplative surrender to God." Adherents to this kind of religion *lived* according to God's will, and in this way communicated their ethical standards to others.[63] Thus, the East Jersey Friends after 1725 exhibited their belief that perpetual slavery was a sin by emancipating their own slaves or by not buying any in the first place, rather than by telling others to free theirs. Despite their firm antislavery position, these Quakers sent no petitions to the Yearly Meeting in favor of strengthening the discipline before 1757, as did the Chester meeting; and even in the 1760s and 1770s when slave buying, selling, and owning were prohibited, Shrewsbury Friends were more concerned with procuring freedom for the slave than with penalizing the slave purchaser or owner. In addition, East Jersey Quakers were reluctant to disown members for other kinds of offenses, especially those like marrying out that violated rules of the Society designed to isolate Friends from people of other religions.

Chesterfield meeting, on the other hand, tended more to the "emissary type of prophecy" that demands that others follow a prescribed moral code.[64] These Friends were not reluctant to disown wrongdoers, and enforced the marriage discipline consistently before 1755. They were slow, however, in accepting the Yearly Meeting's rules against the slave trade and slavery; it is likely that—in accord with their concern about adhering to the behavioral code rather than to the humanistic spirit of Quakerism—Chesterfield leaders assumed a legalistic posture by demanding a sense of the meeting before agreeing that slavery was "wrong." When Chesterfield meeting did enforce the rules against slavery after 1776, on the other hand, they did so with such speed that they appear to have been more interested in ridding the meeting of slave owners than in obtaining freedom for the blacks involved.

Although Weber assigned all Quakers to his "emissary" category, he did note that their religion "contained very strong contemplative

---

[63] Max Weber, "The Social Psychology of the World Religions," in *From Max Weber: Essays in Sociology*, trans. and ed. H. H. Gerth and C. Wright Mills (New York, 1958), 285.

[64] Ibid.

elements" that were common among "exemplary" religions.[65] In fact, Quakerism had characteristics of both types, for as Frost has explained, "one of the reasons why only Friends, of all the sects that sprang up during the Commonwealth period, were able to survive was that they managed to combine the liberty of personal authoritative revelation with a strong system of discipline and church control."[66] The combination of personal revelation and church discipline was not easy to sustain, however. Indeed, George Fox found it impossible to convince all of his co-religionists that a system for supervising behavior was necessary. In the 1660s, John Perrot and his adherents had refused to accept a Society ruling that they should take off their hats during worship services. They maintained that they would not force their principles on others, and so they did not want others to tell them how to worship. In the 1670s, John Wilkinson and John Story led a group that denounced new disciplinary procedures, and eventually split off from the Society. Both rebelling factions believed that the individual's freedom to communicate with God in his or her own way should not be obstructed by "a tyrannical government."[67]

The authority of the church to supervise members' behavior was therefore a question of paramount importance among English Friends in the decades before many of them immigrated to West Jersey and Pennsylvania. It is likely that these Quakers brought with them a concern about the need for church government, but they did not necessarily agree on where to set the balance between discipline and individual conscience. William Penn, in support of Fox, wrote during the Wilkinson-Story controversy that if the church did not have discipline "it would be overrun with lukewarm hypocrites and loose walkers."[68] His associates who became leaders of the Chesterfield meeting probably agreed.

Quakers in East Jersey did not experience this turmoil, and thus had less concern about church government. Their very different past experiences, and especially their unusually favorable association with members of other religions, made them less interested in devising a disciplinary system that would erect boundaries between

[65] Ibid., 291.

[66] Frost, *The Quaker Family in Colonial America* (New York, 1973), 49.

[67] Ibid., 48; William C. Braithwaite, *The Second Period of Quakerism*, ed. Henry J. Cadbury, 2d ed. (Cambridge, 1961), 228-236, 291-297. The Hutchinson and Half-Way Covenant crises among New England Puritans in the 1630s and 1660s contained similar tensions.

[68] Braithwaite, *Second Period*, 299.

themselves and other groups. Many of the Shrewsbury Quakers were among a number of people with Anabaptist and Seeker leanings who had immigrated to Long Island from Lynn, Massachusetts, during the 1640s. They converted to Quakerism after missionaries arrived in New Netherland in 1657, but kept close ties with their Baptist neighbors—some of whom protected Friends from persecution and migrated with them to East Jersey. Shrewsbury Friends did not set up monthly meetings for discipline on their own in the 1660s, but created them only when George Fox visited in 1672. The primary reason for the Quaker leader's journey to America was indeed to encourage Friends there to establish these meetings.[69]

By the mid-eighteenth century, then, Shrewsbury and Chesterfield Friends had fundamentally different points of view on how Quakers should practice their beliefs, which continued to guide their behavior when slavery became an issue. They emphasized separate strands of Quaker tradition, and so had divergent ideas about the identity of Friends within society. The difference in the timing of abolitionism between Shrewsbury and Chesterfield meetings sprang primarily from their different local experiences with the institution of slavery; but their dissimilar views on the fundamentals of Quakerism were important as well in *how* they acted when some move was accepted as being necessary.

Like Quakers elsewhere, members of Shrewsbury meeting did not recognize at first that slavery conflicted with their ideals. Comparatively few blacks lived in Monmouth County before 1710, and Europeans viewed slaves primarily as a source of labor. With the New York slave rebellion of 1712, the rapid increase of blacks imported into the Shrewsbury area after 1710 and the formation of black families, however, Friends had to face up to the fact that slavery violated their beliefs. A system of perpetual bondage necessitated the use or threat of violence within Quaker families and society at large, and negated the belief that all men and women were equal in the eyes of God. And slave ownership, as John Hepburn pointed out so well, encouraged pride and sloth.

The Shrewsbury Quaker slave owners of the early eighteenth century needed help in developing and exploiting their plantations and so they used Africans and Afro-Americans, who were much

<hr />

[69] Jones, *Quakers in the American Colonies*, 216-223; Pomfret, *East New Jersey*, 42-45; Penney, ed., *Journal of George Fox*, 2:226; Frederick B. Tolles, "The Atlantic Community of the Early Friends," *The Journal of the Friends' Historical Society*, Supplement no. 24 (1952), 23.

easier to acquire than white servants in their locality. Thus, while the Friends listened to the urgings of Hepburn, traveling ministers like John Salkeld,[70] and their own consciences, and—unlike most slaveholders of other religions—manumitted their slaves, these East Jersey Friends in the first third of the eighteenth century freed their blacks only after they had obtained the benefits of slave ownership. By freeing their slaves in their wills, they put off proclaiming their disapproval of perpetual servitude until they were near death and deprived their children but not themselves of the slaves' labor. Nevertheless, these early emancipators did establish a precedent for the gradual elimination of slavery that was followed after 1730 by most members of Shrewsbury meeting. Many Friends living in eastern Monmouth County after 1750 avoided owning slaves because they did not need additional labor; but they did so also because they thought that one way in which Quakers could practice their religious ideals was by not owning slaves. Then at mid-century, when the issue of slavery finally caught the full attention of the Yearly Meeting, Shrewsbury meeting still retained the "exemplary" style of the earlier generation by placing more emphasis on obtaining freedom for blacks than on punishing the wrongdoers.

In contrast, Chesterfield Friends relied more heavily on church discipline (particularly in controlling marriage), than on individual commitment to the Quaker ideals like those that underlay antislavery, in order to maintain their separate identity in West Jersey society. As a labor practice, slavery was relatively unimportant in the Burlington County area until after 1740, and so—as in Shrewsbury before 1710—was not considered a danger to the integrity of the Quaker community. Then, during the 1750s and 1760s, while some Chesterfield leaders were concerned about the growth of slavery in their locality, many others relied on slave labor to run their farms, and were reluctant to stop buying Afro-Americans or to free their slaves. Unfortunately for these Friends, they made the move to invest in blacks just as the Yearly Meeting decided that use of slave labor was wrong. When in the mid-1770s Chesterfield finally reached a sense of the meeting in favor of antislavery, after most of its slave-owning leaders died, moved away, or otherwise left positions of power, the meeting acted in a way that was consistent with

---

[70] John Hepburn mentioned that Salkeld spoke against slavery (*American Defence*, 3). Salkeld was a traveling minister who emigrated from England to Chester, Pennsylvania in 1705. He probably visited Shrewsbury on at least one of his journeys between Pennsylvania and New England in 1701, 1702, or 1708-1709. Willard Heiss, ed., *[Quaker] Biographical Sketches* (Indianapolis, 1972), 255-258.

its past disciplinary policy on other issues. Weighty Chesterfield Friends now worked vigorously to rid the meeting of slaveholders, with little regard of the consequences of that policy for the freedom of blacks. Whereas Shrewsbury meeting patiently worked for, and required the manumission of, all slaves its members bought, sold, owned, or hired from non-Quakers, Chesterfield meeting limited its policy to the abrupt disownment of recalcitrant slave owners.

CHESTER AND PHILADELPHIA MEETINGS

The distance between the stances of Chester and Philadelphia monthly meetings on antislavery reform was as great as that between Shrewsbury and Chesterfield. Chester Friends took a very early step in 1711 when they reached a sense of the meeting against buying imported blacks. In that year, in 1715 and 1716, and again in 1729, they sent petitions urging stronger action from Philadelphia Yearly Meeting, which would agree only to censure and not to discipline members who purchased recently imported Africans and West Indian blacks. Chester meeting then fell silent on the issue of slavery after 1730, and took no part in the push against slaveholding in the 1750s. Eventually, in the 1760s and 1770s, Chester Friends dutifully treated with slave purchasers, sellers, and owners, as did most other local meetings in Pennsylvania and New Jersey. By 1780 they had either secured manumissions or disowned those who refused to free their slaves. The meeting dealt with seven members who bought or sold Afro-Americans in the years 1760-1780. Unlike Shrewsbury and Philadelphia, however, until 1773 Chester required only acknowledgments rather than promises of freedom for the injured blacks. The meeting appointed a committee to visit slaveholders in 1765; but at that time they obtained liberty for just one bondsman. Nine years later, a new group of Chester Friends began dealing with slaveholders, and during the period 1776-1780 this committee convinced ten owners to give up their slaves. The meeting eventually disowned two men, Samuel Levis and James Maris, in 1778 and 1780 respectively because they refused to free their blacks.[1]

While Chester abandoned its role as instigator of antislavery reform after 1730, and became one of the local meetings that simply followed the dictates of the Yearly Meeting, Philadelphia moved in exactly the opposite direction. Members of Philadelphia Monthly Meeting around 1700 established a separate meeting of worship for blacks, opposed slave auctions, and formed a committee to request that Quakers in Barbados stop sending slaves to Philadelphia.[2] But the meeting firmly rejected all further measures against slavery and

[1] Chester MM min., 1711-1780; Chester MM mans., 1776-1780.
[2] Phila. QM mins., 30/7M/1698; Phila. MM mins., 29/1M/1700.

disciplined several Friends, including William Southeby and John Farmer, for publishing antislavery tracts without the meeting's approval. The city's Quakers claimed in 1716 that Southeby, an active participant in the meeting from 1686 to 1714, had censured "friends contrary to the minutes of our Yearly meeting"; they believed that the paper he published in 1717 had "a tendency to division."[3] As the most powerful contingent in Philadelphia Quarterly and Yearly Meetings, Philadelphia Friends—along with representatives from the Burlington Quarterly Meeting—blocked acceptance of Chester's petition to prohibit the purchase of imported blacks in 1730 and masterminded the public denunciation of Benjamin Lay in 1738.

Like Philadelphia Yearly Meeting as a whole, Philadelphia Monthly Meeting changed its position on slavery in the 1750s. On 25 January 1754, Anthony Benezet submitted to the local meeting a proposal to publicize Friends' opposition to importing and purchasing imported blacks. The meeting referred the paper first to a committee and then to Philadelphia Quarterly Meeting for consideration. The quarterly meeting acted favorably and sent the tract to the 1754 Yearly Meeting, which issued it under the title, *An Epistle of Caution and Advice*.[4] After 1755, Philadelphia Monthly Meeting, like Shrewsbury, promptly and actively disciplined members who disobeyed the Yearly Meeting's advice against importing or buying slaves. In 1757, the meeting treated with nine Friends, including William and Hannah Logan and William Wishart, and expected them to condemn their errors in purchasing slaves. Philadelphia Friends also attempted to secure promises of freedom for the blacks.[5] By November 1757, the meeting believed that the 1755 advice of the Yearly Meeting must be clarified and strengthened, and so decided that "on Consideration of the Increase of this unjust Practice [slave trading], notwithstanding the Endeavours of Friends to prevent it, it is thought expedient to refer this Matter to the Consideration of the Quarterly Meeting, in order to have the Sense & Judgement of that Meeting thereon, how far Friends may proceed to testify against the Practice, or those who persist therein."[6]

Following the Yearly Meeting's decision of 1758 to discipline slave traders, Philadelphia Friends conscientiously brought buyers and sellers of blacks before the meeting and, like Shrewsbury, went

[3] Phila. MM mins., 27/2M/1716, 3M/1716, 29/9M/1717.
[4] Phila. MM mins., 25/1M/1754; Phila. QM mins., 5/8M/1754; PYM mins., 14-19/9M/1754. See Chapter 1.
[5] Phila. MM mins., 1757.
[6] Phila. MM mins., 25/11M/1757.

even further and attempted to secure freedom for the slaves. Though the meeting usually permitted buyers to regain some of their investment by holding the purchased slaves for a number of years, and also took into consideration the difficulties sellers could encounter in trying to gain freedom for slaves sold to non-Friends, Philadelphia Quakers clearly believed that wrongdoers could not simply condemn their sin but must also provide relief for the blacks involved.[7] However, the meeting did accept the excuses of Mary Robins in 1763 and Joseph Johnson in 1768 that they sold their slaves because they were disruptive in their households and neighborhoods, and hence were unfit for freedom.[8]

Philadelphia Monthly Meeting remained in the forefront of the Quaker abolitionist movement during the 1760s and 1770s. It held quarterly meetings of worship for blacks continuously, beginning in 1756, and in 1770 established a school for the children of free blacks.[9] In 1774, the meeting again helped to initiate action concerning slavery in the Yearly Meeting when a case in which the meeting was obligated to accept the certificate of removal of a man from Wilmington Monthly Meeting who was under discipline (partially disowned) for selling slaves instilled the city's Friends with "a fresh concern that our testimony against the iniquitous practice of buying, selling or keeping Slaves may be further promoted & maintained."[10] In response to the Yearly Meeting's rulings of 1774 and 1776, the local meeting obtained manumissions from most of its remaining slave owners and disowned recalcitrants who refused to free their blacks. By 1779, the meeting could report that most Friends had freed their slaves. Members of the meeting were also active in convincing non-Friends to give up their slaves; beginning in the 1760s John Pemberton and others freed many blacks by paying their owners, by arranging for the slaves to earn money to buy their freedom, or by successfully appealing to the consciences of the slaveholders.[11]

Starting in 1754, then, Philadelphia Monthly Meeting set the pace of antislavery reform in the Yearly Meeting. Unlike Shrewsbury, whose members had opposed slave trading and probably slavery as early as 1730 but through lack of power and perhaps also

[7] Phila. MM mins., 1758-1774.

[8] Phila. MM mins., 29/7M/1763, 27/5M/1768.

[9] Phila. MM mins., 1756-1780. See especially 30/4M/1756 and 30/3M/1770.

[10] Phila. MM mins., 25/2M/1774, 25/3M/1774; Wilmington MM mins., 7M/1772-5M/1773.

[11] Phila. MM mins., 1774-1780, especially 30/2M/1779; Phila. MM mans.

their "exemplary" religious philosophy could not convince the Yearly Meeting as a whole, Philadelphia Friends did swing representatives in the central meeting to their new position against slavery. Whereas the urban Quakers had resisted Chester Monthly Meeting's demands for a ban on purchasing imported blacks during the period 1711-1730, in the 1750s the Philadelphians nudged the now-reluctant rural Friends in Chester and elsewhere to give up their slaves.

Although Chester and Philadelphia meetings followed quite different paths on the issue of slavery before 1776, these divergent actions did not arise from dissimilar interpretations of Quakerism by controlling factions in the meetings, as in the case of Shrewsbury and Chesterfield. Jack Marietta's study of ecclesiastical discipline has shown that *both* meetings participated fully in the 1750s revival of strict enforcement of rules against marrying outside the meeting, dressing frivolously, and taking part in "worldly" activities.[12] Friends who took leadership positions in Philadelphia Monthly Meeting (and the Yearly Meeting) in the early 1750s in fact guided the meeting toward its "tribalistic" reform. At the same time, they agreed to publish the *Epistle* of 1754 that denounced slaveholding and supported the 1758 ban on buying and selling slaves. In Philadelphia, a small number of Friends who held a humanitarian view of Quakerism similar to that of members of Shrewsbury meeting were able to convince men like James and Israel Pemberton II that slavery was wrong. The wealthy ruling reform faction in the city did not rely on black labor as did the dominant clique in Chesterfield, and therefore found no great hardship in adding the prohibition of slave trading to their list of reforms. However, unlike the case in Shrewsbury, the primary thrust of Philadelphia abolitionism was to eliminate the practice among members, not to obtain freedom for slaves. Only in the 1760s did the city meeting begin to require offenders to emancipate or arrange for the emancipation of slaves whom they bought or sold. It seems quite clear that while a few individuals like Anthony Benezet talked the Philadelphia leaders into setting up a school for blacks and otherwise concerning themselves with the Afro-Americans' welfare, most of the elite simply viewed the fight against slavery as part of their drive to rid the Society of worldliness and sin.

[12] Jack Donald Marietta, "Ecclesiastical Discipline in the Society of Friends 1682-1776" (Ph.D. diss., Stanford University, 1968), 136-156, 179-180, 197-199.

EVEN as Chester and Philadelphia shared a style of action when aroused, the *timing* of the two meetings' opposition to slavery was very different. Much of the variation can be explained by changes in the degree of involvement of their members in the institution. As Chapter 3 demonstrated, the socioeconomic circumstances in which Chester and Philadelphia Quakers made their decisions concerning slavery varied considerably over the century before 1780. Slave ownership was at its highest level in Chester before 1700; it plummeted in the 1710s and after 1720 rose back to a plateau with peaks in the 1730s, 1750s, and 1770s (Graph 3.1). The early high point of slaveholding in Philadelphia, on the other hand, occurred a little later—only in the 1710s. Slave ownership among the city's inventoried decedents decreased steadily thereafter, though it went back to a relatively high level in the 1730s and declined at only a slow rate in the 1760s. For most of the century, the percentage of all inventoried decedents (Quakers and others) who owned slaves was substantially higher in Philadelphia than in Chester. Urban residents were on average wealthier; they were closer to the slave market; and they had a greater demand for additional labor that was not always met by indentured servants and free workers. Slaveholding was more extensive in the city also because a much higher percentage of less affluent urban dwellers bought slaves than did relatively ordinary rural people (Graph 3.3).

While economic factors help explain why many Friends and their neighbors invested in slave labor and suggest why some Quakers held on to their bondsmen longer than others, the configuration of slave ownership in Chester and Philadelphia was also the product of changes in the religious character of these localities and the growth of antislavery sentiment there. Slavery declined in Philadelphia after 1720 as increasing numbers of Quakers and Presbyterians either freed their slaves or avoided the institution completely. After the 1730s, the Germans comprised a growing segment of the city's population—one that almost entirely avoided slave ownership. In Chester, on the other hand, slavery increased gradually after the 1710s, despite the growth of abolitionism among Friends by the 1760s, because groups that tended to hold on to their slaves as late as the 1770s—Anglicans, Swedish Lutherans, and disowned Quakers—became proportionally more numerous in the area by the middle of the eighteenth century.

Tables 6.1 and 6.2 compare slaveholding among all decedents who were members of different religions in Chester and Philadelphia

TABLE 6.1. SLAVE OWNERSHIP AND RELIGION AMONG ALL DECEDENTS IN CHESTER MONTHLY MEETING AREA

	1731-1740		1761-1770		1771-1780	
	No.	Slave owners	No.	Slave owners	No.	Slave owners
Quakers	37	21.6%	45	8.9%	38	7.9%
Disowned Quakers	1	0.0	9	0.0	8	37.5
Anglicans and Swed. Luths.	3	0.0	20	35.0	18	55.6
Presbyterians	0	—	1	0.0	2	0.0
Baptists	3	0.0	0	—	0	—
Religion unknown	11	0.0	33	0.0	20	5.0
Total	55	14.5	108	10.2	86	19.8

SOURCES: Probate and church records (see Appendix B and n. 13)

TABLE 6.2. SLAVE OWNERSHIP AND RELIGION AMONG ALL DECEDENTS IN PHILADELPHIA

	1731-1740		1761-1770		1771-1780	
	No.	Slave owners	No.	Slave owners	No.	Slave owners
Quakers	84	21.4%	111	18.0%	92	6.5%
Disowned Quakers	1	0.0	12	25.0	16	18.8
Anglicans and Swed. Luths.	101	29.7	188	29.8	158	24.0
Presbyterians	10	50.0	33	36.4	17	11.8
Baptists	5	0.0	3	33.3	10	10.0
German Luths.	0	—	48	4.2	29	0.0
German Reformed	0	—	19	5.3	25	8.0
Others	0	—	5	20.0	7	14.3
Religion unknown	67	13.4	192	15.6	210	8.1
Total	268	23.1	611	20.6	564	12.4

SOURCES: Probate and church records

in the 1730s, 1760s and 1770s.[13] In both localities in the 1730s, about 21 percent of all identified Quaker decedents owned slaves when they died. This proportion dropped by over one-half in Chester to less than 9 percent in 1761-1780. The decline in Philadelphia was slower, as 18 percent of the city's decedent Friends still owned slaves in the 1760s, but the proportion of urban Quakers who owned slaves then fell sharply in the next decade to only 6.5 percent.[14] To limit the possibility that differences in mean wealth affected the level of slaveholding among the religious groups, Tables 6.3 and 6.4 illustrate slave ownership among only those decedents whose estates ranked in the wealthiest 30 percent of the surviving inventories for each period. Here we see a decline in slaveholding among *wealthy* Friends in Philadelphia that preceded that among *all* Quaker decedents described in Table 6.2. Though the percentage of wealthy Philadelphia Quakers who owned slaves at death was higher than in Chester in both the 1730s and 1760s, in both places the pro-

[13] The number of identified members of each religion does not suggest the approximate proportion of the population who belonged to each religion because records are more complete for some churches than for others. Anglicans and Swedish Lutherans are lumped together because the records of several Anglican churches were kept by Gloria Dei. Separate analysis of the people identified from Christ Church and Gloria Dei records shows little difference in patterns of slaveholding. See Appendix B for more information on how I linked religious and probate records together. The religions of some decedents were identified from references to specific religions or churches in their wills.

Sources of church records for both the Chester and Philadelphia monthly meeting areas include: Phila. MM mins., 1682-1780; Chester MM mins., 1681-1780; Chester MM Births and Deaths, 1677-1780; all located in the Friends Historical Library, Swarthmore College. St. Michaelis and Zion Lutheran Congregation, Burials 1745-1771, Communicants Register 1733-1735, and Marriages 1745-1764; First Reformed Church of Philadelphia, Communicants 1768-1829 and Burials 1748-1809; Old Swedes Church, Gloria Dei, Burial Records 1750-1831; Records of Christ Church, Philadelphia, Burials 1709-1785; all located in the Genealogical Society of Pennsylvania Collections, HSP. Phila. MM Births, Deaths, and Marriages, published in William Wade Hinshaw, *Encyclopedia of American Quaker Genealogy* (Baltimore, 1969), vol. 2. St. Paul's Episcopal Church, Chester, Marriages 1704-1733, published in *Pennsylvania Archives*, 2d ser., 8 (1890), 591-598. First Presbyterian Church of Philadelphia, Marriages 1702-1745 and 1760-1803, published in *Pennsylvania Archives*, 2d ser., 9 (1880), 1-105; and Baptisms 1701-1746, published in *The Pennsylvania Genealogical Magazine* 19 (1954), 277-308. First Baptist Church of Philadelphia, Baptisms, Marriages, and Deaths 1772-1822, published in *PMHB*, 19 (1895), 96-111. Christ Church, Philadelphia, Baptisms 1709-1760, published in *PMHB* 12 to 17 (1888-1893). St. Michaelis and Zion Lutheran Congregation, Baptisms 1745-1755, published in *The Pennsylvania-German Society: Proceedings and Addresses*, 7, 8, and 9 (1897-1899).

[14] The pace of Philadelphia Quakers in abandoning slavery also appears languid in comparison with the rather dramatic shift of the city's Presbyterians away from the institution. See Table 6.2.

TABLE 6.3. SLAVE OWNERSHIP AND RELIGION AMONG WEALTHIEST 30 PERCENT OF INVENTORIED DECEDENTS IN CHESTER MONTHLY MEETING AREA

| | 1731-1740 | | 1761-1770 | | 1771-1780 | |
	No.	Slave owners	No.	Slave owners	No.	Slave owners
Quakers	15	33.3%	16	12.5%	12	16.7%
Disowned Quakers	1	0.0	2	0.0	2	100.0
Anglicans and Swed. Luths.	0	—	9	66.7	7	71.4
Presbyterians	0	—	0	—	0	—
Baptists	0	—	0	—	0	—
Religion unknown	0	—	4	0.0	2	0.0
Total	16	31.2	31	25.8	23	39.1

SOURCES: Probate and church records

TABLE 6.4. SLAVE OWNERSHIP AND RELIGION AMONG WEALTHIEST 30 PERCENT OF INVENTORIED DECEDENTS IN PHILADELPHIA

| | 1731-1740 | | 1761-1770 | | 1771-1780 | |
	No.	Slave owners	No.	Slave owners	No.	Slave owners
Quakers	20	45.0%	37	21.6%	28	3.6%
Disowned Quakers	0	—	4	50.0	7	28.6
Anglicans and Swed. Luths.	28	60.7	45	53.3	35	57.1
Presbyterians	1	100.0	11	72.7	1	0.0
Baptists	2	0.0	1	0.0	5	20.0
German Luths.	0	—	10	10.0	7	0.0
German Reformed	0	—	5	20.0	7	0.0
Others	0	—	1	0.0	3	33.3
Religion unknown	11	36.4	40	40.0	27	22.2
Total	62	50.0	154	39.0	120	25.8

SOURCES: Probate and church records

portion dropped by over one-half over the generation between those two decades. In the 1770s, only one wealthy urban Quaker decedent owned slaves, and he freed them in his will. In Chester in the 1770s, two of twelve wealthy Friends owned slaves when they died.

In addition, many of the Friends who still owned slaves when they died in the 1760s and 1770s freed some or all of their bondsmen in their wills. One-half of all Quaker decedent slaveholders in Philadelphia manumitted their blacks in the 1760s, while in the 1770s two-thirds freed their slaves. In Chester, two of seven Quaker decedent slave owners freed one or more of their slaves in the 1760s and 1770s.

Of particular note in Philadelphia, and quite different from the case in Chester, is that slave ownership among urban Friends whose estates ranked in the lower 70 percent did *not* decline between the 1730s and 1760s. In both decades about 15 percent of the less affluent urban Quaker decedents owned slaves at death; this percentage dropped to only 8.3 percent in the 1770s, which was higher than the proportion of wealthy Friends who owned slaves. Thus, the fact that slave ownership failed to decline significantly among Quaker decedents as a whole in Philadelphia between the 1730s and 1760s can largely be attributed to the fact that the same proportion of less affluent Friends owned blacks in the 1760s as had owned them in the 1730s. Wealthy urban Friends broke a trail in practicing certain religious principles that was not always followed by fellow members whose fortunes were not so secure.

These data from probate records also permit us to compare changes in slave ownership and manumission among Quakers with those among members of other religions. Among all Anglican and Swedish Lutheran decedents, as well as among those who ranked in the wealthiest 30 percent, slaveholding remained relatively high in both Philadelphia and Chester into the 1770s. The proportion of members of these religions who owned slaves scarcely diminished in Philadelphia before the Revolution and even increased in Chester from the 1760s to the 1770s. Among Philadelphia Anglican and Swedish Lutheran decedents whose estates ranked in the lower 70 percent of surviving inventories, slave ownership also rose from 12.8 percent in the 1730s to 22.5 percent in the 1760s; it then declined to 11.2 percent in the 1770s. In Philadelphia in all three decades, about one-half of all decedent slave owners were Anglican or Swedish Lutheran, and in Chester as well, these two groups comprised the majority of slaveholders in the 1760s and 1770s. During these decades, fewer than 10 percent of Philadelphia slave owners of these two religions freed their slaves in their wills. Three of ten Anglican or Swedish Lutheran decedent slaveholders in Chester manumitted their slaves in the 1770s, including William Grantham of Ridley who gave the use of a house and farm to his two black men Caesar and William during their lives.[15]

In Philadelphia, the level of slaveholding among Presbyterians was seemingly even higher than among Anglicans and Swedish Lutherans in the 1730s and 1760s, as five of ten identified Presbyterian decedents in the 1730s owned slaves at death, and 36.4 percent owned slaves in the 1760s. By the 1760s and 1770s, however, members of this religion apparently became convinced that slavery was wrong, since one-third of Presbyterian decedents in the 1760s freed one or more of their slaves in their wills, and both decedent slaveholders of the 1770s freed some or all of their blacks. The drop between the 1730s and 1760s in the frequency of slave ownership among Presbyterians whose estates ranked in the lower 70 percent of surviving inventories was more dramatic than among either their wealthier co-religionists or among Quakers of the same socioeconomic status. Whereas 44.4 percent of these less affluent Presbyterian decedents owned slaves in the 1730s, only 11.8 percent still held blacks in the 1760s. In the 1770s, only one Presbyterian of middling wealth among eleven owned slaves at death and he freed his blacks in his will. Despite this sharp decline over the generation between the 1730s and the 1760s among Presbyterians of middling wealth, however, the level of slave ownership among less wealthy Presbyterians and Friends was quite similar in the 1760s and 1770s, as about 15 percent of the more modest Quaker decedents owned slaves in the 1760s and 8.3 percent still held them in the 1770s.

The religious basis for this movement by Philadelphia's Presbyterians away from the institution of slavery is not totally clear. They may have come to believe that blacks were equal in the sight of God; this concept had currency among many New Lights and was a logical outgrowth of the religious egalitarianism of the Great Awakening.[16] The Synod of New York and Philadelphia considered

[15] One exception among Philadelphia Anglicans was William Broomwich, who freed his blacks and willed them his house when he died in 1763. His children contested the will. Phila. Co. Administrations, William Broomwich, 1763, No. 7. Chester Co. Wills, William Grantham, No. 2881.

[16] Cedric B. Cowing, *The Great Awakening and the American Revolution: Colonial Thought in the 18th Century* (Chicago, 1971), 57-58, 113-115; Winthrop D. Jordan, *White over Black: American Attitudes toward the Negro, 1550-1812* (Chapel Hill, N.C., 1968), 214.

issuing a statement for the gradual abolition of slavery in 1774 but could agree to do so only in 1787.[17] Nevertheless, individual ministers and members evidently adopted antislavery beliefs by the 1770s despite the equivocation of the church.

Two prominent clergymen further illustrate the ambiguity of the Presbyterian position on slavery. George Whitefield, the Great Awakener, in 1740 had warned slaveholders that "Blacks are just as much, and no more, conceived and born in Sin, as White Men are. Both, if born and bred up here, I am persuaded, are naturally capable of the same [religious] improvement." But he held slaves at his Georgia orphanage.[18] Francis Alison, a Philadelphia Presbyterian cleric of opposite, anti-Awakening bent, mixed natural rights theory with his concern that slavery was sin when he wrote to Ezra Stiles in 1768, "I am assured the Common father of all men will severely plead a Controversy against these Colonies for Enslaving Negros, and keeping their children[,] born British subjects, in perpetual slavery—and possibly for this wickedness God threatens us with slavery."[19] Thus, Alison pondered the morality of owning slaves and joined many other Americans in questioning the consistency of denying freedom to blacks while fighting for their own liberty from Great Britain. When he died in 1779, however, Alison still had not made up his mind on the issue of slavery, for he owned five blacks whom he wished freed only when they reached the age of thirty or thirty-one. He wrote in his will that he could find nothing against slavery in the scriptures, but that he was convinced it "leads bad men to inhumanity, injustice, & oppression, & is beneath the benevolence of the Christian religion."[20]

The aversion of Pennsylvania Germans to slavery, whether for moral or ethnocentric reasons, has long been accepted, and the data from wills and probate inventories shown in Tables 6.2 and 6.4 support this view. Fewer than 5 percent of all identified German Lutheran and Reformed decedents in Philadelphia owned slaves at

[17] This statement did not prohibit slaveholding among members of the church. Andrew E. Murray, *Presbyterians and the Negro—A History* (Philadelphia, 1966), 16-17.

[18] Jordan, *White over Black*, 214; Cowing, *Great Awakening*, 114; Stephen J. Stein, "George Whitefield on Slavery: Some New Evidence," *Church History* 42 (1973), 243-256.

[19] Jordan, *White over Black*, 299.

[20] Phila. Co. Wills, Francis Alison, Bk. R, No. 256. Philadelphia Yearly Meeting may have been referring to Presbyterians (among others) when they wrote to London Yearly Meeting in 1773, "we have to observe with great Satisfaction, that the same Disposition [against slavery] prevails with many sober and judicious Professors of Christianity of other Denominations." PYM mins., 27-30/9M/1773.

death in the 1760s and 1770s. This was not because few Germans had sufficient wealth to consider buying a black: only two of twenty-nine (6.9 percent) German inventoried decedents who ranked among the wealthiest 30 percent owned slaves at their deaths in the 1760s and 1770s.

The reasons why Germans eschewed slavery are difficult to assess. There is no evidence that the German Lutheran and Reformed churches discouraged their members from buying blacks,[21] and Owen S. Ireland found that members of these denominations who were elected to the Pennsylvania Assembly in 1779-1787 were much more likely to oppose legislation for the abolition of slavery than assemblymen of any other ethnic group or religion.[22] Many German sectarians, however, were apparently against slavery, as were individuals like Anna Weiss, who carefully insured the freedom of a large family of blacks whom she inherited.[23] It is likely that most Germans who required additional labor simply preferred servants of their own nationality. In the early 1760s, when the availability of German indentured servants became extremely limited, some Germans did evidently turn to black slaves. Christopher Sauer wrote in 1761 that "it is with utmost regret that we learn that the Germans are engaged in the barbarous slave traffic, because they are able no longer to have German servants."[24] However, the number who purchased slaves at that time appears to have been still relatively small.

The decline in slave ownership in Philadelphia after 1720, shown

[21] I am indebted to J. William Frost for this information.

[22] Owen S. Ireland, "Germans against Abolition: A Minority's View of Slavery in Revolutionary Pennsylvania," *Journal of Interdisciplinary History* 3 (1973), 690.

[23] As early as 1662, Cornelius Pieter Plockhoy drew up a plan for a Mennonite settlement that prohibited slaveholding. C. Henry Smith, "The Mennonite Immigration to Pennsylvania in the Eighteenth Century," Part 33 of *Pennsylvania—The German Influence on its Settlement and Development*, published in *Proceedings of the Pennsylvania-German Society*, 35, pt. 2 (1929), 27-28. The Moravians of Bethlehem, Pennsylvania, in November 1742 decided that all servitude hindered conversion and therefore was wrong. Kenneth G. Hamilton, trans. and ed., *The Bethlehem Diary* (Bethlehem, Pa., 1971), 1:105-106. Anna Weiss, widow of George Michael Weiss, a Reformed minister of Upper Hanover Township in Philadelphia County, wrote in her will that her husband had intended to free their family of eleven slaves when he died. She freed them and made sure that they would not be re-enslaved to pay claims on her husband's estate that were being pressed by his family in Germany. Phila. Co. Administrations, Anna Weiss, 1765, No. 89. I am indebted to Marianne Wokeck for this reference.

[24] Quoted from *Pennsylvanische Berichte*, 13 February 1761, in Clair Gordon Frantz, "The Religious Teachings of the German Almanacs Published by the Sauers in Colonial Pennsylvania" (Ed.D. diss., Temple University, 1955), 18.

on Graph 3.1, thus occurred at least in part because increasing numbers of Quakers and Presbyterians freed their blacks before they died or because they decided not to buy slaves in the first place. The percentage of inventoried decedents who owned slaves also decreased because most Germans, who comprised a growing proportion of the city's population after the 1730s, shunned the use of slaves. Only Anglicans and Swedish Lutherans held on to their blacks in force into the 1770s; and just a few decedent slaveholders of these churches manumitted their bondsmen in their wills. In Chester, the rise in slave ownership from the 1730s to the 1770s resulted in part from the increase in the non-Quaker segment of the population. As in Philadelphia, Anglicans, Swedish Lutherans, and disowned Quakers held on to their slaves into the 1770s, though antislavery opinion inspired even one-third of these non-Friends to free their slaves in their wills.

STILL, while many Philadelphia Presbyterians accepted abolitionism by the 1770s and most Germans avoided slavery altogether, the antislavery movement developed first among Friends. By the 1760s, few Chester Quaker decedents owned slaves when they died, and of the twenty Philadelphia Quaker decedents who held slaves at death in that decade, one-half freed some or all of their blacks in their wills. Nevertheless, the process of building support for a ban on slaveholding among Yearly Meeting members was very gradual and drawn out. Even after the 1758 rule against slave trading, slaveowning Friends in Philadelphia, Chester, Chesterfield, and elsewhere continued to resist a total prohibition on ownership. Only gradually did most Quakers come to believe that slavery violated Friends' belief in nonviolence, self-denial, and the brotherhood of man, and threatened the continuation of a society based on these precepts.

As we found in Chapter 5, abolitionism first appeared among Shrewsbury Friends in the early eighteenth century when the high importation of blacks seemed about to create a Barbados-like slave society in East Jersey. Acting in accordance with their humanitarian interpretation of Quakerism by the 1760s, most members of Shrewsbury meeting either freed their blacks or had avoided the institution completely. As the average size of their farms declined in the eighteenth century Friends had much less need for additional labor. In Chesterfield, on the other hand, slavery peaked only after 1740, and even then the local impact of the institution's growth was too limited to instill fear or revulsion in the hearts of any but a few reformers like John or Anthony Sykes. Chesterfield Friends' disciplinary record revealed them to be more interested in keeping distance from members of other religions than in pursuing philanthropic goals. Prominent members of Chesterfield meeting who owned large farms continued to hold slaves into the 1770s and effectively blocked all efforts to prohibit slave trading and owning in their local meeting until that very late decade.

Chester Monthly Meeting's actions on slavery were even more complex than those of Shrewsbury and Chesterfield. Chester was the first meeting to call for strong measures against importing blacks, but its members actually reached a sense of the meeting against slaveholding only in the 1760s. Early on, these rural Pennsylvania Friends evidently feared that the importation of large numbers of Africans and Afro-Americans before 1720 and in the peak years of 1729-1730 would contaminate the "holy experiment." After 1730, however, a large minority of meeting participants owned slaves and prevented the meeting as late as the 1750s from opposing slavery itself.

The timing of Chester's early assaults on the slave trade during the years 1711-1716 and 1729-1730 is not difficult to explain. Slave importation into Pennsylvania relative to the total population was probably highest prior to 1720, and Maryland experienced heavy imports at that time as well.[25] Chester Friends, who lived close to Maryland and could watch the growth of slavery in that colony, feared that Philadelphia merchants would bring into Pennsylvania an excessive number of blacks who would disrupt the Quaker community. Robert Pyle of Concord Monthly Meeting perhaps expressed the views of Friends in neighboring Chester when he wrote in 1698 that blacks "being a people not subject to the truth, nor yet likely so to bee; they might rise in rebellion and doe us much mischief; except we keep a malisha [militia]; which is against our principles."[26]

Despite their early interest in stopping importation, Quakers in Chester never suggested that those who already owned slaves should give them up. As in Chesterfield, slaveholding gradually increased in Chester after 1720 but locally never reached high enough levels in this later period to frighten sensitive Friends. Table 6.5 indicates that about one-fifth of Chester Monthly Meeting participants owned

[25] See Chapter 3.
[26] Henry J. Cadbury, "An Early Quaker Anti-Slavery Statement," *JNH* 22 (1937), 492.

TABLE 6.5. SLAVE OWNERSHIP AMONG CHESTER MONTHLY
MEETING PARTICIPANTS

Date of death	No. participants	Slave owners
1681-1710	16	18.8%
1711-1730	28	7.1
1731-1750	40	17.5
1751-1760	25	20.0
1761-1770	25	8.0
1771-1780	13	0.0
Total	147	12.9

SOURCES: Probate records; Chester MM mins., 1681-1780

slaves at death during most of the period from 1681 to 1760. This percentage dipped to about 7 percent during 1711-1730, which would suggest that the impetus against buying imported blacks originated among a group of Chester Friends currently active in the meeting who were both poorer and less likely to own slaves than the cohorts of leaders who preceded and followed them. However, the Quakers who were active during 1711-1730 included many who died after 1730 and some of these participants owned slaves. As Table 6.6 shows, during the years 1711-1730 nine of seventy-two participants (12.5 percent) who left wills and/or inventories owned blacks, while 13.6 percent of the participants who died before 1711 owned slaves at death. About 17 percent of those participating during 1731-1760 were slave owners, so fewer Chester Friends active before 1731 held blacks than their successors, but the difference was not great.

A look at the percentage of participants in Philadelphia Monthly Meeting who held slaves during the period before 1731 suggests why Chester Friends feared that Pennsylvania would become another Maryland or Virginia. It also explains why the urban Friends resisted Chester's petitions so vehemently. Table 6.7 indicates that over 40 percent of the meeting participants who died during 1711-1730 owned slaves at death; this proportion rose to over one-half in the 1730s. On average, Philadelphia Friends were also a good deal wealthier at death than their rural co-religionists, and so for this reason were more likely to consider buying slaves. In addition,

TABLE 6.6. SLAVE OWNERSHIP AMONG SELECTED COHORTS OF CHESTER MONTHLY MEETING PARTICIPANTS

Participants	No.	No. Slave owners	% Slave owners
Active only			
before 1711	22	3	13.6%
Active 1711-1730	72	9	12.5
Active 1731-1760	89	15	16.9

SOURCES: Chester MM mins., 1681-1760; Probate records

TABLE 6.7. SLAVE OWNERSHIP AMONG PHILADELPHIA MONTHLY MEETING PARTICIPANTS

Date of death	No. participants	Slave owners
1681-1700	36	36.1%
1701-1710	14	28.6
1711-1720	26	34.6
1721-1730	21	47.6
1731-1740	13	53.8
1741-1750	38	42.1
1751-1760	29	34.5
1761-1770	18	38.9
1771-1780	21	19.0
Total	216	37.0

SOURCES: Probate records; Phila. MM mins., 1682-1780

a number of Philadelphia meeting leaders, including Isaac Norris I and Jonathan Dickinson, were actually importers of black slaves.[27]

There are several reasons why Chester Monthly Meeting members quieted down on the question of slavery after 1730. Probably they felt they could do no more to persuade the Yearly Meeting and, in any event, Pennsylvania slave imports declined for several decades after the mid-1730s. Then, when the Yearly Meeting became alarmed over the institution in the 1750s, the issue involved not only slave trading but the abolition of slavery itself. Prominent

[27] Darold D. Wax, "The Negro Slave Trade in Colonial Pennsylvania" (Ph.D. diss., University of Washington, 1962), 372-373.

Chester slave owners like Caleb Cowpland, who was clerk of the meeting for thirty-five years, and Peter Dicks, a member of the meeting of ministers and elders, prevented Chester meeting from taking a leading abolitionist role.[28] Slave ownership among Chester participants reached a high point during the 1750s (Table 6.5). And unlike Friends in Shrewsbury, Philadelphia, and even Chesterfield, apparently not one Chester participant manumitted his blacks before 1760. No man active in Chester meeting freed his slaves in his will (see Table 6.8), though several participants did post £30 bonds in the Chester County Court of Quarter Sessions for slaves they freed during the late 1760s.[29]

After the deaths of influential slaveholders like Cowpland and Dicks by 1760, Chester Monthly Meeting took its place among the great majority of monthly meetings, neither pushing for additional reform nor lagging behind. Slaveholding among all decedent Quakers in the Chester area declined considerably by 1761-1780 (Table 6.1), and only two meeting participants who died after 1760 were slave owners at their deaths (Table 6.5). A total of fifteen slaveholders participated in the meeting during the years 1760-1776. Five of these men stopped serving on committees by 1765 and three more dropped out by 1772. After 1774, with only one exception,

TABLE 6.8. MANUMISSION OF SLAVES IN WILLS AMONG PARTICIPANTS OF CHESTER AND PHILADELPHIA MONTHLY MEETINGS

	Chester MM	Philadelphia MM
1681-1730	0	0 (0.0%)
1731-1740	0	1 (14.3%)
1741-1750	0	6 (37.5%)
1751-1760	0	3 (30.0%)
1761-1770	0	3 (42.9%)
1771-1780	—	4 (100.0%)

SOURCES: Chester MM mins., 1681-1780; Phila. MM mins., 1682-1780; Probate records

NOTE: Percentage of all slave-owning participants who manumitted their slaves in their wills in parentheses

[28] Chester MM mins., 1681-1780; Chester Co. Wills, Caleb Cowpland, No. 1687, and Peter Dicks, No. 1887.

[29] John Minshall posted bond for his slave Oran Hazard on 26 August 1766 and Daniel Sharpless posted bond for his black woman Phillis Menereau alias Hazard (apparently Oran's wife) on 26 May 1767. Chester Co. Quarter Sessions Docket Book A, 1759-1769, Chester Co. Archives.

Chester Friends followed the Yearly Meeting's directive to exclude slave owners, buyers, and sellers from committees for discipline and other meeting business.

As in Shrewsbury and Chesterfield, most of the Chester Friends who rejected abolitionist appeals were relatively large farmers. Table 6.9 shows that the eight slaveholders, buyers, and sellers who had farms in the Chester area and were included on the 1775 Chester County tax assessment list held an average of 265.4 acres. (The other two Quaker slaveholders were mill owners who had relatively small plots of land.) These eight Quaker holdouts not only had farms that were considerably larger than the mean of 112.3 acres for all Chester landholders (Table 3.2), but also had significantly more land on average than all participants in Chester meeting who could be located on the 1775 list.[30] As in Shrewsbury (Table 5.4), the mean acreage in Chester of the eight Quaker slave owners, purchasers, and sellers who farmed was also much larger than that of the Friends who served on antislavery committees.

Abolitionist reform thus followed a distinct and winding path in Chester Monthly Meeting, but the dynamics at work were similar to those found in Shrewsbury and Chesterfield meetings. In all three

TABLE 6.9. LANDHOLDINGS OF CHESTER MONTHLY MEETING
PARTICIPANTS AND SLAVE OWNERS

	No.	% holding land	$\bar{X}$ acres for all	$\bar{X}$ acres for land-holders
All participants on tax list	75	85.3%	153.4	179.8
Antislavery participants	21	81.0%	153.8	189.9
All slave owners, buyers, and sellers	10	100.0%	216.4	216.4
Slave owners, buyers, and sellers who farm[a]	8	100.0%	265.4	265.4

SOURCES: Chester MM mins., 1681-1780; Chester County Tax Assessment List, 1775
[a] Excluding two mill owners

[30] According to the 1760 Chester Co. tax list, thirteen meeting participants who owned blacks had landholdings averaging 259.4 acres. Chester Co. Assessment List, 4 April 1760, Shippen Papers, HSP.

rural areas, wealthy Quakers with large farms tended to hold on to their slaves, and as long as these Friends remained in control, their meetings stayed outside the abolitionist camp. Chester meeting early opposed the slave *trade*, probably in reaction to the high rate of importation and the upsurge in slaveholding in Philadelphia and among the city's Friends, but this rural meeting turned against slavery itself only in the 1760s, after the most powerful members who owned slaves had left the scene.

PHILADELPHIA Monthly Meeting, like Shrewsbury, developed its own impetus against slavery even while a large number of its members owned blacks. The high proportion of meeting participants who bought and held slaves during the 1730s and 1740s appalled sensitive Friends like Anthony Benezet and John Woolman, who worked to convince fellow Quakers that slavery was wrong.[31] They did in fact influence reformers like John, James, and Israel Pemberton II, who took control of Philadelphia meeting in the 1750s, and acted promptly to ensure that a new wave of slave buying in the 1750s and early 1760s would not perpetuate the institution among Friends. The socioeconomic context in which these urban reformers operated was quite different from that of rural Pennsylvania and New Jersey. Nevertheless, as in the other meetings, the underlying struggle occurred between Friends who feared slavery would destroy the integrity of the Quaker community and those who had economic interest in blacks.

As Table 6.7 shows, slave ownership was at its highest among Philadelphia meeting participants during the 1720s through 1740s. It was at this same time that opposition to slavery slowly began to build. To start, Isaac Norris I (d. 1735) freed his Indian slave in his will.[32] In the decades that followed, the percentage of participants who owned Afro-Americans declined slowly as the proportion of slaveholders manumitting their blacks in their wills increased (Tables 6.7 and 6.8). The most substantial decrease came in the 1770s when only 19 percent of decedent participants owned slaves at death—and all freed them in their wills. Thus, abolitionism got its start in Philadelphia Monthly Meeting in the 1730s when slave ownership among active Friends was at its height. It is no wonder that Ralph Sandiford and Benjamin Lay were so outraged—the

---

[31] John Woolman was not a Philadelphia Friend but knew the Philadelphia Quaker elite well and participated very actively in the Yearly Meeting in the late 1740s, 1750s, and 1760s.

[32] Phila. Co. Wills, Isaac Norris, Bk. E, No. 412.

slaveholders they denounced in the 1730s were leading members of Philadelphia meeting. Conversely, given the very deep involvement in slavery of weighty Friends during this period, it is no surprise that they cast Sandiford and Lay out of the meeting.

Slave ownership remained high among participants in Philadelphia Monthly Meeting who died as late as the 1760s, but a closer look at when these slave owners were active in Quaker affairs helps explain the timing of the meeting's involvement in antislavery reform. Of the twenty-one meeting participants who owned slaves and died after 1750 leaving wills and/or inventories, eight either died or became inactive in the meeting by 1754, and five more either died or stopped participating by 1758. Only four of these twenty-one decedent slave owners remained active after 1764, and all were gone by 1773. In addition, six of the eight slaveholders who died after 1758 agreed by the time of their deaths that blacks should not serve life terms; each of these participants except John Armitt (d. 1761) and Anthony Morris (d. 1763) manumitted his slaves in his will.[33]

These decedent Quaker participants were not the only men active in Philadelphia Monthly Meeting who held slaves, for fifteen others who participated in the period after 1758 are known to have manumitted slaves in the 1770s.[34] Interestingly, however, only three of these men remained in Philadelphia Monthly Meeting after 1772 when the city meeting divided into three parts: seven went to Southern District Monthly Meeting and five went to the Northern District. Thus, Philadelphia Monthly Meeting was able to reach a sense of the meeting in 1774 to prohibit slaveholding among Friends because the vast majority of slave owners who were active in the meeting by that time either died or removed to other meetings.

This decline in slave ownership among meeting participants explains why Philadelphia Friends could reach agreement by 1774 to ban slave ownership, and the continuing presence of owners until that time suggests why the decision took so long. The most perplexing question still unanswered, however, is why did the city meeting come to oppose slave trading in the 1750s? The explanation of the Friends themselves in 1754 was that slavery had "of late increased amongst us."[35] But why did they think this was so if slavery was decreasing among meeting participants (Table 6.7),

[33] Phila. Co. Wills, John Armitt, Bk. M, No. 176; Anthony Morris, Bk. N, No. 25.
[34] Phila. MM mans.
[35] PYM mins., 14-19/9M/1754.

among all urban Quaker decedents (Table 6.2), and among Philadelphia's decedents as a whole (Graph 3.1) over the long term from the 1730s to the 1770s? Probably because divestment of slaves among Philadelphia's Quakers did not proceed evenly among all socioeconomic groups. While wealthy Friends who had come to believe that slavery was wrong refrained from investing in blacks and could do so because they could afford the steep price of wage labor during the Seven Years' War, many less affluent Philadelphia Quakers turned to blacks during the 1750s and early 1760s because German and Scots-Irish immigrants were temporarily unavailable as a source of labor at that time.[36] The first battle over slavery won by the abolitionists in Philadelphia Monthly Meeting—the struggle over the ban on slave trading in 1757-1758—involved sides from socioeconomic backgrounds that were virtually the reverse of comparable alignments found in the rural meetings. Whereas abolitionists in Shrewsbury, Chester, and Chesterfield were on average less wealthy and owned smaller farms than the Friends who traded in and held on to their slaves, in Philadelphia the slave buyers, sellers, and owners dealt with in the 1750s, 1760s, and 1770s tended to be less affluent than those who opposed slavery. As we saw earlier, slave ownership did not decline between the 1730s and the 1760s among decedent Quakers in Philadelphia whose estates ranked in the lower 70 percent of all surviving inventoried estates, while slaveholding did drop by one-half among wealthy Friends (Table 6.4).

The record of discipline on slave trading and slaveholding in Philadelphia Monthly Meeting indicates that on average (of those located) the offenders were less wealthy than the committee members who dealt with them. Of fifty-seven Friends taken before the meeting for slavery offenses from 1757 to 1780, twenty-eight could be identified with reasonable accuracy on the 1772 Philadelphia tax list. The mean assessment for these offenders was £57.3 sterling (Table 6.10). In contrast, the mean assessment for members of antislavery committees was £97.2, or almost twice as much. Perhaps less startling is the difference in mean assessment between offenders whose acknowledgments the meeting accepted or whose cases it dropped (£97.4) and that of Friends whom the meeting either disowned or barred from participating in meetings for business (£35.0).

[36] Marianne S. Wokeck, "A Tide of Alien Tongues: The Flow and Ebb of the German Immigration to Pennsylvania, 1683-1776" (Ph.D. diss., Temple University, 1983), ch. 3; see also Chapter 3 of this study. It should be pointed out that this evidence shows that Gary Nash was correct in arguing that slaveholding persisted among Philadelphia Quakers of more average wealth during this period. Gary B. Nash, "Slaves and Slaveowners in Colonial Philadelphia," *WMQ*, 3d ser., 30 (1973), 254.

TABLE 6.10. TAX ASSESSMENTS OF PHILADELPHIA MONTHLY
MEETING PARTICIPANTS AND SLAVE OWNERS

	No.	$\bar{X}$ Assessment
All participants on tax list	142	£62.8
Antislavery participants	52	£97.2
Members disciplined for owning, buying, or selling slaves	28	£57.3

SOURCES: Phila. MM mins., 1682-1780; Philadelphia Tax Assessment List, 1772, computer printout by Billy G. Smith

These data are problematic because only about half of the slave buyers, sellers, and obstinate owners could be found on the tax list. They do, however, add further evidence that many middling urban Friends, swayed by their need for labor, found antislavery ideals more difficult to accept than did their co-religionists who already enjoyed affluence.

Statements made by slave buyers who acknowledged their errors in Philadelphia meeting further suggest that many purchased blacks because they needed labor in their shops and businesses. Though James Logan was an affluent merchant and certainly could have afforded to hire free workers if he desired, his acknowledgment describes conditions in the labor market during the Seven Years' War that were experienced by many. He wrote in 1757 that "I had been unsuccessful (as well as many others) in white Servants several having enlisted & prov'd bad & I found it difficult to hire Persons suitable to my Occasions & so determin'd to buy a Negro thinking he would answer my purpose better." Robert Hopkins in the same year pleaded "the Necessity of his Business," and in January 1760, Nathaniel Brown, a blacksmith, wrote that his apprentices had joined the army and he could get no journeymen, so he had bought a black because otherwise he would have had to "drop" his business. Benjamin Mifflin and Samuel Massey explained in 1762 that they had some years ago started a baking business "which it is well known cannot be carried on but by a constant & steady sett of hands." So they bought a slave, whom they subsequently sold when they closed their shop.[37]

[37] Phila. MM mins., 26/8M/1757, 25/11M/1757, 25/1M/1760, and 27/8M/1762.

In Philadelphia Monthly Meeting, then, Friends who believed that slavery violated basic Quaker beliefs were upset in the 1730s and 1740s by the large number of Quakers (including leaders) and Philadelphians of all persuasions who owned blacks. As long as the slave-owning clique controlled the city meeting, however, the abolitionists had little chance to obtain a ban on slave trading or slaveholding within the Society. But soon after 1750 a new group of wealthy reformers took control. While these men saw the purification of the meeting, not ameliorating the plight of slaves, as their chief objective, they agreed that slaveholding was a sin and should be eradicated from their religion. They hoped to set Friends apart from religious groups like the Anglicans and Swedish Lutherans, who together numbered about one-half of all decedent slave owners in Philadelphia and who continued to buy and hold on to their slaves as late as the Revolution. Many of the leaders of the 1750s reform in Philadelphia had occupations that permitted them, if they desired, to employ slaves just as domestic labor; for these men slaveholding was a form of ostentation that could be easily shunned.

Like Shrewsbury and Chesterfield meetings, Philadelphia Friends and their allies in the 1750s reform movement lend credence to J. William Frost's suggestion that there were two kinds of reformers in the Society of Friends, those who focused on eliminating slavery and those who worried most "about the corruption of Quaker practices symbolized by marriages out of unity." Frost found no evidence from their writings that Woolman and Benezet wanted strict enforcement of the discipline, and discovered little concern about slavery among reformers such as John Churchman, the Pembertons, Samuel Fothergill, Catherine Payton, Sophia Hume, John Griffiths, and Mary Peisley. John Churchman, a minister from Nottingham Monthly Meeting and one of the primary reformers in the Yearly Meeting, did not mention slavery in his journal until 1756, when he concluded that God had brought war to Pennsylvania to punish Friends for holding slaves. The correspondence of John, James, and Israel Pemberton II provides no hint that they were instrumental in convincing the Yearly Meeting to publish the *Epistle* of 1754 or to adopt the 1758 ban on slave trading.[38] And the English reformer Samuel Fothergill, who toured the colonies during the years 1754-1756 urging Friends to adhere more closely to the discipline, mentioned slavery only in a letter written to English Friend

[38] J. William Frost, "The Origins of the Quaker Crusade against Slavery: A Review of Recent Literature," *Quaker History* 67 (1978), 56-58.

James Wilson in November 1756. In this letter, Fothergill decried the ruinous effect of slaveholding on Friends in Maryland, Virginia, and North Carolina, but did not mention slavery in Pennsylvania or New Jersey.[39]

It seems quite clear, then, that the impulse for abolition came from one small group of Friends, while the drive for purification arose from another. Woolman, Benezet, members of Shrewsbury meeting, David Ferris of Wilmington, and others, regarded the Quaker testimony that all people are equal in God's eyes, which mandated emancipation, as the central tenet of their religion. The more tribalistic reformers, on the other hand, were less interested in abolition at first, though they eventually came to view slaveholding as one kind of worldly behavior that must be purged from the meeting. Nevertheless, there was enough overlapping in membership of the Yearly Meeting committees that dealt with these two kinds of reforms in the 1750s to show that, while each group had its particular focus, each supported the other type of reform. For example, seven of the twelve men who approved the publication of the *Epistle* of 1754 also served on the committee of weighty Friends appointed in 1755 to visit local meetings to urge greater enforcement of the discipline. Four of the five men appointed in 1758 to deal with slave owners had also served on the 1755 visitation committee: of John Woolman, John Sykes, John Churchman, John Scarborough, and Daniel Stanton, only Sykes was not a member of the 1755 committee, probably because he was absent from the Yearly Meeting at that time. John Churchman's participation on the 1758 committee to visit slaveholders is evidence that his concern about slavery had grown since 1755. Somewhat later, John and James Pemberton also took more interest in abolitionism, as John actively sought manumissions from non-Friends in the 1760s and 1770s, and James, beginning in 1787, served first as vice president and then as president of the Pennsylvania Abolition Society.

The dissimilar stances of Chester and Philadelphia meetings on slavery therefore did not arise from divergent interpretations of Quakerism. Most members of both meetings adhered to what Max Weber called the "emissary" form of prophecy: they both strongly supported the 1750s drive to purify the meeting and to separate Friends from the larger society. The new reformers of Philadelphia Monthly Meeting did listen to abolitionists like Woolman and

---

[39] George Crosfield, ed., *Memoirs of the Life and Gospel Labours of Samuel Fothergill* (New York, 1844), 281-283. J. William Frost provided this reference.

Benezet, however, and were convinced that slavery was a sin. Primarily wealthy merchants, they associated slaveholding with conspicuous consumption and were determined to root the practice out of the meeting—which was one way of making them "better" than and distinct from other wealthy Philadelphians. Other city Quakers, both men and women, depended more directly on outside help to run their shops and yards, and found giving up their slaves much more difficult. Skilled blacks would be valuable to craftsmen in any case, but the timing of the reformers' ban on slave trading—intended at this time to ensure that a new wave of slave buying would not perpetuate the institution among Friends—was especially inopportune for more ordinary Quakers. Their opposition to the 1758 prohibition and the continued participation of slaveholders in Philadelphia meeting until 1772 delayed any move to ban slaveholding itself among members until 1774. In Chester, antislavery reform followed a different course, although the same basic dynamics of moral concern and economic interest were at work. These rural Friends opposed the high importation of blacks into Pennsylvania in the early eighteenth century, but failed to agree to ban slave owning within their religion until the 1760s. As in the two rural meetings in New Jersey, Chester Friends who had large farms tended to hold on to their slaves. As long as these wealthy Quakers held influence in the meeting, Chester resisted abolitionist reform.

CONCLUSION
THE LIMITS OF QUAKER
REFORM

The century-long struggle over slavery within Philadelphia Yearly Meeting was essentially a journey over unmarked ground. The Society of Friends had no rule against enslaving blacks when Quaker missionaries proselytized in the New World and British Friends immigrated to America. Thus, like affluent adherents of other religions, many Delaware Valley Quakers invested in slave labor, apparently without thinking about the implications of buying and owning fellow human beings. Over the years individual Friends pointed out that slavery was inconsistent with the Society's beliefs in nonviolence, the equality of all people in the sight of God, and the sinfulness of ostentation, but they were unable to convince the Yearly Meeting. Though Pennsylvania and New Jersey Friends agreed to discourage slave importation as early as 1696, they could not reach a sense of the meeting to prohibit slaveholding until eighty years later, primarily because a considerable number of leading members owned slaves until that time.

The process by which Friends forged their collective opposition to slavery was complex. Local meetings moved against the institution at different times during the eighteenth century, each meeting reacting to a distinct set of socioeconomic conditions and each interpreting Quaker ideals in its own way. Some meetings prodded the Yearly Meeting to prohibit slaveholding, while others held it back. The central meeting avoided disciplining slave traders until the most powerful local meeting, Philadelphia, consented to that change, and the Yearly Meeting postponed the ban on slaveholding until most weighty slave-owning Friends had either died or left influential positions.

Such analysis of the eighteenth-century Friends' path-breaking decision to cleanse their Society by eradicating slavery sheds light on the way in which a "conscience" reform movement is born and grows. The humanitarian interpretation of Quaker beliefs accepted by Shrewsbury Friends and individual members of other meetings provided the basis for antislavery thought. The reformers, with methods that ranged from serving as good examples by manumitting their slaves to writing diatribes in the manner of Benjamin Lay, urged fellow members, whose view of Quakerism was more inward-

173

looking, to oppose slavery. Some of those more tribalistic Friends did in fact accept abolitionism, but only as part of a more general effort to purify the Society. The primary concern of those general reformers was not justice for enslaved blacks. Rather they believed that slavery—and perhaps the slaves themselves—polluted their religion and Delaware Valley society as a whole. Still other Friends failed to see that slavery was inconsistent with Quaker thought at all. As their numbers decreased and the Yearly Meeting tightened its rules on slavery, these members had to choose between giving up their slaves and separating from the Society. Friends who invested in slaves during the late 1750s and early 1760s because they needed labor found this decision most difficult.

It is not really possible to distinguish precisely between the two kinds of reformers active in Philadelphia Yearly Meeting. The wings must be seen as tendencies that emanated from different traditions in the church (the humanitarian and the separatist), not as two firmly entrenched, opposite camps. Of the four local meetings examined above, Shrewsbury tended most toward Max Weber's "exemplary" type. The East Jersey Friends backed away from disciplining children for marrying out and were extremely conscientious in obtaining freedom for blacks. Chesterfield, Chester, and Philadelphia more closely fitted the conventional portrait of tribalistic Friends. All three participated fully in the post-1754 purge of members who broke the more strictly enforced rules of endogamy, simplicity, and nonviolence. However, within these meetings (especially Philadelphia) were Friends who cared deeply about abolitionism and who convinced others that elimination of slavery must be part of the general drive for reform.

Evidence of the humanitarian tradition in Philadelphia Yearly Meeting is scattered, but it is now possible to trace accurately its influence on the growth of antislavery reform. Early Friends who, in the face of solid opposition, pushed for emancipation and decried the conditions in which blacks lived, must be viewed in this light: William Southeby, John Hepburn, Ralph Sandiford, and even Benjamin Lay. Members of Shrewsbury Monthly Meeting in the 1730s and 1740s quietly created their abolitionist policy on an individual basis by freeing their slaves before their deaths or in their wills (or by not owning any blacks in the first place). John Woolman and Anthony Benezet are both well known for their influential writings against slavery. Woolman spent much of his adult life traveling throughout the colonies urging Quaker masters to give up their slaves. Benezet was one of very few eighteenth-century figures who believed that blacks were as capable of learning as whites. In 1750 he began holding evening classes for blacks in his home, and in 1770 he convinced Philadelphia Monthly Meeting to open an "Africans' School." The first class included twenty-two girls and boys, evenly divided in gender. Later, older black men and women also came. All of the children studied reading, writing, and arithmetic. The girls learned sewing and knitting from a mistress, while boys did more advanced academic work. Though the school had trouble keeping schoolmasters, and also had difficulty in maintaining regular attendance of pupils who often had to help support their families, a total of 250 black students received some instruction between 1770 and 1775.[1]

Friends who are less famous than Woolman and Benezet also took an interest in the welfare of blacks. David Ferris, probably the spirit behind Wilmington Monthly Meeting's early stance against slavery, realized that slaves freed by Quakers were in peril of being captured and sold into bondage by unscrupulous whites. He began recording manumissions over a decade before other meetings adopted the practice. Thomas Harrison, a member of Philadelphia Monthly Meeting and quiet linchpin of the Pennsylvania Abolition Society from 1775 to 1815, worked tirelessly to emancipate blacks and ease their way into society as free men and women.[2]

The bond that tied together all of these men (as well as others) was their ability to view slavery as a social evil, not simply as a sin. They were concerned about its effects on the enslaved blacks as well as on the Quakers who held them. John Hepburn and Benjamin Lay denounced bad treatment of slaves and John Smith of Philadelphia and Burlington awakened to the horrors of black bondage when he watched a beaten slave jump into the Delaware River and drown.[3] Whereas in the 1750s and early 1760s other meetings

---

[1] Nancy Slocum Hornick, "Anthony Benezet and the Africans' School: Toward a Theory of Full Equality," *PMHB* 99 (1975), 399-421.

[2] Wayne J. Eberly, "The Pennsylvania Abolition Society, 1775-1830" (Ph.D. diss., The Pennsylvania State University, 1973), 208-209; David Brion Davis, *The Problem of Slavery in the Age of Revolution, 1770-1823* (Ithaca, N.Y., 1975), 216.

[3] In his diary, John Smith wrote, "as I was sitting at my door this afternoon I perceived a Bricklayer who works at Building Capt. Dowers's house & his negro differing—saw the master strike him upon which the negro ran down to the End of the wharf—& several after him—when he got there he swore if his master struck him again he would jump off & drown himself—which the master unhappily doing—the fellow was as good as his word—jumped off & perished before anybody could save him—this affair affected me very much." John Smith's Diary, vol. 5, entry for 28/4M/1748, Library Company of Philadelphia; on deposit at HSP.

accepted the acknowledgments of slave buyers and sellers that they had acted wrongly, Shrewsbury and Wilmington monthly meetings required each member who bought or sold a slave to go further and secure freedom for the blacks involved. To this extent, the growth of abolitionist thought was cumulative. As Friends and members of other religions released their slaves one by one over the eighteenth century, a community of free black people grew. They went to Friends meetings and Christ Church, were married by the Anglican and Lutheran ministers, and attended Benezet's school or those opened by William Sturgeon and Bray's Associates at Christ Church.[4] In Philadelphia the number of ex-slaves was quite sizable by the 1770s; they provided support for each other and offered assistance to enslaved blacks who wanted to be free. We know that one black woman Dinah, a grandmother, asked for freedom in 1776 from her owners, the Quakers William and Hannah Logan. That her daughter was already free and she could fall back if necessary on the free black community for moral and financial support gave this older woman the courage to make her demand.[5] As more and more blacks gained their freedom from sympathetic masters, earned their own livings, learned to read and write, went to church, married and had families—in essence, as they followed the same path taken by European indentured servants and free immigrants—slavery became very hard to justify in the minds of Friends and other Americans who cared to think about its implications. Meanwhile, emancipation of some blacks bred discontent among the rest. It also showed that Afro-Americans would become productive members of Anglo-American society. Abolitionists like Benezet, Woolman, Ferris, and Harrison perceived this, and knew that slavery was wrong. The challenge facing them was to convince their fellow Friends.

Abolitionism thus got its start in Philadelphia Yearly Meeting with Friends who thought that blacks were equal with whites before God and must be free. By 1750 the leaders of Shrewsbury meeting and individual Quakers elsewhere were convinced. Then during the 1750s these true opponents of slavery persuaded many other Friends, including the new dominant faction in Philadelphia Monthly Meeting, that slaveholding was wrong and should be purged from the Society. Reformers like Samuel Fothergill and John

[4] Richard I. Shelling, "William Sturgeon, Catechist to the Negroes of Philadelphia and Assistant Rector of Christ Church, 1747-1766," *Historical Magazine of the Episcopal Church* 8 (1939), 388-401.

[5] Jean R. Soderlund, "Black Women in Colonial Pennsylvania," *PMHB* 107 (1983), 49-68.

and George Churchman, whose interest in blacks was secondary to their desire to purify the Society, added slave trading to their list of proscribed practices to be strictly enforced as part of the reformation of 1755.[6] They urged that the Seven Years' War was God's punishment for Friends' worldly, sinful, selfish behavior during the first half of the eighteenth century and insisted that Quakers stop marrying out, indulging in frivolous activities, and buying and selling slaves.

While the inclusion of the antislavery component in the general reform movement broadened the appeal of abolitionism to Friends, at the same time it diluted the impact of action taken on the lives of blacks. Most reformers viewed slaveholding as a sin to be banned from the Society, not as a condition from which Afro-Americans must be delivered. Thus they believed their job was finished once all Friends had either freed their slaves or been disowned. That Philadelphia Yearly Meeting followed for the most part the tribalistic rather than the humanitarian reform tendency had unfortunate results for relationships between Quakers and blacks. The refusal of the meeting to accept black members until the 1790s is only the most glaring example of Friends' clannishness. Their inward retreat and withdrawal from government during the Seven Years' War and the Revolution also prevented them from participating in Pennsylvania's legislative abolition of slavery or from pushing more effectively for an emancipation law in New Jersey. After 1780 Friends went little farther than to lobby Congress for an end to the slave trade.[7] The main concern of the meetings in the 1780s was to treat with members who had not yet freed their slaves or who inherited them after 1780, and to visit ex-slaves to find out how they were faring in freedom.

THE ways in which Delaware Valley Quakers dealt with freed blacks illustrate both the humanitarian and tribalistic reform traditions. Friends who viewed slavery as a social ill knew that simply eradicating the institution from their religion was not enough: blacks often needed legal assistance and protection from corrupt or unfair whites, and should be paid restitution and helped financially to begin

[6] J. William Frost, "The Origins of the Quaker Crusade against Slavery: A Review of Recent Literature," *Quaker History* 67 (1978), 56-58.

[7] Henry J. Cadbury, "Negro Membership in the Society of Friends," *JNH* 21 (1936), 151-213; Thomas E. Drake, *Quakers and Slavery in America* (New Haven, Conn., 1950), 90-113.

their new lives. Older and disabled blacks who could not work must be supported, and everyone should learn to read and write.

On several occasions before 1782, members of the Society attempted to secure freedom for the relatives of freedmen or to protect the liberty of blacks emancipated by Friends. In 1770, the Yearly Meeting became involved in an intricate case concerning the administration of the estate of James McCarty, a mulatto who had lived in Shrewsbury, New Jersey. McCarty had been freed in 1744 by George Williams I, a leader of Shrewsbury meeting, and had amassed a fairly large estate before he died intestate. Friends decided that his money should be used to buy the freedom of his half-sister Catherine and her five children who were owned by a non-Friend, and went to considerable trouble over a period of five years before McCarty's next of kin were finally freed.[8] In 1781, Western Quarterly Meeting attempted to free a young black who had been manumitted several years earlier by Daniel Mifflin of Duck Creek Monthly Meeting but was seized and sold as a slave by the sheriff of Accomack County, Virginia, when Mifflin refused to pay a war tax. In this case, Friends were not able to liberate the boy.[9]

Quakers also provided financial assistance to blacks in a variety of ways. Some meetings tried to ensure that elderly ex-slaves would have enough support for the rest of their lives, and required manumitting owners to provide maintenance for blacks who could no longer work.[10] Jonathan Harned of Woodbridge, for example, promised to provide his black woman Mary with those necessary supplies, including meat, drink, apparel, washing, and lodging "as will render her Life comfortable." The three sons of William Paxson, late of Middletown (Bucks), promised in their manumission of their father's black woman Matillo, that they would each pay a third of "a reasonable expence for supporting her as a free woman from year to year during her natural life."[11]

Other Friends gave their ex-slaves a financial start by paying restitution for the years they worked as slaves after reaching ma-

---

[8] Shrewsbury MM mins., 1769-1774; Shrewsbury QM mins., 1769-1774; Friends of Shrewsbury Reports, 1770, and Burlington MM mans., David Cooper and Samuel Allinson, 1777, Burlington Co. Abolition Society Papers, BCHS.

[9] Western QM mins., 19/2M/1781, 19/11M/1781, and 18/2M/1782.

[10] Pennsylvania and New Jersey law of course required manumission bonds of £30 and £200 respectively for the same reason. The Friends avoided lawsuits initiated by local governments by providing adequate support for their ex-slaves.

[11] Woodbridge MM mins., 18/9M/1776; Bucks QM mans., William, Joseph, and Mahlon Paxson, 1776.

turity. An early instance of restitution involved John Woolman's brother, Abner, who in 1767 asked Haddonfield Monthly Meeting to determine how much he should pay two black men his wife had inherited from her father. He wanted to pay them, from his share of his father-in-law's estate, the amount by which their labor had increased his inheritance.[12] A few owners paid their slaves freedom dues when they set them free. William Rogers of East Nottingham, for instance, compensated his mulatto woman Dinah for the seven years she served him after she reached age eighteen, with bedding for herself and two daughters, a house, free firewood, and a half acre of land rent-free for eight years.[13] In the early 1780s, the quarterly and monthly meetings discussed the question of restitution more frequently than before. Western Quarterly Meeting reported in 1780 that there was an "Increasing Concern" to make compensation in several monthly meetings; and in 1782 the same meeting found that some Friends "near the close of their Day" had a desire to do blacks full justice by paying them for past labor. Bucks and Burlington quarters also mentioned that some Friends desired to make compensation. In Burlington, the meeting decided that the proper procedure for payment was for "indifferent" Friends to ascertain the sums to be paid; in a case in which the black was deceased, the money was to be divided among his or her next of kin.[14]

Restitution, however, was not often made; and meetings were sometimes unsuccessful in convincing former owners to support their freed slaves who were unable to take care of themselves. In the face of that problem, the meetings themselves sometimes provided assistance. Chester Quarterly Meeting in 1779 for example suggested "that a Subscription be made as Occasion may require by the Members of each Monthly Meeting to pay for Schooling [free blacks'] children, and to Assist in Things necessary for their going to School, and for the relief of such Negroes who by reason of old age & infirmity cannot support themselves; and such young ones whose Parents are dead or cannot Provide for themselves."[15]

[12] Haddonfield MM mins., 13/7M/1767 and 10/8M/1767.

[13] Nottingham MM mans., William Rogers, 1775.

[14] Western QM mins., 21/8M/1780 and 19/8M/1782; Bucks QM mins., 29/8M/1782; Burlington QM mins., 25/8M/1783. As early as 1767, David Ferris of Wilmington Monthly Meeting thought that owners should pay their freed blacks £12 for each year they had labored in bondage past maturity. David Ferris to Samuel Feild and wife, 20/9M/1767, Ferris Collection, FHL; excerpt published in J. William Frost, ed., *The Quaker Origins of Antislavery* (Norwood, Pa., 1980), 186.

[15] Chester QM mins., 9/8M1779.

The Committee of Free Negroes of Concord Monthly Meeting provided aid in 1779 to two black families, an aged couple who needed their daughter's help at home but could not provide for her education or training, and a mother with two young children whose husband was still a slave. Several other meetings—Philadelphia and Abington were among them—set up schools for black children using the Society's funds.[16]

In 1778 Philadelphia Yearly Meeting as a whole recognized that some freed blacks needed assistance, urging

> Friends in their Quarterly and Monthly Meetings, seriously and attentively to consider the Circumstance of these poor People, and the Obligation we are under to discharge a religious Duty to them; which being disinterestedly pursued, will lead the professors of Truth to advise and assist them on all occasions; particularly in promoting their Instruction in the principles of the Christian religion and the pious Education of their Children, and to advise them in respect to their Engagements in Wor[l]dly concerns as occasions offer.[17]

This directive, however, made it clear that the meeting thought Friends should do more than just dispense financial aid to freed blacks: they should teach the ex-slaves religious principles and be sure that they knew and followed the rules of right conduct. Western Quarterly Meeting, a few months before this Yearly Meeting directive, was even more forthright in this respect. A committee of Western Quarter reported that

> a Concern was opened & spread in the minds of Friends on behalf of such of those People, who have been, or may be released from a state of Bondage by Friends, within the Compass of this Quarter; with desires, that a proper care & Exercise may be attended to, for their Religious Instruction & Encouragement, in a life of Sobriety, & the Fear of God; as also to encourage them to an Honest, Industrious Care, for the Necessaries of this Life; which may be a means to preserve them from the Corruptions that these poor People have been to much indulged in.[18]

Thus when the Society took up the ideas of some of its more humanitarian members to help blacks start their lives as freed persons,

[16] Concord MM mins., 4/8M/1779; PYM mins., 22-28/9M/1770; Abington MM mins., 26/7M/1779.
[17] PYM mins., 26/9M-5/10M/1778.
[18] Western QM mins., 17/2M/1778.

it incorporated aspects of the system of "caring and control" that united the Quaker community.[19] The Friends extended their network of mutual aid and supervision to Afro-Americans freed by their members because they regarded them as part of their community (without formally being part of the meeting). This dual nature of the Friends' concern toward blacks was of long standing. Even the 1696 minute of the Yearly Meeting, which for the first time told Friends to avoid importing slaves, advised members to bring the blacks they already owned to meetings and to prevent them from "Rambling abroad on First Days or other times." Also, a prominent section of the query on slavery that meetings answered regularly after 1755 asked if Friends educated their slaves in the Christian religion and gave them sufficient food, clothing, and shelter. The *Epistle* of 1754, in addition, urged slave owners to educate and train their slaves in preparation for liberty.[20]

The Quaker meetings, guided by reformers of the sectarian strain, therefore adapted the humanitarian impulse for aiding blacks to fit their well-practiced system of supervising and caring for members. Friends probably felt responsible for the ex-slaves, fearing that they would bring disrepute to the Society, and also wanted to ensure that the blacks would not become burdens on the towns or counties where they lived. In arguing against emancipation, non-Friends held that blacks were innately lazy, vicious, and incapable of supporting themselves or their families if freed.[21] In February 1774, for example, a group of non-Quaker "Inhabatants Freeholders and Owners of Negroes" in Middletown, Monmouth County, petitioned the New Jersey Assembly against the proposed law to liberalize manumission in the colony, contending that "in the Abovesd Township there is a Great Number of Negro men women and children being Slaves and are Daily Increasing in Number and Impudence that we find Them Very Troublesome by Runing About All Times of Night Stealing and Taking and Riding people['s] horses & Other Mischeifs in a Great Degree Owing to their having a Correspondence and Recourse to the Houses of them Alread[y] Freed."[22] Many of the

---

[19] See Valerie Gladfelter, "Caring and Control: The Social Psychology of an Authoritative Group, the Burlington Friends Meeting, 1678-1720" (Ph.D. diss., University of Pennsylvania, 1983) for a discussion of the development of this system of mutual assistance and supervision in Burlington Monthly Meeting during the early colonial period.

[20] PYM mins., 23/7M/1696, 14-19/9M/1754, and 20-26/9M/1755.

[21] Copy of Dr. T. R. Chandler's Letter to Stephen Crane, 27 January 1774, Burlington Co. Abolition Society Papers, BCHS.

[22] Petitions to the New Jersey Assembly from Residents of Middletown Township, Monmouth County, 2 February 1774, MSS, Division of Archives and Records Management, Trenton, New Jersey.

freed slaves these East Jerseyans were complaining about had undoubtedly been released by Friends of Shrewsbury Monthly Meeting. Since members of the Society were highly suspect as a result of their neutral or pro-British stance prior to and during the Revolution, they did their utmost to keep the slaves that Friends manumitted in line. Spokesmen like the Burlington Quaker Samuel Allinson argued in 1773, in favor of a New Jersey law eliminating the required surety bond for manumission, that free blacks would lead peaceful and productive lives under the law.[23] The Quaker meetings sent committees to visit black families to make sure that they did.

The local Committees on Free Negroes began their work in 1778 and 1779. A committee from Concord Monthly Meeting in 1779 visited all but three or four single persons within the compass of that meeting. It inspected and settled accounts between the free blacks and their employers, and recommended that those who had large families put out their children as apprentices. Wilmington Friends were well satisfied to discover that most of their ex-slaves were able to provide for themselves and their families "with frugallity," and Burlington Quarterly Meeting reported that several black families maintained themselves "with Reputation." The New Garden Monthly Meeting committee found that most of the freed blacks continued to live among Friends and that they were successful in finding jobs of some sort. This committee, evidently concerned previously that some of the blacks had not been behaving properly, was pleased to report that one or more of the emancipated men and women had recently achieved an "amendment in life & Practice."[24]

Some local meetings, including Bucks and Burlington quarterly meetings, and Philadelphia, Wilmington, and Nottingham monthly meetings, reinforced the home visits by holding special monthly or

[23] "Reasons in favor of a Law, 'for the more equitable Manumission of Slaves in N Jersey &c'," 24/12M/1773, MS, Burlington Co. Abolition Society Papers, BCHS.

[24] Concord MM mins., 4/8M/1779; Wilmington MM mins., 14/7M/1779; Burlington QM mins., 26/8M/1782; New Garden MM mins., 5/5M/1781. Thomas Milhouse of New Garden Monthly Meeting joined the Wilmington Monthly Meeting Committee on Negroes to visit blacks in the Wilmington area in March 1779. In a fragmentary report of which he was almost certainly the author, Milhouse wrote that the blacks received the committee well, though the visits to some were more "comfortable" spiritually than to others. In most of the homes the Friends sat in worship with the freed men and women. Milhouse did not report on the economic well-being of the blacks, though he noted that several of the houses were very neat and clean. [Report of Thomas Milhouse], ca. 12 March 1779, MS [incomplete], Miscellaneous Slavery Papers, Chester County Historical Society; Wilmington MM mins., 16/6M/1779.

quarterly meetings of worship for blacks. At these meetings, Friends conducted the service in order to "promote Piety and Virtue amongst them, and impress in their Minds, a Sense of the Nature of Spiritual Worship and Adoration to the Author of their being."[25] Blacks apparently spoke at these meetings on rare occasions. In a letter probably written in 1762, Sally Armitt of Philadelphia thought it was newsworthy (along with the latest gossip about several upcoming marriages and a friend's death) to tell Susanna Wright that a free black had stood up and said a few words in the last Philadelphia meeting for blacks.[26] The Quakers had mixed feelings about the results of these meetings. The Committee on Free Negroes of Bucks Quarter reported in 1783 that a meeting "for the most part was a favoured opportunity" and that the blacks in the main had behaved in a "becoming manner," while Philadelphia Quarter could report in 1781 that blacks there were "excited to a sober orderly deportment, a steady attention to the duty of divine worship, and a pious regard to the well-being of their Offspring in that respect." The Chesterfield Monthly Meeting committee, on the other hand, reported after a religious meeting that it believed most blacks who attended had "but little savour of true Religion."[27] This sour comment probably had its source in the particularly antiblack attitudes of many Chesterfield Friends, displayed in other evidence of their reluctance to free slaves. In addition, the fact that these Quakers took so long to discipline slave buyers and obtain manumissions hardly endeared local blacks to the Society of Friends. It is also possible that the ex-slaves in Chesterfield had little interest in Quaker-style Christianity, because—in an area where slavery among Quakers was strong rather late in the colonial era—many blacks were relatively recent arrivals from Africa and the West Indies.

The freed blacks who were the recipients of the Quakers' attentions apparently did react in varying ways to the visits and meetings conducted by Friends. Nottingham Quakers found in 1779 that their advice "appear'd to have some weight" with the freed blacks, and they believed that "a continuance of care over and towards them may be both acceptable and useful." The Wilmington Committee on Free Negroes thought that the blacks they visited were both

[25] Bucks QM mins., 29/11M/1781.

[26] Sally Armitt to "Susy" [Susanna Wright], undated [1762], Society Collection, HSP. Alan Tully provided this reference.

[27] Bucks QM mins., 28/8M/1783; Phila. QM mins., 6/8M/1781; Chesterfield MM mins., 5/8M/1779.

"free and open to Receive Friends Company."[28] However, not all ex-slaves accepted the solicitude of Quakers gladly. The committee of the Western Quarter found that most blacks in Duck Creek received the "Care & Labour of Friends with respect" but that some Friends "who have been engaged in this Service, have frequently hinted that Obstructions have appeared in their Way, by reason of the Injuries & Injustice done that People; which hath been affecting to them." Evidently, the assistance of Friends was not welcomed by some freedmen in this area of Delaware; and at least some contemporary Quakers believed that the blacks' antipathy arose from their experience in slavery.[29] The Burlington Quarterly committee reported several times that its meetings for blacks were not well attended, and John Drinker summed up the reaction of Philadelphia Quarter's committee when in 1779 few free blacks asked for their help or advice. He wrote that "a backwardness of forwarding this business [prevailed] with some of that People; which we hope, nevertheless, may not discourage Freinds, so as to divert them from a continuance of Christian care towards them: believing that the labour of the honest hearted therein will find a sure reward, and the pious purpose of the Yearly Meeting be thereby measurably answered."[30]

From the perspective of the blacks involved, then, Quaker philanthropy was less than satisfactory. Friends meetings extended financial help when needed, but exacted a price for that aid in supervising the binding out of children and the drawing up of contracts between blacks and their employers. In accepting monetary help, freed men and women discovered, as do recipients of public assistance today, that they lost independence in making decisions concerning their own families. And beyond financial matters, the Friends also expected the blacks to conform to white Christian (perhaps Quaker) standards of morality, attend special Friends meetings held for blacks (but conducted by whites), and send their children to special schools set up for blacks (but again controlled by white Quakers). Blacks benefited from the Friends' system of mutual aid and endured, with varying degrees of patience, their paternalistic concern. Not permitted to join the Society until the 1790s, Afro-Americans formed a separate (and unequal) segment of the Quaker community.

[28] Nottingham MM mins., 27/2M/1779 and 29/7M/1780; Wilmington MM mins., 10/2M/1779.

[29] Western QM mins., 21/8M/1780.

[30] Burlington QM mins., 25/2M/1782 and 26/8M/1782; Phila. QM mins., 2/8M/1779.

The gradualist, segregationist, and paternalistic approach of Friends set the tone for the white antislavery movement in America from 1780 to 1833. Friends played a guiding role in establishing the Pennsylvania Abolition Society and similar groups in New York, New Jersey, Delaware, Maryland, Connecticut, and elsewhere, which were the chief agencies through which white Americans opposed slavery before William Lloyd Garrison and others launched the American Anti-Slavery Society to push for immediate emancipation. The efforts of the early abolitionist organizations both to care for and to control blacks were very similar to those of Philadelphia Yearly Meeting. They petitioned Congress for prohibition of slave importation and for the gradual, not immediate, abolition of slavery. The abolitionists endeavored both to obtain liberty for Afro-Americans who were legally free but who were detained as slaves and also to prevent the re-enslavement of free blacks; they represented freedmen in both predicaments in court. The Abolition Society also arranged for education and apprenticeships, and gave monetary assistance to mothers of dependent children and the aged.[31] As with blacks freed by meeting members and supervised by the meetings, however, the actions and attitudes of the abolitionists toward the freed women and men were paternalistic and geared toward monitoring their behavior. The Pennsylvania Abolition Society admitted only one black man—the light-skinned Robert Purvis—during the entire period from 1775 to 1859; and The American Convention for Promoting the Abolition of Slavery and Improving the Condition of the African Race (an informal federation of the state abolition societies) counseled slaves to be patient and advised free blacks to live within their means.[32] The concerns of the members of the abolition society in Burlington County, New Jersey, are quite evident from their lists of slaves and free blacks living in several townships there in the late 1790s. The census-takers not only recorded the number of persons in each freedman's family, but also wrote down the value of each family's property and whether or not the head of household was "sober" and "industrious."[33] Although David Brion Davis' thesis that the abolition societies were manned by incipient capitalists who hoped to exploit the obedient masses—

[31] Benjamin Quarles, *Black Abolitionists* (London, 1969), 12; Davis, *Problem of Slavery in the Age of Revolution*, 225.

[32] Quarles, *Black Abolitionists*, 9-12, 254. Wayne Eberly believed that the Pennsylvania Abolition Society's worst failure was in not establishing closer ties with black abolitionists. See Eberly, "Pennsylvania Abolition Society," 212.

[33] Lists of Freed Blacks and Slaves Living in Several Townships of Burlington County, ca. 1797, MSS, Burlington Co. Abolition Society Papers, BCHS.

both black and white—is open to question, he summed up well the attitude toward free blacks of the early abolitionists whose *modus operandi* developed in the struggle over slavery within the Quaker meeting. He concluded that "liberation from slavery did not mean freedom to live as one chose, but rather freedom to become a diligent, sober, dependable worker who gratefully accepted his position in society."[34]

REFORM in America has blossomed in many forms. Every issue involving social change fosters debates on which ends should have highest priority and which methods would serve the purpose best. Radical reformers, in particular, have had to make tough choices between adhering firmly to their plans for changing American social structure and governmental policies, and diluting their demands in order to garner wide support. The eighteenth-century Quaker abolitionists of the Delaware Valley faced this dilemma. The earliest radicals like William Southeby, Benjamin Lay, and Ralph Sandiford lambasted the slaveholding elite of Philadelphia Yearly Meeting and were condemned or expelled. Later, when fewer members of most local meetings owned or needed slave labor, abolitionists obtained a more kindly reception. Reformers then held sway in the Yearly Meeting, both abolitionists like John Woolman, John Sykes, David Ferris, and Anthony Benezet, and men like John Churchman and Israel Pemberton who had less concern about the social evil of slavery. This leadership was determined to reform the Society by enforcing more rigorously the rules against marrying persons of other religions, swearing oaths, supporting military measures in any way, and behaving or speaking in a frivolous or profane manner. The abolitionists managed to convince the meeting in 1758 to proscribe slave trading, and eighteen years later, when rather few participants still owned slaves, they obtained a complete ban on slaveholding itself. The antislavery reformers therefore finally attained their goal, but it took nearly a century after 1688 and it was accomplished only on terms that most Quakers could accept. Abolition became part of the inward-looking, self-conscious drive to purify the Society: slaveholding was a sin to be purged from the corporate body. If the meetings helped blacks through their Committee on Free Negroes, their purpose, in addition to philanthropic motives that some members certainly had, was to ensure that the ex-slaves would give outsiders no reason to criticize Friends.

[34] Davis, *Problem of Slavery in the Age of Revolution*, 254.

It is clear, then, that no single factor or circumstance accounts for the origins and growth of eighteenth-century Quaker abolitionism, just as the sources of every reform movement in American history are complex. Radical, "conscience" reformers pushed for an end to slavery because they believed blacks were equal in God's eyes and should not be oppressed. Before 1750 these abolitionists had little success in the Yearly Meeting, however, because many powerful leaders owned slaves. Only when the number of Friends who relied on slave labor declined drastically was the Society able to ban the institution. Some local meetings moved earlier than others: decreasing farm size as well as their humanitarian interpretation of Quakerism fostered Shrewsbury's early antislavery stance, while the continued demand after 1750 among large Quaker farmers in Chesterfield and Chester deterred those meetings from accepting abolition. The pivotal local meeting was Philadelphia. Few of the wealthy reformers who led the city meeting in the 1750s owned slaves—the holdouts in this meeting were much less powerful middling craftsmen who turned to blacks during the Seven Years' War, when the supply of white labor diminished. The Yearly Meeting adopted abolitionism during the 1750s as part of its drive to cleanse the Society of worldliness. Increasing numbers of Friends came to believe that slaveholding was a sin to be eliminated from their religion, but abolitionists were only partially successful in convincing fellow Quakers to go further than expelling slave owners and to work strenuously to end oppression for all American blacks. In the end, Philadelphia Yearly Meeting accepted abolition, but the process and result of the struggle were quite different from what early abolitionists had envisioned. At the same time Friends adopted abolitionism they turned inward and renounced the leadership of Pennsylvania that they had held when William Southeby and Benjamin Lay demanded emancipation for blacks. After 1780, individual Quakers, not the Yearly Meeting or a political presence of Friends in state government, worked for an end to slavery through the Pennsylvania Abolition Society and similar groups. Under their influence, the white abolitionist movement continued forward into American history the gradualist, segregationist, and paternalistic policies developed for almost a century within the Society of Friends.

APPENDIX A
QUAKER ORGANIZATION
AND DISCIPLINE

When Friends immigrated to the Delaware Valley, they brought with them the organization and practices that George Fox had established in the 1660s and 1670s. The new settlers in Pennsylvania and New Jersey remained within the verge of London Yearly Meeting; they simply extended its purview to another part of the world.

The Society of Friends had a hierarchical structure of meetings.[1] At the lowest level were the local *meetings for worship* that met at least twice weekly and were held in a member's home until a meeting house was built. At these gatherings, Friends and anyone else who desired to attend waited in silence for God to inspire someone— usually a seasoned minister but on occasion a young person or other less-experienced speaker—to preach or pray. Men and women attended meetings for worship together, but sat on opposite sides of the room.

The next higher meeting was the *monthly meeting for business*, which was composed of Friends from several local meetings for worship in the same township or group of adjacent townships. All adult Friends who were not under discipline (see below) could take part. Some meetings for worship established *preparative meetings* to decide what business should be presented to the monthly meeting. Men and women held separate monthly meetings, and only the men could disown, or expel, members from the Society. Though in Quaker theology women were considered spiritually equal with men, their role in making policy and enforcing discipline within the meeting was quite limited.[2] The women's meeting normally investigated the behavior and marital status of women before approving marriages or writing removal certificates to another meeting. They

[1] The following discussion of Quaker organization and practice relies upon my own reading of the minutes of Philadelphia Yearly Meeting, all quarterly meetings, and many monthly meetings in the Delaware Valley for the period 1681-1780; J. William Frost, *The Quaker Family in Colonial America* (New York, 1973); L. Hugh Doncaster, *Quaker Organisation and Business Meetings* (London, 1958); and Howard H. Brinton, *Guide to Quaker Practice* (Wallingford, Pa., 1952).

[2] This ambivalence of Friends concerning the proper role of women in the Society was reflected also in their attitudes about where blacks fitted into the Quaker community.

also provided poor relief and *treated* or *dealt with*[3] women for offenses such as marrying out of unity, fornication, and backbiting or slander. Whenever they believed a woman should be disowned, most women's meetings referred her case to the men.

Indeed, the men's monthly meeting had a wider range of powers and concerns. It disowned unrepentant members for disciplinary offenses, discussed and made decisions on issues such as antislavery reform and the participation of Friends in government, provided poor relief on a larger scale than the women's meeting, mediated disputes among members, controlled the meeting's property, managed the schools, investigated the behavior and marital status of men before approving marriages or writing removal certificates, and often supervised inquiries into the conduct of women as well. *Weighty Friends*, the Society's most respected members who included *ministers*, *elders*, and *overseers*, performed most of the meeting's work. The overseers were charged specifically with monitoring the behavior of the congregation; but committees assigned to treat with miscreants usually included ministers and elders as well. The chief duty of ministers, of course, was to preach. They were unpaid except for expenses when they traveled. Elders were appointed to ensure that both ministers and more ordinary members were guided by the Light.

Though practices of disciplining members varied from one meeting to another, typical procedures can be described. Generally, an overseer advised the monthly meeting that a Friend of his meeting for worship had committed an offense. The misdeeds brought to the attention of the meeting most often were marrying a non-Friend or not following Quaker rules for marriage; fornication; drunkenness; assault; indebtedness and bad conduct in trade; oath-taking; participating in military activities or paying fines for not attending training; lying, profanity, and slander; taking part in frivolities like horse-racing, card-playing, and lotteries; and acting in other ways considered unbecoming to a member of the Society and labeled "loose conversation." Cases that occurred much less often but show the range of the meeting's concern included concealing the birth and burial of an infant, incest, disruption of meetings, living off one's father, not caring for grandchildren, receiving stolen goods, and attempted rape.

---

[3] These were the terms used for visits made to inquire about a reported misdeed and to convince a member of her or his wrongdoing if the report proved true.

Following the report of the offense, the monthly meeting usually appointed two men to visit the accused, hear his explanation or excuses, and endeavor to bring him to a sense of sorrow for his wrongdoing. These committees usually took a number of months to finish their business; some cases continued for years. One of the visitors might be out of town or ill, or the offender might be away on business or even refuse to receive his callers. Alternate members were sometimes appointed when the original committee felt they could do no more to convince the sinner of his transgression. The amount of patience shown varied from one meeting to the next, and was affected by the nature of the offense and the accused's former standing in the meeting—and probably by his social status as well.

A Quaker under discipline had several choices. If he had not committed the same offense before, he could usually acknowledge and express sorrow for his mistake and remain a member in good standing. The Friends either required a person to acknowledge his sin orally before the meeting or told him to submit a written admission that would be read at the monthly meeting or at a local meeting for worship. Many Quakers who married non-Friends continued to belong to the Society and some were able to bring their children under the meeting's care. While the tightening of enforcement of discipline after 1755 meant that most meetings were less forgiving than formerly, many Friends continued to marry out and yet stay within the religion by acknowledging their guilt. Quakers were considerably less lenient with members who had committed the same mistake before and often testified against, or disowned, such persons after only one visit. First offenders who refused to make acknowledgment after more prolonged dealings were also excommunicated. If a person felt he had not received justice he could appeal to the quarterly meeting, but few did. The higher meetings almost always upheld the stands taken by the monthly meetings.

The meetings also used two other punishments for certain kinds of offenses, including slave trading. As noted above, Philadelphia Yearly Meeting stipulated before 1755 that Friends who imported or bought imported blacks should be admonished. This probably meant that the offender was simply reprimanded orally, because there is no record in monthly meeting minutes prior to 1757 of any Friends being censured or otherwise disciplined for slave trading. The penalty for importing or purchasing blacks instituted by the Yearly Meeting in 1758, a status of partial disownment in which the accused could not participate in business meetings or contribute funds to the Society, was also used against Friends who continued to hold political offices during the Seven Years' War. This was also the situation in which all persons accused of misbehavior were held until they either acknowledged their guilt or were disowned.

Quakers in monthly meetings—and in quarterly and yearly meetings as well—reached decisions concerning discipline, slavery, building new meeting houses, and other business, by coming to a *sense of the meeting*. Friends did not vote, nor did they follow majority rule. Rather, the *clerk* (the presiding officer who also kept the minutes) determined and recorded the resolution of the meeting after a subject had been discussed fully. Quakers believed that, ideally, guidance came from the Light which revealed itself to everyone in the meeting in the same way. In practice, however, Friends disagreed often—especially over the issue of slavery—and therefore either postponed decisions or made compromises. For the eighteenth century, it is impossible to know from a meeting's minutes if decisions represented the wishes of the whole meeting or the will of just a few of the weightiest Friends. The number of members participating in a decision probably varied from one group to another. One result of resolving issues by sense of the meeting was that one or two eminent, but also obstinate, Quakers could prevent a meeting from taking an important stand.

The *hierarchy of Quaker business meetings* went from preparative to monthly, then to quarterly, and finally to the Yearly Meeting. The monthly meetings sent representatives every three months to the quarter, which in turn sent delegates to the annual meeting. In the Delaware Valley, there were six quarterly meetings until 1758 when Chester Quarterly Meeting was split in half. Map 1 illustrates the geographic distribution of the local meetings within the compass of Philadelphia Yearly Meeting, and Table A.1 lists these meetings along with a means for estimating their approximate size. The relationships among meetings at different levels, and between Philadelphia and London yearly meetings, were complex. For the most part, questions of policy reached Philadelphia Yearly Meeting when a monthly meeting encountered a problem that it could not solve by itself or when a member raised an issue that the meeting believed should be discussed by the entire Society. The local group sent the question with its delegates to the quarter. If that meeting in turn could not resolve the problem or thought the topic had merit, it sent the inquiry to the Yearly Meeting. The central body then either reached a decision or referred the problem elsewhere. Philadelphia Friends often asked London for counsel early in the colonial period, as the Yearly Meeting in England was considered "first among equals."[4] Yearly meetings in Britain, Europe, and America kept in contact with each other by writing epistles at least once a year. These epistles described how Friends were faring in each region or country and asked for advice on problems of import to the entire Society. On controversial questions like slavery, Quakers in one part of the world waited until others generally agreed before they moved forcefully to change the discipline.

When a yearly meeting did resolve to change a rule, it called upon the constituent meetings to implement the new policy. After 1743, Philadelphia Yearly Meeting required its local meetings to answer a list of questions, or *queries*, that inquired about the general state of each meeting and asked whether Friends were adhering to the discipline. While monthly meetings were supposed to enforce the central body's decisions, some groups would not follow instructions. Sadsbury Monthly Meeting permitted some members to marry non-Friends until 1761[5] and Chesterfield and Deer Creek meetings refused to punish slave purchasers according to the 1758 rule until the 1770s. Most meetings did follow the lead of the annual meeting, but the speed and strictness with which they responded varied widely.

Philadelphia Yearly Meeting performed most of its business each year by appointing ad hoc committees that considered problems and drafted reports which were then discussed by the entire body. The meeting maintained continuity, however, by choosing a number of officers and standing committees who served from one year to the next. These officials included the clerk, collectors of the yearly stock (or treasurers), correspondents to London Yearly Meeting, overseers of the press, and after 1756, representatives to the Meeting for Sufferings. (See Table A.2 for lists of Friends who held most of these posts during the years 1681-1780.)

The *overseers of the press* deserve special mention because these men examined the writings of Friends and decided if they should be published. They could make substantial changes in any work to ensure that it reflected the views of the Society. The overseers of

---

[4] Frost, *Quaker Family*, 4.
[5] Sadsbury MM mins., 22/4M/1761.

the press held considerable power because they could prevent individual Quakers who wished to remain in good standing from issuing tracts on disputed topics such as slavery. In England, the Morning Meeting of men ministers supervised Friends' books. Their rejection of one of George Fox's papers and his reaction illustrate the scope of their control. He wrote in 1676:

> I was not moved to set up that meeting to make orders against the reading of my papers; but to gather up bad books that was scandalous against Friends; and to see that young Friends' books that was sent to be printed might be stood by; and to see where every one had their motion to the meeting that they might not go in heaps; and not for them to have an authority over the Monthly and Quarterly and other Meetings or for them to stop things to the nation which I was moved of the Lord to give forth to them.[6]

Philadelphia Yearly Meeting appointed the first committee to cooperate with the printer William Bradford in 1691, and then assigned Philadelphia Monthly Meeting to handle the press for several years. In 1709 the Yearly Meeting specifically appointed a committee to censor members' writings; until 1756 new overseers were added periodically as death took its toll. After that date, Philadelphia Meeting for Sufferings, which was established in 1756 to deal with problems arising from the crisis of 1755, assumed a number of executive functions of the Yearly Meeting including control of the press.[7]

Few censuses or membership lists exist for the local meetings of Philadelphia Yearly Meeting during the eighteenth century. However, the assessments in Table A.1, taken from the meeting minutes, provide an approximate measure of the size of the quarterly and monthly meetings. Presumably, the Yearly Meeting determined the amount the local meetings were required to contribute to the Yearly Stock according to their number of members, although the ability of local Friends to pay probably affected the quotas as well. As a guide to how these assessments may translate into number of members, the total membership of Philadelphia Monthly Meeting in 1760 was 2,250.[8]

---

[6] William C. Braithwaite, *The Second Period of Quakerism*, ed. Henry J. Cadbury, 2d ed. (Cambridge, 1961), 280.

[7] PYM mins., 1691-1780.

[8] Joseph Oxley, "Philadelphia in 1771," *The Friend* 71 (31 July 1897), 10.

TABLE A.1. ASSESSMENTS OF LOCAL MEETINGS OF
PHILADELPHIA YEARLY MEETING

Meeting	Assessment	
Philadelphia Yearly Meeting: 1757[a]		
Pennsylvania, Delaware, Maryland, and Virginia:		
Philadelphia Quarterly Meeting	£32.5	
Chester [and Western] QM	25.0	£67.5
Bucks QM	10.0	
New Jersey:		
Burlington QM	£17.5	
Gloucester-Salem QM	11.0	£32.5
Shrewsbury QM[b]	4.0	
	£100.0	
Philadelphia Quarterly Meeting: 1763[c]		
Philadelphia MM	£33.0	
Abington MM	15.0	
Gwynedd MM	6.0	
Radnor MM	5.0	
Exeter MM	3.0	
Richland MM	3.0	
	£65.0	
Bucks Quarterly Meeting: 1739[d]		
Falls MM	£1.5	
Buckingham MM	1.5	
Wrightstown MM	1.0	
Middletown MM	1.0	
	£5.0	
Chester Quarterly Meeting: 1753[e]		
Goshen (Pa.) MM	£2.70	
Chester (Pa.) MM	2.60	
Concord (Pa.) MM	2.50	
Nottingham (Pa. and Md.) MM	2.15	
Newark (Del.) MM*	1.85	
New Garden (Pa.) MM*	1.75	

TABLE A.1. (*cont.*)

Meeting	Assessment
Wilmington (Del.) MM	1.40
Darby (Pa.) MM	1.30
Bradford (Pa.) MM*	1.00
Duck Creek (Del.) MM*	1.00
Sadsbury (Pa.) MM*	1.00
Hopewell (Va.) MM*	.25
Fairfax (Va.) MM*	.25
Warrington (Pa.) MM*	.25
	£20.00
Burlington Quarterly Meeting: 1763[f]	
Burlington MM	£50.0
Chesterfield MM	40.0
Little Egg Harbor MM	10.0
	£100.0
Gloucester-Salem Quarterly Meeting: 1757[g]	
Haddonfield MM	£45.0
Salem MM	45.0
Egg Harbor and Cape May MM	10.0
	£100.0

[a] PYM mins., 23-29/9M/1758. The assessments of individual meetings that follow do not have a direct relationship to this assessment. Meeting assessments should be compared with others on the same list only, unless they are adjusted according to the quarterly meeting quotas on the Yearly Meeting list.

[b] In July 1761, Woodbridge Monthly Meeting contributed £1.75 to the Yearly Meeting stock, which probably means that Shrewsbury MM's share was £2.25. Woodbridge MM mins., 16/7M/1761

[c] Phila. QM mins., treasurer's accounts for 30/7M/1763 to 25/9M/1763, located after minutes for 4/2M/1771

[d] Bucks QM mins., 30/6M/1739

[e] Chester QM mins., 13/8M/1753. This list includes meetings that became part of Western QM in 1758; these meetings are marked with an asterisk.

[f] Burlington QM mins., 28/2M/1763. This assessment was to help finance construction of a meeting house at Hardwick. Hardwick MM was small, but was assessed £100.0 because the assessment was for its own building.

[g] Gloucester-Salem QM mins., 25/3M/1757

TABLE A.2. OFFICERS OF PHILADELPHIA YEARLY MEETING, 1681-1780

Office	Quarterly meeting	Dates of service or date appointed
Clerk[a]		
Phineas Pemberton	Bucks	1696-1701
Griffith Owen	Phila.	1702
Anthony Morris I	Phila.	1704, 1710
Caleb Pusey	Chester	1704
Isaac Norris I	Phila.	1711-1729[b]
Samuel Preston	Phila.	1722
John Kinsey II	Phila.	1730-1749
Israel Pemberton II	Phila.	1750-1759
John Smith	Burlington	1760
James Pemberton	Phila.	1761-1781[b]
George Churchman	Western	1767
Isaac Jackson	Western	1777
Correspondent with London Yearly Meeting		
Isaac Norris I	Phila.	1713
Samuel Carpenter	Phila.	1713
Richard Hill	Phila.	1714
Israel Pemberton I	Phila.	1730
John Kinsey II	Phila.	1735
Samuel Preston	Phila.	1735
Treasurer[c]		
Samuel Jennings	Burlington	1702-1708
Griffith Owen	Phila.	1702
Edward Shippen	Phila.	1702
Anthony Morris I	Phila.	1706-1718
Thomas Raper	Burlington	1708-1712, 1714
Peter Fretwell	Burlington	1711
Samuel Preston	Phila.	1714,1716-1742
Samuel Smith I	Burlington	1714-1717
Daniel Smith I	Burlington	1715, 1718-1741
Caleb Raper	Burlington	1718-1744
Anthony Morris II	Phila.	1743-1762
Richard Smith II	Burlington	1745-1751
Samuel Smith II	Burlington	1752-1775
John Reynell	Phila.	1763-1780

TABLE A.2. (*cont.*)

Office	Quarterly meeting	Dates of service or date appointed
Overseer of Press		
Alexander Beardsley	Phila.	1691
John Delavall	Phila.	1691
James Fox	Phila.	1691
Samuel Jennings	Phila. (in 1691)	1691
Anthony Morris I	Phila.	1691, 1706, 1709, 1717
Griffith Owen	Phila.	1691, 1709
Thomas Griffith	Phila.	1706
Richard Hill	Phila.	1709, 1717
William Hudson	Phila.	1709, 1717
Isaac Norris I	Phila.	1709, 1717
Caleb Pusey	Chester	1709, 1717
Thomas Story	Phila.	1709, 1717
Nicholas Waln I	Phila.	1709, 1717
Joseph Kirkbride	Bucks	1717
David Lloyd	Chester	1717
Samuel Preston	Phila.	1717
John Wright	Chester	1717
Thomas Chalkley	Phila.	1722
Thomas Griffitts	Phila.	1722
Thomas Lightfoot	Chester	1722
James Logan	Phila.	1722
Israel Pemberton I	Phila.	1722
Richard Smith	Burlington	1722
John Bringhurst	Phila.	1730
Robert Jordan	Phila.	1736
John Kinsey II	Phila.	1736
Caleb Raper	Burlington	1736
John Evans I	Phila.	1743
Michael Lightfoot	Chester (in 1743)	1743
Anthony Morris II	Phila.	1743
William Morris	Burlington	1743
Isaac Norris II	Phila.	1743
Israel Pemberton II	Phila.	1743
Richard Smith II	Burlington	1743
Anthony Benezet	Phila.	1752
Owen Jones	Phila.	1752
Samuel Preston Moore	Phila.	1752

Office	Quarterly meeting	Dates of service or date appointed
John Smith	Phila. (in 1752)	1752
Samuel Smith II	Burlington	1752
Mordecai Yarnall	Phila. (in 1752)	1752
John Armitt	Phila.	1756
William Brown	Chester (in 1756)	1756
John Churchman	Chester	1756
William Logan	Phila.	1756
James Pemberton	Phila.	1756
John Pemberton	Phila.	1756
Joseph White	Bucks	1756
John Woolman	Burlington	1756

ᵃ Not clearly identified in the minutes before 1711
ᵇ With interruption
ᶜ Called Collector of the Yearly Stock before 1736

APPENDIX B
SOURCES AND METHODS

QUAKER MEETING RECORDS

Quakers are justly famous for keeping excellent records. Their *minutes* of meetings for business on the monthly, quarterly, and yearly meeting level permit historians to study the ways in which Friends dealt with religious and social concerns both locally and throughout the entire Delaware Valley region. These records are not trouble-free, however, and must be used with considerable caution. One mistake that several scholars have made is to assume that all monthly meetings acted in concert with Philadelphia Yearly Meeting. Instead, my earliest survey of these minutes showed that—for example—local meetings came to oppose slavery at quite different times in the eighteenth century. In order to choose a few meetings that would best represent the range of positions taken, and also to discover which meetings probably stimulated or hindered the development of abolitionism in the Yearly Meeting as a whole, I read the minutes of all seven quarterly meetings and over three-fourths of the monthly meetings in the Delaware Valley. Evidence from the quarterly meetings suggested that looking at the minutes of the remaining monthly meetings would provide little additional insight. Thus the four monthly meetings chosen for close scrutiny—Philadelphia, Chester, Chesterfield, and Shrewsbury—were selected on the basis of a systematic survey of the stances on slavery of the overwhelming majority of local meetings in Philadelphia Yearly Meeting.

After choosing representative congregations, the next task for investigating the growth of abolitionism among Friends was to decide where individual members of the meetings stood on this issue of reform. Omission of the details of discussion of all types of concerns from all Quaker minutes leaves a serious gap in interpreting the process of decision-making: when deliberations ended, clerks wrote down only what they believed the entire group had decided. Thus it was necessary to identify in other ways which members supported and opposed antislavery reform. The meeting minutes, records of manumissions kept by local meetings, probate records, and tax lists all provide information about whether or not Friends held, bought, and sold slaves. Those who served on committees to treat with slave buyers, sellers, and owners can be considered opponents of slavery;

other abolitionists made their positions clear in tracts, diaries, and personal correspondence. Proslavery Quakers can be identified from those who held on to their blacks until death or until the meeting dealt with them for slaveholding in the 1770s. This group also included members who were disciplined for buying or selling slaves after 1757.

Another problem is the dearth of membership lists for the Society of Friends during the eighteenth century. Most Quakers can be identified only from records of birth, death, marriage, removal, and discipline—and some Friends never show up in these documents. Of greater concern for the investigation of policy-making in local congregations and in the Yearly Meeting itself, however, is the lack of lists of participants in meetings for business. I overcame this deficiency by extracting the names of all men assigned to committees in the Yearly Meeting and in the four monthly meetings studied closely. This way, I could determine who played a role in the meetings, how significant their participation was, and the length and dates of their service. The meeting minutes also usually noted the appointment and resignation of officers.

Friends Historical Library, Swarthmore College, Swarthmore, Pennsylvania, has originals and/or microfilm copies of the men's meeting minutes of Philadelphia Yearly Meeting and its constituent quarterly and monthly meetings. I used the following minutes:

Philadelphia Yearly Men's Meeting (1681-1780).

Men's Quarterly Meetings: Bucks (1684-1792), Burlington (1686-1783), Chester and Concord (1684-1783), Gloucester-Salem (1682-1780), Philadelphia (1682-1781), Shrewsbury and Rahway (1705-1782), and Western (1758-1782).

Men's Monthly Meetings: Abington (1692-1780), Bradford (1737-1781), Buckingham (1720-1780), Burlington (1681-1780), Chester (1681-1781), Chesterfield (1684-1783), Concord (1684-1780), Darby (1684-1781), Deer Creek (1760-1780), Duck Creek (1705-1780), Egg Harbor and Cape May (1726-1780), Evesham (1760-1780), Exeter (1737-1780), Goshen (1722-1781), Gwynedd (1714-1784), Haddonfield (1710-1781), Kingwood (1744-1780), Little Egg Harbor (1715-1780), Middletown (Bucks) (1683-1780), New Garden (1718-1781), Nottingham (1730-1781), Philadelphia (1682-1781), Sadsbury (1737-1780), Salem (1676-1780), Shrewsbury (1732-1780), Uwchlan (1763-1781), Wilmington (1750-1781), and Woodbridge (1686-1780).

The *manumission records* kept by local meetings provide the names and places of residence of slaveholders, their occupations (in most cases), and the number and kinds of slaves they owned. They also normally give the names, ages, and gender of the freed blacks, and state whether they were "Negro" or "mulatto." These documents sometimes describe family relationships among the ex-slaves, and can suggest how long they had lived in the Delaware Valley. However, most meetings did not record manumissions until 1774, and so we cannot learn from them about slave ownership among Friends who died or freed their slaves before that very late date. Thus I have searched for (and found) earlier evidence of slaveholding and manumission in wills and inventories. Also, Quaker records of manumissions apparently survive for only about one-half of the monthly meetings in the Delaware Valley. Those that have been located for meetings in New Jersey and Pennsylvania and were utilized in this study are:

Abington Monthly Meeting Manumissions (1765-1784), Quaker Collection, Haverford College, Haverford, Pennsylvania; Bucks Quarterly Meeting Manumissions Book (1776-1793), Friends Historical Library, Swarthmore; Burlington Monthly Meeting Manumission Book (1771-1781), Burlington County Historical Society, Burlington, New Jersey; Chester Monthly Meeting Manumissions (1776-1780), FHL; Chesterfield Monthly Meeting Manumissions (1774-1796), FHL; Concord Monthly Meeting Manumissions Book (1777-1789), FHL; Exeter Monthly Meeting Manumissions (1777-1787), FHL; Goshen Monthly Meeting Manumissions, recorded in the monthly meeting minutes (1775-1777), FHL; Kennett Monthly Meeting Manumissions (1776-1780), FHL; Manumission Book for the Three Philadelphia Monthly Meetings (1772-1796), Arch Street Meeting House, Philadelphia; and Salem Monthly Meeting Manumission Committee Report (27/4M/1777), Stewart Collection, Glassboro State College, Glassboro, New Jersey.

PROBATE WILLS AND INVENTORIES

The risks of using data from probate records are now well known. For discussion of these potential problems, see Gloria L. Main, "Probate Records as a Source for Early American History," *WMQ*, 3d ser., 32 (1975), 89-99; and Daniel Scott Smith, "Underregistration and Bias in Probate Records: An Analysis of Data from Eighteenth-Century Hingham, Massachusetts," *ibid.*, 100-110.

At the same time, however, careful utilization of evidence from inventories has permitted scholars to explore aspects of colonial society that would otherwise remain obscure. The recent work of Lois Green Carr, Paul G. E. Clemens, P.M.G. Harris, Allan Kulikoff, Gloria Main, Russell R. Menard, and Lorena S. Walsh, for example, has illustrated the usefulness of probate records in examining the development of a plantation society in seventeenth- and eighteenth-century Maryland. By weighting their data for likely biases, they have been able to suggest in great detail how local economic and demographic changes contributed to the growth of a society based on tobacco and slaves and on mixed farming close to that practiced in southeastern Pennsylvania and southern New Jersey.

Use of probate records was indispensible for this study if it was to include comparison of slave and servant ownership and wealth in specific localities in Pennsylvania and New Jersey over a century in time. Tax lists that enumerate blacks survive only for the late colonial period and do not include the same information for both provinces. A few censuses—for 1726, 1738, and 1745—provide population data by county in New Jersey, but none exists for pre-revolutionary Pennsylvania. Thus, evidence on slaveholding, wealth, and economic activity from inventories is clearly superior to aggregate data available from other sources for several reasons: we can compare rather better the results of analysis of probate records in different localities because the source materials are the same; we can trace changes in patterns of slave ownership over time and thus place the still-life images provided by tax assessment lists and censuses into long-term perspective; and we can pinpoint specific local areas for study of slaveholding and economic life instead of relying on county- or province-wide data.

The major drawback in using inventories to compare levels of wealth and slave and servant ownership among different localities is that the percentage of decedents whose estates were inventoried (or whose inventories have survived) sometimes varied substantially from one geographic area to another, and also perhaps from one decade to another within the same locality. In places and periods for which relatively few inventories exist, wealth biases are likely to be more pronounced than in areas for which a greater number of inventories are extant relative to the number of adults likely to be dying.

The number of inventories that survive for decedents in each of the four local areas are provided in Table B.1. Rough estimates of the percentage of *total* decedents in each area for whom inventories exist are given in Table B.2. The number of heads of household

TABLE B.1. TOTAL NUMBER OF INVENTORIES

Decade	Chester	Chester-field	Shrews-bury	Philadel-phia
1676-1690	6	6	20	22
1691-1700	10	22	15	77
1701-1710	18	27	13	104
1711-1720	30	36	32	165
1721-1730	42	58	19	182
1731-1740	55	69	41	207
1741-1750	82	115	59	353
1751-1760	84	104	64	378
1761-1770	104	134	72	512
1771-1780	79	122	32	401
Total	510	693	367	2,401

TABLE B.2. ESTIMATED PERCENTAGE OF TOTAL DECEDENTS WHO WERE INVENTORIED

Decade	Chester	Chester-field	Shrews-bury	Philadel-phia
1676-1690	—	—	—	—
1691-1700	83%	73%	33%	64%
1701-1710	86	56	21	75
1711-1720	100	56	42	60
1721-1730	100	72	20	44
1731-1740	95	62	36	38
1741-1750	100	86	38	54
1751-1760	88	59	40	34
1761-1770	90	62	43	48
1771-1780	67	48	18	30

who could be expected to die per decade in each area was calculated from tax lists and census data. I interpolated in decades for which no evidence survives, and used a crude mortality rate of fifteen per thousand per year in the three rural areas and a rate of between thirty-three and forty-seven per thousand per year in Philadelphia (derived from Billy G. Smith, "Death and Life in a Colonial Immigrant City: A Demographic Analysis of Philadelphia," *The Journal of Economic History* 37 [1977], 863-889). For the earliest decade in each area no percentages could be reasonably determined.

While Table B.2 has some particular fluctuations that need to be kept in mind, the first observation to note is that up to 1770 the estimated percentage of total decedents who were inventoried stayed fairly level in the three rural areas. Chester stayed at 85 to 95 percent, Chesterfield remained around 60 to 65 percent, and Shrewsbury was usually close to 35 to 40 percent. After 1720, Philadelphia also remained fairly steady at about 40 to 45 percent. The decline from a higher level at 60 to 65 percent in 1691-1720 will make Philadelphia decedents seem wealthier during the later period than they actually were; the drop in the 1770s in all four localities will have this effect everywhere. In terms of certain specific decades where caution is advised, two periods stand out because the percentage of decedents inventoried fell while slave ownership rose. These were in Shrewsbury in the 1720s and in Chester in the 1770s. In Shrewsbury, the slaveholding level may be somewhat too high, but the percentage owning slaves was probably at least equal with the 1710s and 1730s. For instance, Graph 3.2 shows that the level of slaveholding among the wealthy did not drop much during the 1720s. The rise in slave ownership in the Chester data in the 1770s may simply reflect the increased importation of blacks into Pennsylvania in the early 1760s.

The colonial exchange rates compiled by John J. McCusker in *Money and Exchange in Europe and America, 1600-1775: A Handbook* (Chapel Hill, N.C., 1978), 314-317, were used to change the values that were reported in the inventories in Pennsylvania or New Jersey currency into £ sterling. This procedure standardizes the values, permits comparisons between the two colonies, and eliminates distortion caused by fluctuations in the value of these provincial currencies. However, it does not correct for inflation or deflation that occurred generally throughout the Atlantic economy (see Chapter 3, n. 9). For the years 1776-1780, those estates that were assessed in inflated continental currency were adjusted to the 1775 level and then changed into £ sterling.

Most inventories in New Jersey and Pennsylvania included only personal wealth. The value of real estate has been subtracted from those that included real wealth.

The New Jersey probate records are located in the Division of Archives and Records Management, Trenton. The Chester County records are in the Chester County Archives, West Chester, although most of the wills and inventories before 1715 are included with the Philadelphia records. The original Philadelphia County inventories (for wills and administations) are located in the Register of Wills office in the basement of City Hall Annex, Philadelphia, but those of most testate decedents are on microfilm in the Register of Wills office in Room 185, City Hall. The Historical Society of Pennsylvania has photostat copies of probate records of testate decedents (wills and inventories) for Philadelphia County, 1682-1724. Bucks County wills and inventories are kept in the county court house in Doylestown and Delaware probate records are located at the state archives in Dover.

TAX ASSESSMENT LISTS

On the whole, tax lists for Pennsylvania and New Jersey are much less useful than probate inventories, in a large part because relatively few tax lists exist. They are also not as reliable a source for comparing absolute levels of wealth because only real estate, some livestock, and certain categories of personal property were taxed, whereas all personal property, business inventories, debts due to the estate, livestock, and crops on hand at the time of death were supposed to be evaluated in probate records. In addition, it would be difficult if not impossible to use tax lists to compare absolute levels of wealth between residents of New Jersey and Pennsylvania because different items were assessed and rates of taxation were not the same. Thus in Chapter 2, I ranked the leaders of Philadelphia Yearly Meeting who came from various parts of the Delaware Valley by their relative standing on their own particular county tax lists in order to compare their economic statuses across counties, colonies, and different eras of tax legislation.

For Friends and their neighbors still living in 1780, however, tax lists provided information on slave ownership, wealth, and landholding that could be found nowhere else. Probate records could yield little information on slaveholding among Quakers active in meetings in the 1760s and 1770s because members who wished to remain in good standing and who died after 1780 had already given up their blacks by the time of their deaths. In addition, deeds could be of little help on land ownership, at least in New Jersey, because only about one-fourth of that province's land records survive.

Thus I was forced to consult tax lists to detect slave and servant ownership among Friends still living in the 1770s. These tax records were of uneven value, however, because the date of the earliest extant lists varies from one locality to another and because the kinds of slaves enumerated differed in Pennsylvania and New Jersey. The earliest lists that include slaves and servants are: Chester County,

1760; Philadelphia County, 1767; part of Lancaster County, 1750s; part of Bucks County, 1776; West Jersey, 1773 and 1779; and East Jersey, 1779. Tax lists available for New Castle County (Delaware) for the 1770s do not enumerate slaves. In Pennsylvania after 1764, tax assessors counted both male and female blacks aged twelve to fifty years, and all white servants aged fifteen to fifty years. In New Jersey, only male slaves and servants who were sixteen years or older were taxable. (James T. Mitchell and Henry Flanders, comps., *The Statutes at Large of Pennsylvania from 1682 to 1800* [Harrisburg, 1896-1915], 6:358; Samuel Allinson, comp., *Acts of the General Assembly of the Province of New-Jersey from . . . 1702, to . . . 1776* [Burlington, 1776], 320.)

Most of the New Jersey tax ratables lists are located in the Division of Archives and Records Management, Trenton. Those used in this study include:

Burlington County: Burlington (1773), Chester (1774, 1779), Chesterfield (1774, 1779), Evesham (1773, 1774), Mansfield (1774, 1779), New Hanover (1774, 1779), Northampton (1774, 1779), Nottingham (1774, 1779), Springfield (1774, 1779), and Willingboro (1773).

Cumberland County: Fairfield (1773, 1774), Greenwich (1773), Hopewell (1773, 1774), and Stow Creek (1773).

Essex County: Elizabeth (Town Ward) (1779, 1780), Elizabeth (Rahway) (1780), and Elizabeth (Westfield Ward) (1779, 1780).

Gloucester County: Deptford (1779), Galloway (1773), Gloucester (1773, 1774, 1779), Great Egg Harbor (1773), Newton (1779), and Waterford (1779, 1780).

Hunterdon County: Trenton (1779).

Middlesex County: Piscataway (1780), Windsor (1779), and Woodbridge (1778, 1779).

Monmouth County: Middletown (1779), Shrewsbury (1779), and Upper Freehold (1778).

Salem County: Elsinboro (1773, 1774), Lower Alloways Creek (1774), and Mannington (1773, 1774).

Somerset County: Western Precinct (1779).

In addition, the Stewart Collection at Glassboro State College, Glassboro, New Jersey, has the tax ratables list for Cape May County, Upper Township (1773).

In Pennsylvania, the Bucks County Historical Society, Doylestown, has the Bucks County tax assessment lists for 1779 and 1783. Of the long series of tax lists available for Chester County, I used the tax rates for the years 1722, 1747, 1749, 1750, 1753, 1756,

1757, 1758, and 1759, and the tax assessment lists for 1760, 1765, 1774, and 1775. All of these are held by the Chester County Archives except the 1760 tax assessment list which is located in the Shippen Papers at the Historical Society of Pennsylvania. The Lancaster County tax assessment lists for 1771 and 1773 are located at the Lancaster County Historical Society, Lancaster. The Philadelphia County tax lists are located in several libraries. The Rare Book Room of Van Pelt Library, University of Pennsylvania, has the Philadelphia County tax assessment list for 1767. The Historical Society of Pennsylvania has the Philadelphia County tax assessment lists for 1769, 1772, and 1774. The Philadelphia City Archives, City Hall Annex, has the Constables' Returns of 1775.

Linking Religious Records, Probate Wills and Inventories, and Tax Lists Together

Religious affiliation and property-holding of individuals were matched in this study for two purposes: 1) to determine wealth, slave ownership, occupation, and landholding of the Yearly Meeting elite and participants in Chester, Chesterfield, Shrewsbury, and Philadelphia monthly meetings; and 2) to identify insofar as possible for comparative purposes the religions of all decedents in the four localities whose estates were probated during the 1730s, 1760s, and 1770s.

Toward the first of these objectives, I was able to locate information about slaveholding and wealth for over 85 percent of the Yearly Meeting elite. In the local meetings, the proportion of all participants who could be found in the probate records or on the tax lists, or who are known to have left the meeting because they requested certificates of removal, are: Shrewsbury-80.9 percent; Chesterfield-86.2 percent; Chester-88.2 percent; and Philadelphia-78.3 percent. There are several reasons why the rest were not found. Probate records do not exist for all decedents (though Quakers were required to prepare wills and appear to have had their estates inventoried more consistently than people of other religions); and some participants in the meetings were not heads of households when the tax lists were made either because they had turned their property over to their sons or because they themselves were sons still living in their fathers' households. Also, similarity of names made identification impossible in some cases.

My attempt to discover the religions of decedents who left inventories in the 1730s, 1760s, and 1770s from the four localities was somewhat less successful because comprehensive records survive for few churches. It is also true, however, that an unknown but by the eighteenth century probably large proportion of colonists had no active religious affiliation. The numbers of decedents for whom religion could not be identified are included in each of the relevant tables in Chapters 5 and 6. The names of wives and children in wills and on administrative bonds aided identification, but duplication of names still made linkage difficult, especially in Philadelphia.

INDEX

Delavall, John, 198
Delaware River, 67, 175
Dicas, Mary, 62
Dickinson, Jonathan, importing slaves, 163
Dicks, Peter, 164
Dinah (a slave), 82n, 176
Discipline, Book of (1719), 21
disowned Quakers, 152-53, 160; and slavery, 130
Doughty, Daniel, 129, 132n, 134
Doughty, Jacob, 129
Douglass, Frederick, 13
Drake, Thomas E., 9
Drinker, John, 184
Duck Creek (Del.), 15
Duck Creek (Del.) Monthly Meeting, 93, 97
Dury, Mary, 133
Dutch Reformed church, and slavery, 130
Dutch settlers, 67, 114

Eaton, Joanna, 122
Eaton, John, 114
Eaton, Joseph, 69
Eberly, Wayne, 185n
Edmundson, William, 3
Emlen, George, 82n
Epistle of Caution (1754), *see* Philadelphia Yearly Meeting
Evans, John, 198
Evans, Joshua, 98-99
Evans, Philip, 73
Evilman, William, 72
Exeter (Pa.) Monthly Meeting, 88, 106

Fairlamb, Nicholas, 43
"Falls, the," 69
Farmer, John, 22, 35, 149
Farrington, Abraham, 132
Fenwick, John, 67
Ferris, David, 45, 95-96n, 99-100, 171, 175, 176, 179n, 186
Field, Benjamin, 136
Finns, 67
"First Publishers of Truth," 6
Fishbourn, Elizabeth, 83n
Fishbourn, Ralph, 69
Folwell, John, 94

Forman, Barzillai, 136
Forman, Isaac, 134n
Fothergill, Samuel, 170, 176-77
Fox, George, 5, 6; and church government, 144, 145, 189; and Morning Meeting, 194; and slavery, 3; visit to Shrewsbury, 113-14
Fox, James, 37, 198
free blacks, *see* blacks
French and Indian War, *see* Seven Years' War
French Protestant church, 119-20
Fretwell, Peter, 197
Friends, Society of, *see* Society of Friends
Frost, J. William, 140, 144, 170
Furly, Benjamin, 42n

Gardner, Thomas, 37
Garnet, Henry Highland, 13
Garrison, William Lloyd, 13, 185
German Lutherans, *see* Germans
German Reformed church, *see* Germans
Germans, 57, 61, 65, 76, 77, 82; and slavery, 152-53, 158-60; immigration of, 82n, 168; in Pennsylvania Assembly, 159
Germantown petition (1688), 4, 18
Gloria Dei Church (Phila.), records of, 154n
Gloucester-Salem (N.J.) Quarterly Meeting, 50, 51, 89n, 104, 110; and slave trade, 23, 25; slave ownership in, 47-48, 49n
Godwyn, Morgan, 3n
Golden Rule (Luke 6:31), 18, 20, 27, 30, 94, 117
Goshen (Pa.) Monthly Meeting, 90, 94, 104, 106
Great Awakening, 10, 157
Green, Theophilus, 6n
Griffith, Thomas, 198
Griffiths, John, 170
Griffitts, Thomas, 198
Grimké, Angelina, 13
Grimké, Sarah, 13
Gwynedd (Pa.) Monthly Meeting, 28, 89

Haddonfield (N.J.) Monthly Meeting, 179

LIBRARY OF CONGRESS CATALOGING IN PUBLICATION DATA

Soderlund, Jean R., 1947–
Quakers & slavery.

Includes bibliographies and index.
1. Slavery—United States—Anti-slavery movements.
2. Slavery and the church—Society of Friends.
3. Quakers—United States—Political activity—
History.   4. Abolitionists—United States—History.
I. Title.   II. Title: Quakers and slavery.
E441.S7   1985   973'.0496   85-42707
ISBN 0-691-04732-4 (alk. paper)

Jean R. Soderlund is Curator of the
Swarthmore College Peace Collection.